Get the eBook FREE!

(PDF, ePub, Kindle, and liveBook all included)

We believe that once you buy a book from us, you should be able to read it in any format we have available. To get electronic versions of this book at no additional cost to you, purchase and then register this book at the Manning website.

Go to https://www.manning.com/freebook and follow the instructions to complete your pBook registration.

That's it!
Thanks from Manning!

Design for Developers

Design for Developers

STEPHANIE STIMAC
FOREWORD BY AARON GUSTAFSON

MANNING
SHELTER ISLAND

Manning Publications Co.
20 Baldwin Road
PO Box 761
Shelter Island, NY 11964

Development editor:	Sarah Miller
Technical development editor:	Kris Athi
Review editor:	Aleks Dragosavljevic
Production editor:	Deirdre Hiam
Copy editor:	Alisa Larson
Proofreader:	Melody Dolab
Typesetter:	Gordan Salinovic
Cover designer:	Marija Tudor

ISBN 9781617299476
Printed in the United States of America

For Mr. Birrer, Mr. Carroll, and Mr. Steigleder (Stiggy), whose guidance encouraged me to write and keep writing.

And to my dog, Vogue, who both patiently and impatiently sat by my side while I wrote.

brief contents

contents

x

CONTENTS

foreword

I've worked on the web for a long time. When I say a long time, I mean a *long* time—as in *my first browser was on the command line* old. As in *my first backend development was a CGI script* old. With my nearly three decades of building dozens upon dozens of projects for the web, the one skill I've found most valuable is the ability to bridge the gaps between the worlds of design, user experience, and development.

Each of these fields attracts practitioners from different education and/or hobbyist backgrounds. This can be a point of tension, as folks in each camp tend to see their own field as having the greatest influence on a web project's success. The reality is that the web exists in the nexus of these fields, relying equally on what each of these practices brings to the table. I have found that the most valuable people in any web project are those who understand enough of each field to be able to operate in that nexus, ensuring each team is communicating effectively with the other teams and that everyone is working together toward a shared goal.

This brings me to Stephanie Stimac's *Design for Developers*. This book is an invaluable resource for developers looking to level up their understanding of what it takes to build for the web today. It provides a crash course in design and user experience in a way that will both improve your fluency on these topics and give you the necessary skills to become productive in these spaces. Beyond that superficial perspective, however, this book provides the foundation for leveling up your career and becoming the person who thrives in the space between design, user experience, and development.

Stephanie is the perfect person to provide you with these insights. Not only is she an excellent communicator, but she also has years of working experience as a designer, developer, user experience practitioner, and educator. She's even worked behind the scenes on web browsers and the web standards they implement, giving her an incredible depth of understanding of the web and the tools we rely on to build it.

Whether you're a long-time developer looking to grow a new branch on your skill tree or you're starting out and looking to get a solid foundation in what it takes to build for the web, *Design for Developers* is sure to provide you with a wealth of knowledge to help you on your way.

—AARON GUSTAFSON
AUTHOR, *ADAPTIVE WEB DESIGN:*
CRAFTING RICH EXPERIENCES WITH PROGRESSIVE ENHANCEMENT

preface

I started designing for the web long before I went to university. I discovered a love of customizing things like Myspace and LiveJournal, and I started figuring out how to use Photoshop and make edits to my web pages with CSS. This was a hobby when I was a teenager, and I didn't consider graphic design as a career path until my senior year of high school. I had actually wanted to go into fashion design, but my portfolio was more suited for graphic design.

In university, I went into the design program with a specialty called "new media design," which covered the web, interactivity, video, and special effects. While I do recall learning the basics of HTML and CSS, the primary tool I'd spent so much time in was Adobe Flash and the language ActionScript 3.0. How perfectly timed was my graduation in 2010, which was right before Flash died as a medium for the web.

My first two design jobs were short stints before I moved on to a role that was the catalyst for diving into frontend development. I did user experience research, user experience design, visual design, and frontend development, working with a developer for more complex backend functionality and JavaScript. In the frontend role and in relationships with full-time developers, I encountered the problem of designers having grand ideas that, at the time, were not implementable, therefore changing the design.

I spent four years in this role before moving on to the Microsoft Edge team, where I found myself doing the same kind of work but with a different sort of freedom. I had more room to learn and more time to spend with developers to understand the developer experience and the problems they encounter. I learned how to use Git and push changes (and often needed help resetting things with Node and npm—thanks, Anton, for fixing those for me). I designed developer tools, built experiences for developers, and started to get involved with standards and web platform features, leading to work as a developer relations product manager.

I often find myself at an intersection, and a busy one at that—a designer who became a designer who could code, who became a product manager designing and building tools for developers, who became a product manager evangelizing web platform and browser features while still designing and developing the bits I needed to do that job. But ultimately, I view myself as a link between developers and designers. I understand and empathize with both.

In my time as a developer relations product manager, I found that some web developers wished they could design what they built better. A common theme I heard was that they could build a site, but it never looked quite right, and that working with color was hard. I tucked these things away; they weren't problems to solve at the time.

And one day, someone from Manning was in my inbox, and suddenly those design problems for web developers were my problems to solve.

acknowledgments

I started writing this book at the end of 2020 when it seemed like I would have plenty of time to write, and I did. However, life often gets in the way, and at times, it was a struggle to juggle so many life changes and a book over the last two years.

I want to thank my friends—you know who you are—who encouraged me on many Zoom calls, in our Slack group, and in person. You're my soul family and continuously brighten my life with your creativity.

To my family, who supported me through this project and checked in to ask how things were going, I love you. And although she'll never be able to read this, thanks to my dog, Vogue, who sat in my lap many nights while I wrote and kept me in check if I'd been on the computer too long.

Next, I want to thank my editor at Manning, Sarah Miller. Thank you for your patience and understanding as I navigated multiple hurdles while writing this book. We tackled several challenges as this book unfolded as it's not your typical technical book, so thank you for being so open when I pushed back and for all of your guidance throughout this process. I also want to thank the rest of the staff at Manning: my technical development editor, Kris Athi; my review editor, Aleks Dragosavljevic; my production editor, Deirdre Hiam; my copy editor, Alisa Larson; and my page proofer, Melody Dolab.

Thank you to all the reviewers and those who provided feedback along the way to help shape a better narrative for the book: Adrian Rossi, Al Krinker, Alain Couniot, Alex Lucas, Andres Sacco, Arun Kumar, Bang Nteme, Bruno Sonnino, Cass Petrus, Daniel Couper, Daniel Carl, Danilo Zekovic, David Cabrero Souto, David Krief, Frans

Oilinki, Harald Kuhn, Harrison Maseko, Håvard Wall, Jereme Allen, Jose San Leandro, Katia Patkin, Marcin Sęk, Martin Tidman, Miguel Isidoro, Nick Rakochy, Oliver Korten, Phillip Sorensen, Ramaa Kandasamy, Rodney Weis, Sezin Çağıl, Simeon Leyzerzon, Søren Dines Jensen, Steve Albers, Steve Prior, Tanuj Shroff, Tanya Wilke, Viorel Moisei, and Weyert de Boer.

And finally, to my web community online and those I know in person. If it weren't for your encouragement, I never would have started speaking at conferences, and I certainly wouldn't have even thought about writing a book. I am blessed to know so many amazing people I consider friends in my line of work. Thank you for all your support and encouragement.

about this book

Design for Developers was written to teach design fundamentals, user experience fundamentals, and the key elements of design that bring a website to life and give it character. It teaches how design elements can be used to convey a tone and message and how that tone and message can be changed through those design elements. This book is laid out in the order of a typical project cycle. It begins with the absolute core design principles needed before either the user experience or visual design phase is started. It goes into the user experience phase, covering both research and design, where you lay the foundation for applying visual design elements in the following chapters. It wraps up with testing your design, the iterative cycle, and development, which is core to the design process as it brings the design to the web and makes it usable. It is core to the entire user experience of a website.

Who should read this book

Design for Developers is written for web developers building websites and web apps who want to learn the basics of what makes a website or web app look well designed and how to make design decisions and choices with confidence. Whether you are a freelance developer or work on a team with designers, the content in this book will give you the tools and vocabulary to talk to your clients or design team about design and how it relates to your job as a developer, whether you're entry level or advanced.

This book focuses on teaching developers about visual design and user experience fundamentals within the context of the web and how to apply those fundamentals to their current or future role. The term *web developer* can mean many different things in

xix

today's professional environment. The type of developer who will benefit most from this book is the one who writes code that ultimately affects the frontend of a website or what the user sees. These developers will have job titles such as full-stack developer, frontend developer, and web app developer.

We won't focus heavily on code, but as this book is about design and user experience for the web, there will be some code references. Most people who will benefit from this book will come from a strong code background in JavaScript or PHP and will have an understanding of HTML and CSS with little or no knowledge of design or user experience fundamentals.

How this book is organized: A roadmap

Part 1 covers the benefits of understanding design principles and what the main design principles are. Chapter 1 discusses why developers should learn design fundamentals and the positive effect it can have on communication between teams. Chapter 2 goes in depth into what the core design principles are. They are fundamental to understanding what makes a design seem polished and well organized.

Part 2 begins the cycle of design with user experience fundamentals. Chapter 3 is an introductory overview of the many facets of user experience, including research, copywriting, and design. Chapter 4 covers the research phase, giving an overview of why user research is necessary, the different types of data you can collect, and some of the most common exercises to gather data. In chapter 5, we start to lay the foundation of our design by organizing content and figuring out user flows, focusing on the user experience design phase.

Part 3 introduces more ways to think about layout and how to layer on the core design elements to bring your foundation from chapter 5 to life. Chapter 6 covers common layout types, how to set up a grid, reading patterns, and layout considerations when designing the responsive version of your site or app. Chapter 7 dives into animation, how you can enhance your layout and UI by incorporating animation, and why it shouldn't be an afterthought. Chapter 8 is where we explore typography basics and how your type choices have the ability to change the tone of your website. Chapter 9 focuses heavily on color and touches on choosing imagery depending on your color palette. Chapter 10 is where we bring it all together and use what you've learned from chapters 4 through 9 to build and design a homepage with a layered approach that follows the chapters of this book.

Part 4 wraps up the design cycle, which covers testing designs and why development is the backbone of user experience on the web. Chapter 11 is about testing your designs and confirming that they achieve your site's goals. Chapter 12 ends the book with user experience and development connections and considerations.

liveBook discussion forum

Purchase of *Design for Developers* includes free access to liveBook, Manning's online reading platform. Using liveBook's exclusive discussion features, you can attach comments to the book globally or to specific sections or paragraphs. It's a snap to make notes for yourself, ask and answer technical questions, and receive help from the author and other users. To access the forum, go to https://livebook.manning.com/ book/design-for-developers/discussion. You can also learn more about Manning's forums and the rules of conduct at https://livebook.manning.com/discussion.

Manning's commitment to our readers is to provide a venue where a meaningful dialogue between individual readers and between readers and the author can take place. It is not a commitment to any specific amount of participation on the part of the author, whose contribution to the forum remains voluntary (and unpaid). We suggest you try asking the author some challenging questions lest her interest stray! The forum and the archives of previous discussions will be accessible from the publisher's website as long as the book is in print.

about the author

STEPHANIE STIMAC is a product manager with design experience spanning over a decade who focuses on building products for developers. She has spoken at web conferences around the world on web development and design topics, bridging the gap between design and development in many of those talks. When she was working solely on design projects, she worked with companies such as Safeway, MBARI, Microsoft Azure, Microsoft Office, Windows, T-Mobile, and Blue Cross Blue Shield. She joined the Microsoft Edge team because she had a passion for the web, design, and development. She worked on developer tools, such as webhint.io and the Edge browser DevTools, and on other web platform initiatives such as the Web We Want (webwewant .fyi), working with a developer experience mindset. She spent six years on the Microsoft Edge team before moving on to pursue more developer experience product management work in the startup space.

Part 1

Design basics

In the opening part, I set the stage for the rest of the book and introduce design principles that are essential to understand before you start the visual design phase of a project.

In chapter 1, I establish the purpose of this book and why it's beneficial to you as a developer to understand design fundamentals. Chapter 2 creates the book's foundation and the design principles we will explore. Every principle discussed in this chapter is vital for understanding how to establish relationships among pieces of content, which are introduced in part 2. These principles can be applied to all visual elements, which we will do in part 3. The more comfortable you get with design principles, the more radically you can apply these principles to create even more standout designs. By the end of this part, you'll be ready to start the user experience phase of the design cycle.

Bridging the gap between design and development

This chapter covers

- The entirety of the web design process covered in this book
- The evolving role of web developers
- Benefits to both freelancers and full-time developers of understanding design fundamentals and user experience processes

The web is a place of change. New technologies and frameworks are introduced every year. HTML and Cascading Style Sheets (CSS) remain the foundations for building websites and web applications, and they continue to grow, accommodating the needs of developers as designs evolve.

Part of building for the web is keeping up to date with the technologies used to build it. But how does this work for design? Although tools change over time, a lot of the underlying concepts are timeless. What you see is a shift in trends over time.

Familiarity with web development has been invaluable to me as a specialist in web design. When asked, "Should designers learn to code?" my answer is *yes*. An understanding of what's possible on the web is a great asset. It makes communication between designers and developers much easier. In tech, the communication gap between designers and developers is commonly considered one of the hardest to bridge. A less-asked question is, "Should developers learn to design?" Again, my answer is *yes*, at least when it comes to understanding design fundamentals.

Empowering developers with design skills allows them to quickly update a user interface when a design team may be more focused on solving user experience flows than making small adjustments to pixels. A CEO once shared feedback with my development team that the user interface of one of our tools didn't feel as efficient as some of our competitors. What he meant was that there was too much whitespace between components. The user interface wasn't as refined as it could be. One of the developers reduced the spacing around components and tightened up the design. He didn't need a designer to provide mock-ups; instead, he was able to make a change, show it to a designer to make sure the teams were aligned on what had changed, and then push the UI changes.

When a developer can compare your product with another design, identify the difference—in this case, the use of whitespace—and make a change, you, as a designer, are able to focus on solving more complex experience problems. A good developer understands that small visual changes positively affect the creation of a polished design.

1.1 How design and user experience fundamentals benefit developers

Designers and developers usually speak different languages and have different skill sets. Designers focus on the user and building out the visuals. Developers focus on translating visuals into something interactive for customers. However, the two areas intersect because developers recreate what a designer has built with code, usually with CSS, which brings styling to web interfaces. Understanding the *what* and *why* behind what you're bringing to life makes you a better developer and gives you the skills to feel confident in making design decisions when you don't have a design counterpart.

Design is much more than visuals and aesthetics. While these are important and the first thing customers notice when landing on your website, the rest of the experience is just as important. If the site is slow to load or people aren't completing the primary tasks you expect them to, like buying an item, aesthetics aren't enough. You need to understand how to make user experience decisions that will inform visual design decisions. The typical workflow for a website project when I started my career over a decade ago was as follows:

1   The designer would research a project against the websites of their client's competitors and assess what was done well versus what wasn't.
2   The designer would produce a few user personas of the type of person the project was trying to target and provide a solution on the website to a particular need (such as providing information, buying a product, booking an appointment, comparing hotels, etc.).

3   Taking the competitive research, user personas, and business requirements, the designer would build wireframes, simple diagrams of the website showing content placement, and then get approval from the client on those wireframes to move forward.

4   The designer would finally move into the visual design phase of the project, provide pixel-perfect mock-ups to the client for review, revise the mock-ups, get approval, and then hand the project off to the developer to code the website.

5   The developer would take the static mock-ups and build the interactive website.

6   After quality assurance testing checked for bugs or problems, the site was launched.

All these steps still happen today, and this workflow is largely the scope of what this book covers: the project cycle from the start of the user experience phase through user experience design (wireframes) and application of visual design elements to make the design come to life. However, we'll adjust this project cycle to focus on modern workflows that encourage more iterative design and development, closer working relationships, and constant testing and research to improve a design.

The workflow I've laid out in the previously listed steps is divided between the designer and the developer. A user experience designer may focus solely on competitive research and wireframing while working with a visual or interaction designer who focuses on design decisions such as typography, color, spacing, and animation—all the visual aspects of a website that we'll explore in this book. Nonetheless, the work is still split between the designers and developers, with developers not being involved until the handoff occurs.

This way of working doesn't allow for a collaborative approach. Developers have insight and knowledge that designers don't typically have, and involving developers earlier in the process is beneficial to the project cycle. Whether it's to reduce unnecessary work if a design feature can't be implemented or to get a different perspective that can influence the creative direction, it's a win for both sides.

1.1.1   Improving collaboration and communication

Designers don't expect their developer counterparts to become design experts, just as developers don't expect designers to become experts in JavaScript. We are each in our roles for a reason, but the work we do is intertwined. What code developers write can affect the design, and what designers create can affect what choices developers need to make with code. Sometimes there's also a limit to what can be built by a developer due to either technical limitations or a code solution that would negatively affect the user experience, such as an animation that causes the web page to load slowly.

Understanding the fundamentals of what decisions drive design choices can help make collaboration and communication between designers and developers more efficient and reduce the amount of back and forth because of those technical limitations. When developers are equipped with the tools and vocabulary, they can provide more actionable feedback and ask the right questions of designers. They can begin to understand the *why* behind design decisions.

This book is intended to help give developers the terminology and understanding to communicate more effectively with a design team throughout the process of a project. Even if you're not part of a company with a design team, reading this book will give you the confidence to make design decisions that result in a polished-looking end product. Perhaps you're a freelance developer who wants to be able to make visual adjustments to a website, and you don't have the budget (or you just don't want) to hire a designer. It all comes down to understanding these few design principles and how to apply them.

1.1.2 *Understanding the why behind design decisions*

I led a project whose target audience was developers. It was a tool that analyzed a website or web application's code and provided suggestions for improving things like a website's accessibility, performance, and security. Although the project was open source, most members of the team working on it were Microsoft employees. I knew that, in general, web developers' perception of Microsoft was not always positive, and when Microsoft put out another tool for developers, they would scrutinize every bit of it. I had decided that, similar to other developer tools, our branding would include an illustrated mascot that we could use in the graphics on the website.

My intention with the mascot's design was to purposely evoke a feeling of empathy in the people using our site. One placement of a particular illustration in the website's user flow, as shown in figure 1.1, was critical to achieving this feeling. The first few iterations of the website placed users into a queue to have their code analyzed because our backend could only handle so many URLs at once. Humans are impatient beings when it comes to the web, and developers, even more so.

I hypothesized that there would be complaints about the waiting queue, so the illustration I placed on that page was of our mascot in a dark room behind a desk with a lamp, her face dripping with sweat as she worked away to make her way through the queue of URLs.

My hypothesis was later validated when I was talking to a developer about the tool and the website, and they told me, "I wanted to be mad I had to wait, but I just felt bad for your mascot."

BUILDING EMPATHY FOR THE TARGET AUDIENCE TO PROVIDE ENHANCED EXPERIENCES

By understanding and having empathy for our website's target audience, I was able to make design decisions to help mitigate future complaints. Eventually, the backend was upgraded to handle more code analyses simultaneously. This example serves as a perfect illustration of how developer decisions and user experience are intertwined. In this case, the initial setup of the backend led to a poor experience for the website's users by making them wait, so that poor experience had to be temporarily patched with some design thinking. With lightning-fast data speeds available today, people are less inclined to wait for a webpage to load before quickly moving on to the next option. Getting that experience right is vital to business metrics.

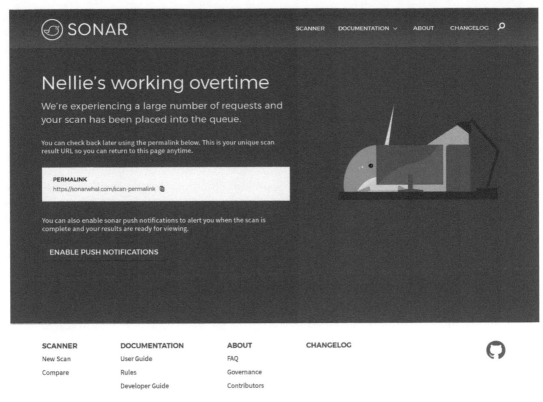

Figure 1.1   The waiting queue for the website scanner showed the narwhal mascot that was working overtime to get a website scan done for a developer.

Improving the user experience is where a developer's understanding of their target audience and being able to empathize with them become incredibly valuable. There were multiple solutions a developer could have implemented without input from a designer in the case of the code analysis website. They could have implemented a loading animation or an intermediary page with a message that said, "Check back later for your results." While these are not necessarily bad experiences, they are standard, baseline experiences that fail to consider the target audience and what that audience has little tolerance for while using a tool, especially a new tool that needs to make a good impression on first use.

TECHNICAL DECISIONS ARE USER EXPERIENCE DECISIONS
Understanding the fundamentals of the *why* that drives design and user experience can help expand a developer's understanding of how their choices, from the code stack to how code gets compiled to the hosting provider, all ultimately affect the end-user experience of a website or web application. The technical decisions are as much a part of the design of the site as the visuals are, which is why being able to talk about the design choices made by a designer from the viewpoint of development is so important.

Let's say a designer is envisioning a site that features a lot of animation via user interaction. The developer's perspective of how that will affect the site's performance is critical feedback to provide the designer early on in the process. Is all the animation a necessary part of the user experience of the site? If not, having that conversation before coding begins can help save time and provides an opportunity for the designer and developer to work together closely to figure out solutions that achieve the desired result without negatively affecting the site's user experience.

1.1.3   *Writing better code by understanding visual design fundamentals*

Understanding some visual design fundamentals provides a few other benefits for developers, beyond better collaboration and communication with their design counterparts. The first, which affects the developer directly, is that understanding how different elements fit together can lead to more organized and cleaner code, which is easier to maintain in the long run.

Breaking down and understanding how an entire page is laid out can affect how the code is written for a cleaner responsive experience with fewer hacks for coding for smaller screens. Developers can also identify the spots where a component or layout may break or be insufficient on smaller screens—for example, a button isn't tall enough when viewed on a mobile phone—and feel empowered to make or suggest visual adjustments.

On a more scoped scale, understanding how the different individual elements, such as headings and buttons, get reused across multiple user interface components also affects how code gets grouped, especially in a CSS file. Identifying those reusable bits can mean more shared code between components resulting in less code served to the end user, which is always a win on the performance side of the web.

Design can also inform backend code decisions. Some databases may need to be queried from a certain form, or data may need to be stored. Understanding the user flows in these scenarios means this work can start earlier instead of waiting for the design handoff. Both communication and project speed improve, and again, everyone benefits.

1.1.4   *Better code (and design) through less dependency on third-party frameworks*

Many developers I know use a third-party component library or frontend framework as a quick way to implement many of the user interface pieces that they'll need for a project. They're fast to set up and start using, and if you don't trust your design skills as a developer, the pieces are all there to provide an experience better than what you think you may be able to deliver. But there are multiple disadvantages to using those third-party libraries from both a design and code perspective.

More often than not, you'll be serving up a library of code with more code than your site will actually use. Also, it's not code that you've written, so how the different UI components are intertwined or reused may not be clear, and attempting to remove or alter code that you think you won't use may lead to bugs in the UI. In addition, you are now dependent on the framework authors to ensure that the framework code is up to date with new web standards and best practices.

By having the confidence and understanding of visual design principles and how those are applied to the web through layout and UI components, developers can build their own component system and serve minimal code to the end user. This codebase can be easier to maintain, iterate, and add new components to, and developers don't get locked into a specific ecosystem beyond their control.

Third-party frameworks offer some very common patterns for entire web page layouts. Usually, there's one layout with a big hero image at the top and horizontal bands to divide up the page content and another with the hero image and three columns of content underneath it, like in figure 1.2.

Figure 1.2 An example of one of the commonly provided templates supplied by third-party frameworks

These aren't inherently bad layouts. They serve a function and purpose, but they only really address the main landing page, so you may end up with a home page that looks well-designed but with subpages that don't feel quite as polished. They're also incredibly common, and if you want the website that you're building to stand out a bit more, utilizing these templates straight out of the box won't get you that.

Developing a well-designed website or web application is much more than just picking a good template for the layout. Understanding design principles, such as how to apply color theory and use typography and space within a layout, can lead to a much more polished experience for users. It also means that rather than trying to fit the content of your website into someone else's generic template, you can understand how to build and tailor your website's structure for your users. The layout and flow of an e-commerce store would be much different than that of a news website or a blog.

But we live in a very fast-paced world, and depending on the client, development projects may be on a tight timeline, and you may not have a choice between using a template and building your site from the ground up. Knowing how to use color, typography, and space can still be applied to any templates you may need to use and can enhance the design significantly.

1.1.5   *User experience and development*

Design as a whole is a vast subject to tackle. There are so many different areas to specialize in, and user experience is perhaps one of the broadest parts of web design, which can be broken down into specialties like user research and interaction design. So much of user experience is focused on the design aspect of the specialty, but every choice a developer makes is also a user experience choice. Some aspects of the user experience process don't necessarily tie into a site's actual code development. However, knowing the fundamentals can help developers understand the decisions made for users and make technical choices that will most benefit them.

The evolving role of the developer means understanding and connecting with the target audience to build a solution that meets their needs. User experience methodologies can provide a footprint for developers to begin to understand how to build with their users at the forefront. Again, this can affect how developers write their code or what tools they adopt to accomplish their goal.

For example, let's say a developer at a smaller company is working on a product, which could be a website or web application, and they're going to implement a new feature. Because the company is small, it doesn't have a dedicated user researcher or the budget to conduct formal user research. So, it plans to release the feature without user testing and see how usage of the feature goes. Still, some plan for testing must be in place for this experiment to be successful. Understanding how to test a design and gather feedback to iterate on a feature is critical in product design.

Every decision a developer makes affects the user experience of the website or application. Understanding the importance of each of the different areas of user experience and how they fit into the project's lifecycle can help developers become more user-centered and identify problems in an experience before too much time is spent in development. For example, ironing out details and feature functionality in the prototyping phase will ensure features work as expected and can lead to fewer bugs on the website or web application production code, which, in turn, leads to a better end-user experience.

User experience and web development are deeply intertwined, and with the push for developers to become more knowledgeable about the business and the business's customers, it's beneficial to understand user experience fundamentals and how they connect with the development phase. Ultimately, this information can help developers write better code, ship code with fewer bugs, and keep their users in mind when making technical decisions. If done correctly, understanding user experience fundamentals will not only positively affect the end business goals but also give developers the tools to pivot and iterate quickly if something doesn't perform as expected before it can have a negative effect.

1.2 *The path to understanding better design and user experience*

Both visual design and user experience are extremely broad subjects, with many individual areas of expertise that allow for deep specialization. With user experience, some roles focus on the design aspects like wireframing and interaction design, and some focus solely on research. There are many different paths and areas to specialize in, and people spend years developing the skills for these specialties. However, everyone starts with the foundational principles in each area, which we'll touch on in this book, all within the context of the web.

The core areas for visual design will focus on composition, layout, color, and typography and how all those things work together to create a page's visual hierarchy. We'll look at layout basics, like the principles of symmetry, and explore layouts based on common reading patterns identified by researchers. With color, we'll explore the basics of the color wheel and how to build a color palette. Even with tools that can generate a color palette for you, a guide to understanding how to apply those colors across a website is not provided, which can result in overly colorful websites that don't feel as refined as other websites.

As for user experience, entire careers are made out of different areas of specialties, but we'll touch on information architecture and how to define the user flow of a website. Regarding user experience, understanding the different types of user testing and ways to gather feedback, even without access to an extensive budget, is highly requested among the developers I interact with. How to incorporate feedback into a project and know when something is "good enough" to test is another common question that comes up for developers.

1.2.1 *The design process this book covers*

The design process in this book is focused on an iterative process. An iterative process is a continuous cycle of releasing a product—in our case, a website or web application—and continuing to make incremental changes to improve it. However, this process also works with projects that aren't ongoing. The same phases apply; they just won't be continuous. Each phase is laid out in figure 1.3.

The first phase we'll discuss is the user experience (UX) research phase, where we are given a problem from a client to solve. Thus, you would build a website or web app that solves that given problem. Your initial research should identify what the user needs your website to fulfill and the targeted audience. Also, depending on what you're building, this phase could mean you're making sure that the problem you're solving is actually a user problem that needs to be addressed.

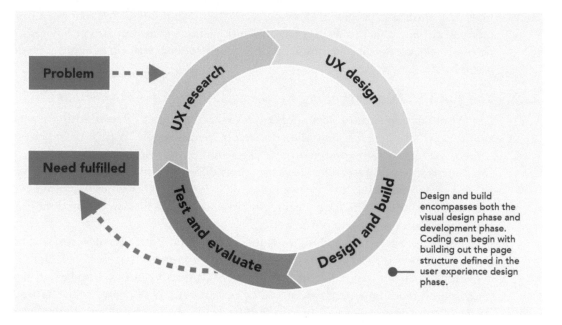

Figure 1.3 The iterative process this book covers for a web design or web application project—from identifying the problem to user research, user experience design, design and build phase, and test and evaluate

Phase 2 is user experience design. You take the client and business requirements for your project, combine those with the needs you identified in your user research phase, and start to form a plan for your website. In this phase, you lay the foundation for the visual pieces you will apply in the next phase. The focus is on figuring out page layout, content placement, and the flow of the pages (how users get from point A to point B).

Phase 3 includes the design and build phases. These two phases consist of applying visual design elements such as color, typography, and plans for any animation you want to include and the actual development process with code, respectively. I've purposefully grouped these together because most modern teams I've encountered do not work siloed like they used to. Development can start after the website's structure is agreed upon in the user experience design phase. Visual choices like color, images, and typography can be added and adjusted as those decisions are made.

Phase 4 is where the iterative part of the process comes in. You want to ensure that what you've built meets your users' needs efficiently. If it doesn't, you must restart the process to dig into why it doesn't and make refinements from there. Depending on the type of project you're working on, you could be continually adding new features and updating in iterations. With smaller projects or freelance projects—for example, a one-off marketing website—you'll most likely launch the website and then make sure it's functioning and meets all the business requirements. If you hand off the site to a client, they can manage the testing and evaluation phase to make sure it's performing how they want it to, and if not, they can start the process again to make adjustments.

The phases of this cycle can be broken into two categories: (a) user experience fundamentals, which focus on researching, building the scaffolding of the project (how it's laid out and connected), and testing and (b) visual design fundamentals. These visual elements are applied on top of the scaffolding built in the user experience phase to bring character and hierarchy to the experience through colors, spacing, typography, and animation.

USER EXPERIENCE FUNDAMENTALS

User experience isn't just one part of the project; often, user experience is tied to the design phase, yet it goes beyond that phase. Business requirements, design, and web development all come together to create the user experience of a website or application. This book will focus on understanding the importance and purpose of the different phases: research, planning, and wireframing, which we will cover in the first few chapters, and prototyping and testing and how these intersect with web development, which we'll cover in the last few chapters of the book.

User experience can be broken down even further into a subset of experiences, like developer experience, which is how a developer interacts with your product. However, the scenarios become much more niched and specific. Knowing the foundations of user experience methodology will help you understand how to build for your different users and what other experiences may apply to your website or application if your target audience isn't only consumers.

While every choice in web development ultimately affects user experience, we'll touch on some of the most specific technical choices a developer must make that can alter users' visual experience of the website or application. We will also look at choices that can affect the experience of users who don't interact visually. Being aware of these choices and the effect they have will help developers evolve their understanding of their product's target audience and how to build a better experience by empathizing with this target audience.

VISUAL DESIGN FUNDAMENTALS

Design is a visual communication language that can be taught. It's a way to solve a problem or provide information through visuals. Understanding the fundamentals will give you the tools to make design decisions and communicate the reasons behind those decisions. One thing I hear from developers when it comes to design is that many feel they're not good at it because they're either not creative or they can recognize a good design but don't know how to achieve that same result themselves.

Before we can even start to pick our typography and colors and consider how to lay things out, we need to start with our foundational design principles. These cover things like proximity, contrast, symmetry, and alignment. Understanding these principles is vital before the user experience phase, which is why the next chapter will start with these design principles. They are the basis for establishing relationships between content on the page, building hierarchy, and laying out content that draws people to the page. Once you know these principles, you can confidently go into the user experience design phase before moving on to the visual design phase, which involves color, typography, and animation.

A few different areas of visual design come up consistently when I ask developers what they struggle with the most: color theory and how to pick a color palette and apply it to a website or web application, typography, and layout—specifically, what makes a good layout. In the next chapter, we'll examine design fundamentals in the context of a website or web application. In later chapters, we'll dive deeper into each design element. Knowing how to use these different elements of design—color, type, and space—cohesively and mix them to create the hierarchy of a page or to create components on a page are skills that can be learned and are not dependent on whether you think you're the creative type.

1.2.2   Design experts vs. designing smart

Like web development, design is an area with many paths and specialties. This book isn't intended to replace formal education or even informal education, like the boot camps that many designers attend. Also, it doesn't replace the cumulative experience of working in the design field. Some design experts work in niche areas like typography and animation, which can certainly become whole roles for people, while others maintain component libraries and design systems.

This book will not make you a design expert. It will not impart all the knowledge about the different areas of design, logos, and branding, nor will it even dive deep into the different areas of design and user experience as they relate to the web. It is not a ploy to turn developers into designers. Design and web development are two complementary professions that frequently overlap. Just as it's beneficial for designers who design for the web to have some knowledge of code, I believe it's equally beneficial for developers to have some knowledge of design.

1.2.3   Putting it all together

In the following chapters, you'll learn about the foundational principles behind graphic design within the context of the web and how to use the different principles to establish the hierarchy of a web page. Following that, you'll learn about the user experience process, where visual design fits in, and how this knowledge coincides with the web development process, which will improve how you work as a developer.

Summary

- Understanding the design process and how to apply both user experience and visual design fundamentals allows you to create more polished-looking web experiences on your own and be more involved with the process, communicate better, and even write better code.
- Knowing the fundamentals and how they affect the user experience can help you understand from a developer's perspective why certain design decisions are made.

- Knowing the design terminology will make you a better communicator with your team or a client. When working with a team, you can more confidently be involved early in the project to help make decisions that reduce project churn that comes from miscommunication or a designer's lack of understanding that a design isn't possible.
- Instead of relying on third-party frameworks for a design system, you can use design principles to build a design system that solves your project's needs and is more lightweight. Shipping less code means better performance in the browser, which positively affects user experience.
- Visual design fundamentals start with the most basic concepts around creating the hierarchy and relationships between content. Understanding these concepts before the user experience design phase is vital so you clearly understand how to create relationships between content.
- User experience fundamentals are focused on research and validating user needs, which will inform the user experience design phase. The user experience design phase sets the foundation on top of which the visual design elements are applied.
- Visual design concepts, such as typography and color, are the parts of the visual design phase that bring a design to life. They are layered on top of the foundation, and you can further apply the core design principles discussed in the next chapter to enhance a website's design.

Design fundamentals

The layout is the most critical piece of a website's design. It is quite literally the foundation for the remaining pieces that will eventually be added to the website. Let's consider building a house rather than a website for a moment. Before you can start picking out windows and blinds or even the type of bathtub you want, you need to have the plans for the structure and layout of the house. The size of the bathtub can certainly influence the choices you make about the house's structure, but you can't put a bathtub in before the other foundational elements are built.

There needs to be some sort of blueprint that defines the structure and lays out a plan. Without a plan, there's a possibility that things just get built as you go, and then you could have windows and doors that are all very different sizes or rooms that are oddly shaped, resulting in something feeling off about the house. It could be difficult to navigate or unpleasant to look at. Even after those finishing touches are added, some things may still not quite flow well with the house. It feels unfinished or unpolished. It's also the same when writing code with HTML, CSS, and JavaScript: it has to adhere to a certain structure to work properly.

Now let's say a house goes up next door that was well thought-out and had a plan. The doors are all the same size, and the windows, though some may be different sizes, are not all individually different. They share proportions and look like they go together. The rooms are not oddly shaped, and the structure is well-defined. Overall, it feels easier to navigate that home than the one next door, built without a plan. If both houses go up for sale at the same time, which do you think would be likely to sell quicker or for more money? Probably the house that was built with a plan and that has a well-defined structure.

In the case of a website's layout, it's a similar situation, especially if a website is intended to sell a product or a service. Imagine a user lands on your website and, at first glance, is overwhelmed in some way. Perhaps there's too much content sized the same, the navigation isn't clear, or they simply can't cognitively determine their next step on the website. They'll most likely abandon your website. If you're selling something, this equates to lost sales because the user leaves your website before they reach the checkout page. In some instances, users will wade through a poorly laid-out website and add items to their cart but then become so frustrated that they abandon the site because the cart layout page is too difficult to follow.

The basic design principles this chapter covers are crucial to good design. These guiding principles establish a sense of order through alignment, keep your users oriented through repetition, drive hierarchy with contrast, and make a design feel centered through balance. Proximity, alignment, repetition, contrast, and balance within the context of a website's layout will help you build a strong foundation for your website's design. Once you establish the main structure, these five principles become vital as you add the smaller components. They are all relevant to each piece of a website, from the main layout down to how a piece of text and a button are grouped together, and can be mixed and matched to make a design more interesting

These principles are important to understand before you reach the visual design stage, even before you start building a wireframe in the user experience phase. Wireframes are the blueprints or schematics for your website that define its skeletal structure, where you start to group and arrange the different pieces of content for the website. It's where the initial layout of a website happens, and the first use of these principles comes into play when we place content and establish relationships between each piece. We'll look at wireframing in greater depth in the coming chapters.

2.1 The principles of design

Although design is a vast subject area that is distilled down into many different disciplines and areas that people can specialize in, from print and packing design to video game design, a few fundamentals apply across all areas. Understanding these principles will lay the foundation for visual design and help you understand why designers make some of their decisions and how to apply these principles when you don't have access to a designer. You don't need to be a design expert to make a website look well-designed or make design modifications; these principles are at the core of how to do those things.

Depending on whom you talk to, the number of design fundamentals differs. For the sake of this book and getting down the absolute basics, we'll discuss five fundamentals: proximity, repetition, alignment, contrast, and balance and symmetry. None of these are necessarily more important than the other, and they are rarely used alone. They are all part of an interconnected system to create the visual hierarchy of a page and draw the eye through the content. These fundamentals are not exclusive to the web; they are used throughout print and packaging design. But because we are web builders, we'll assess each one in the context of the web.

2.1.1   *Proximity*

Proximity, or closeness, is the design principle of relationships. The closer items are placed together, the more they are seen as related or as part of the same group. Applying proximity to group different elements together is, at its core, how we organize information. When elements appear closer to one another, we perceive them to be part of a group or related. Take the two different rows of circles in the graphic in figure 2.1.

Figure 2.1 Adjusting the space between shapes establishes smaller groups of two instead of one large group of circles in the second line.

The first row of circles is evenly spaced, so all circles are perceived as part of the same group. In the second row, when we move two circles closer together throughout the row and increase the space between each pair, the proximity of the two circles in each pair creates five separate groups. Using whitespace between elements is a key to grouping content on the web and creating a meaningful distinction for your users. With easily identifiable groups of content, users will be able to more easily scan your website or application. Elements related to or part of the same section or component should be grouped together and appear physically close to each other on the screen.

The principle of proximity is key to organizing content into groups. In figure 2.2, even though the elements have different shapes, it's still clear that there are two unique groupings.

If we ignored the use of other principles and relied only on proximity to create distinction, we would still be able to identify which elements go together and form a unit.

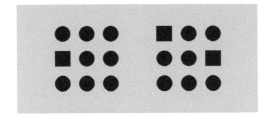

Figure 2.2   Although made up of different shapes, there are two distinct groups of shapes due to the large space between them.

Let's look at figure 2.3 as an unstyled list of blog post titles with an introductory text snippet below each title.

What the heck is an Origin Trial?
In this blog post I'll explain what an origin trial is and how it's vital...
Browser font rendering inconsistencies
Let's take a look at what's happening across different browsers when...
How to use the CSS "appearance" property properly
The "appearance" property has been used by developers to hack their...
Diving into building apps for dual screen devices
Dual screen devices have finally hit the market, but how can we start...

Figure 2.3   A list of blog post titles and a preview of the blog post copy without styling, spacing, or a clear hierarchy

Much like the evenly spaced horizontal row of circles, this vertical list of blog post titles with their corresponding article previews is evenly spaced. Upon first glance, these items appear to be a part of the same group; only upon closer inspection would a viewer

What the heck is an Origin Trial?
In this blog post I'll explain what an origin trial is and how it's vital...

Browser font rendering inconsistencies
Let's take a look at what's happening across different browsers when...

How to use the CSS "appearance" property properly
The "appearance" property has been used by developers to hack their...

Diving into building apps for dual screen devices
Dual screen devices have finally hit the market, but how can we start...

Figure 2.4   Blog titles and preview copy are grouped into pairs and separated by white space to show the relationship between the pieces of content. Each grouping is a separate piece of content.

realize differently and probably even be a bit confused about the content being presented to them. Because of the even proximity between each item, the list appears to be one large group. Let's increase the white space below each text preview in figure 2.4 without altering the space below the blog post title to group each item into pairs.

Once we add some space between each paired title and text snippet, our groups become more distinct. Now, when we scan the list, it's clear that there are four separate chunks of content due to the whitespace between each grouping.

Whitespace in design isn't something to be afraid of; it is extremely vital in creating a design that is easy for your website users to consume. Many design beginners want to fill up as much space on a page as possible. Also, I've often had clients give feedback that there's too much whitespace, and they want to fill it all in by making elements bigger and reducing the space between them. On the web, usability is reduced when related items aren't grouped together appropriately, which makes scanning content more difficult. For example, let's look at the blog post list again but alter the style of the title to make it more distinct (figure 2.5).

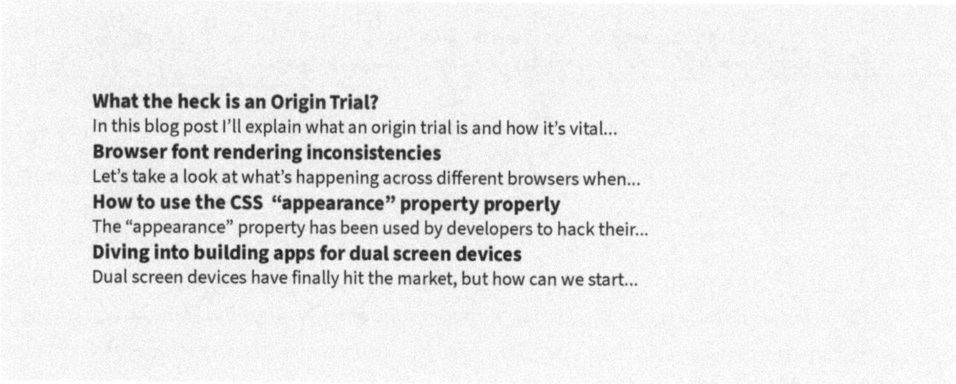

What the heck is an Origin Trial?
In this blog post I'll explain what an origin trial is and how it's vital...
Browser font rendering inconsistencies
Let's take a look at what's happening across different browsers when...
How to use the CSS "appearance" property properly
The "appearance" property has been used by developers to hack their...
Diving into building apps for dual screen devices
Dual screen devices have finally hit the market, but how can we start...

Figure 2.5   The blog post title is now emphasized in bold lettering, making it stand out from the copy below it.

While emphasizing the blog post title helps create some distinction, there still isn't a clear relationship between the items since everything is still evenly spaced. Adding the extra emphasis on the blog post titles isn't enough to indicate that there are supposed to be four separate groups of content. So, let's again add space below each nonemphasized line of text in figure 2.6 to create our groups of content.

AVOID CONFUSION BY KEEPING UNRELATED ITEMS APART

More often than not, the users coming to your website are trying to complete a task, so they're focused on finding what they need as quickly as possible. It's important to keep in mind that while some items on your page may look similar and function the same way, this doesn't always indicate that they should be grouped together.

Figure 2.6   Adding space helps create groups of content and establish clearer relationships between content. The bolded headline shows that it is separate from the copy below it, but the proximity to the line below indicates it is still part of the same group.

Thus, what goes into a grouping should be carefully considered. For example, if you have one style for buttons on your website and one of your pages has two distinct and unrelated groups of buttons, like navigation buttons and buttons that perform an action (such as Delete or Edit), ensure that enough space exists between the two groups. Don't mix the buttons together, as this can create a confusing experience for your users, who don't want to spend extra time thinking about the different actions the buttons may perform (figures 2.7 and 2.8).

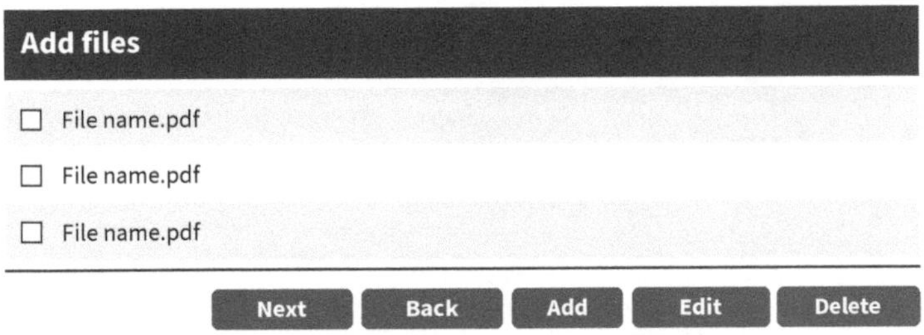

Add files

☐ File name.pdf

☐ File name.pdf

☐ File name.pdf

[Next] [Back] [Add] [Edit] [Delete]

Figure 2.7   In this piece of UI, all the buttons for navigating through the form are grouped together and look similar. It takes the user time to find the action button they're looking for.

Add files

☐ File name.pdf

☐ File name.pdf

☐ File name.pdf

[Next] [Back]   [Add] [Edit] [Delete]

Figure 2.8   A better solution is to group the action buttons and navigation buttons on different sides of the page.

CREATING EASILY SCANNABLE WEB PAGES WITH THE PRINCIPLE OF PROXIMITY

Proximity is also important when it comes to how you decide to group and space your content to design an easily scannable web page. Let's look at an example of a page where items are not grouped; they're just spaced evenly apart (figure 2.9).

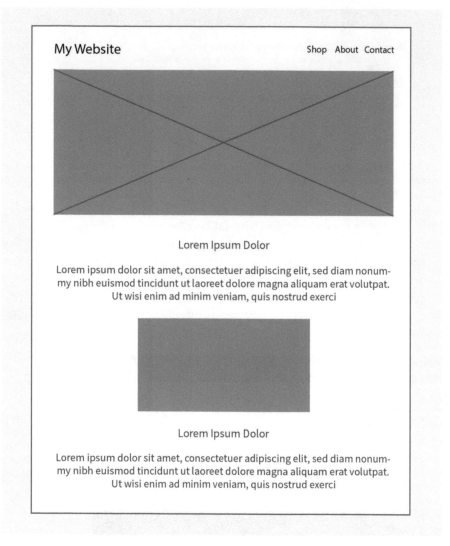

Figure 2.9 In this example, every piece of content is spaced evenly, so we don't know whether the images (the rectangles) are related to the content below or above them.

In this example, everything on the page is evenly spaced, and proximity isn't used to group content together. So, we don't know whether the top rectangle relates to the text below it or whether the bottom rectangle relates to the text above or below it.

In figure 2.10, we use the principle of proximity to move related items closer to each other and create groups that are distinguishable on the page. The top rectangle isn't directly related to the content below it, but the bottom rectangle has been grouped closer to the first set of text, and the paragraph of text has been moved closer to the related heading so we can identify each separate group of content.

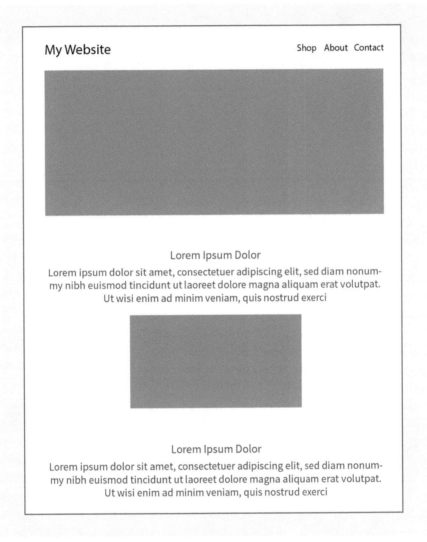

Figure 2.10   In this example, we establish relationships between the content by using proximity to group related content together on the page and create "chunks" or sections of content.

Look at an example from the webhint.io website in figure 2.11. If we remove all of our margin and padding from the content, we get one block of content on the right side that is hard to parse. All the pieces of content sit on top of one another and are close

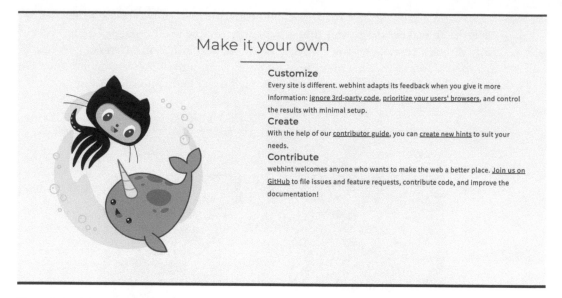

Figure 2.11   This example doesn't use space or proximity, thus creating a wall of text.

together. While some headings are larger, the relationship between the different lines of content isn't clear.

But by using proximity, in figure 2.12, we create groups of content by moving the text blocks closer to their respective headings and increasing space between each

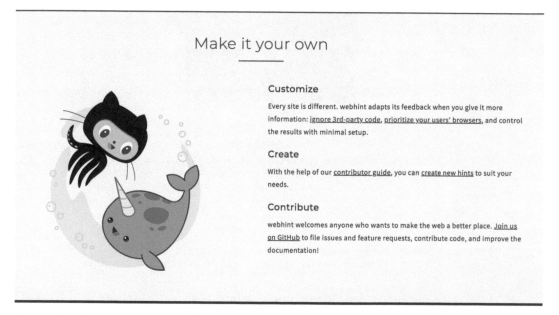

Figure 2.12   After we group the headings and text blocks together, the individual groups of content become easier to scan and parse.

group. The page becomes much clearer and more scannable when the content is broken up into groups.

When you apply the principle of proximity to the different user interface elements on your page, the goal is to create easily identifiable sections of content for your users. You want to reduce the cognitive load and create a user interface that isn't overwhelming. Forms are another area where proximity can help alleviate users feeling like they're staring at a wall of content. Figure 2.13 shows an order form with line after line of input fields.

It's a bit overwhelming to look at visually. If we were to look at the code, we'd find line after line of HTML text inputs with the occasional HTML `<select>` element. But if we chunk the form out into different sections, like in figure 2.14, it becomes less overwhelming. We create related groups within the form that provide a natural stopping point for a user if they need to pause and return later to complete the form.

Providing this grouping also brings some clearer organization to our frontend code. The two sections, the billing and payment information, would be grouped into their own `div` containers in the code. Instead of one giant list of HTML inputs, the code will also be visually formatted to indicate two separate sections, reducing cognitive load on the developer when scanning through the code to make edits in the future.

The goal is to reduce how much your user needs to think about how to interact with your page. Establishing clearly identifiable relationships by grouping items together is the first step toward creating a clean interface for your users.

PROXIMITY: THE PRINCIPLE OF RELATIONSHIPS

Proximity is the principle of relationships and is perhaps the most important fundamental to understand. It comes into play when planning and organizing your website, before you even start to think about visual design and style treatments. When you reach the wireframing stage of a project, precision and nailing down visual design details should be ignored. Focus instead on grouping and organizing content and components and figuring out the rough placement of content on the web page to ensure that the relationships between the larger chunks of content make sense. Embrace whitespace between unrelated groups of content to make the page more scannable for users and to avoid confusion or uncertainty when they're focused on completing a task.

Grouping related content when we haven't applied any other design principles to our content is the most basic and fundamental way to create some distinction between groups of content. The example in figure 2.4 shows this concept on the most basic level, with nothing but space between each blog title and article snippet group. Defining relationships between content with proximity before any other principles are applied will help establish the site structure and ensure relationships are clear before moving on to apply the appropriate principles that will further establish a hierarchy in a web page's layout.

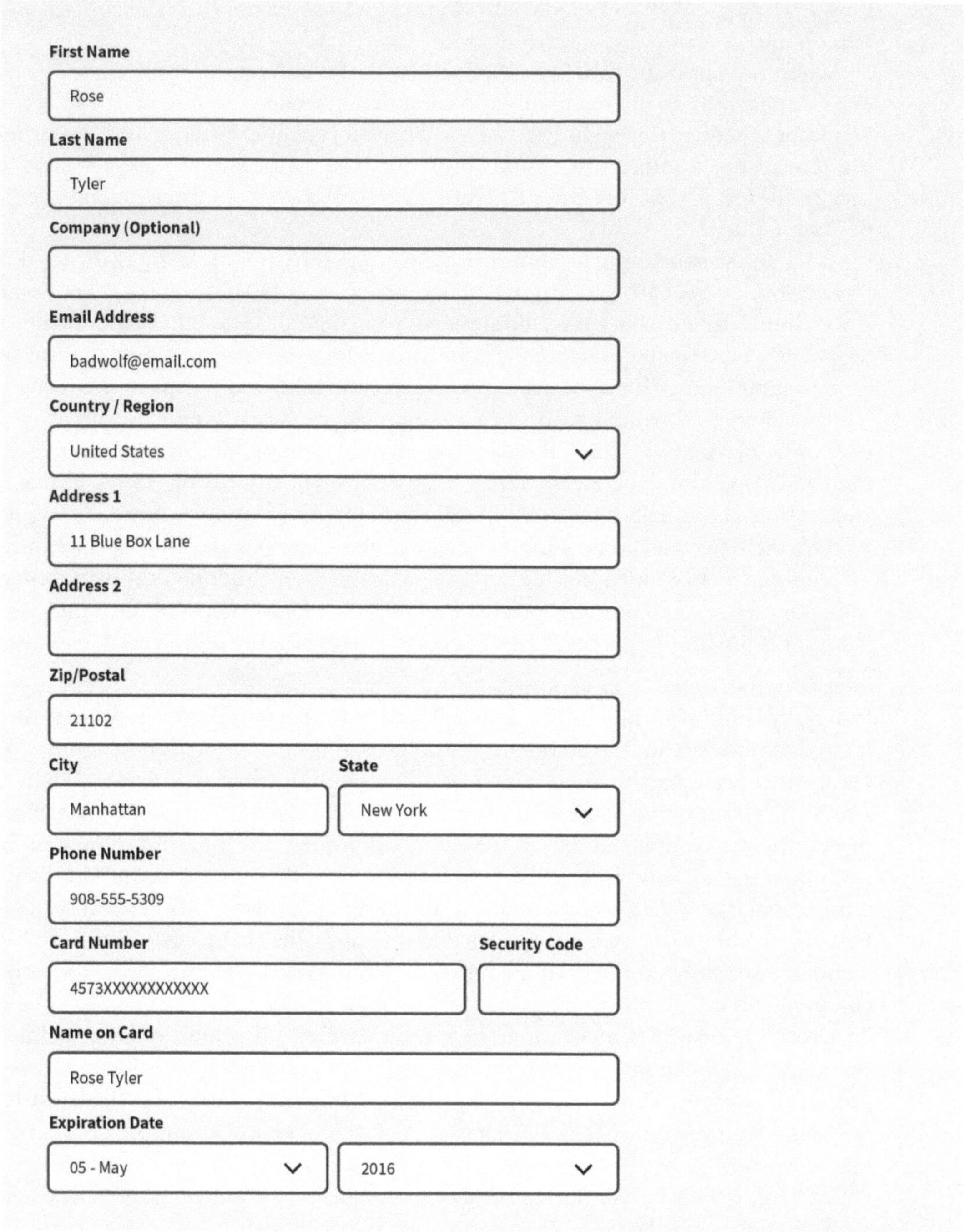

First Name

Rose

Last Name

Tyler

Company (Optional)

Email Address

badwolf@email.com

Country / Region

United States

Address 1

11 Blue Box Lane

Address 2

Zip/Postal

21102

City

Manhattan

State

New York

Phone Number

908-555-5309

Card Number

4573XXXXXXXXXXXX

Security Code

Name on Card

Rose Tyler

Expiration Date

05 - May

2016

Figure 2.13 This checkout form is just line after line of input fields, and the information needed isn't clear.

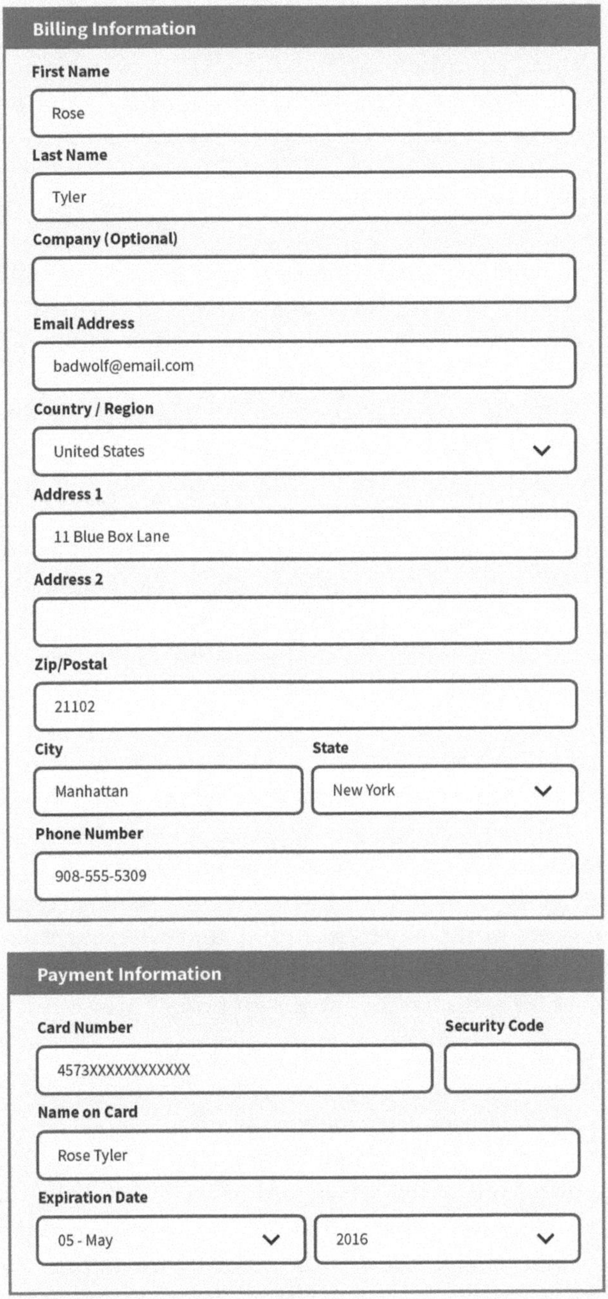

Billing Information

First Name

Rose

Last Name

Tyler

Company (Optional)

Email Address

badwolf@email.com

Country / Region

United States   ⌄

Address 1

11 Blue Box Lane

Address 2

Zip/Postal

21102

City   State

Manhattan   New York   ⌄

Phone Number

908-555-5309

Payment Information

Card Number   Security Code

4573XXXXXXXXXXXX

Name on Card

Rose Tyler

Expiration Date

05 - May   ⌄   2016   ⌄

Figure 2.14   If we group related input fields and add section headings, the checkout form becomes easier to parse when scanning it.

2.1.2   *Alignment*

The term *alignment* may bring to mind a number of different CSS properties for developers and how to position elements on the page with CSS. Or perhaps it brings to mind one of the most common layout problems in the history of the web: aligning text vertically and centered on a web page or in a `<div>`. Alignment on the web pertains to positioning elements along different axes, aligning groups of elements in a particular way to form a cohesive unit, and text alignment, such as flush right or justified text.

When designing for the web, alignment of elements is a bit more rigid compared with print design. In the software we use for print design, it's unconstrained. On the web, in a browser, we're constrained by the web platform and the code we write to define our layout. Arguably, it's harder to place an element randomly on a web page in the same way we could randomly place an element when designing something for print. Even with drag-and-drop layout editors for web pages, the dragging and dropping are constrained to the overall outline of the predefined site. You can drop random elements in, but you can't place them randomly.

As a developer, you're familiar with how to use code to align different elements on the page, but a level of structure to alignment is already built in via the web platform when using something like CSS Grid or Flexbox to define your page's layout. For example, if I set `display: flex;` on a parent element that has two child elements, the web platform now has a blueprint for how that layout would render with just that line of code. But if you're designing a website, you're most likely not going to use `display: flex;` on its own on one line of content. Here, understanding the principle of alignment is vital because alignment establishes order on the page.

Alignment is another way to organize and establish relationships between items on a page by aligning them along an invisible line. This alignment helps create the structure of a page and is also a key to readability. Even if you were to create a layout for a website that broke away from some of the more common patterns on the web today and appeared to be a bit more random and unstructured, the alignment of certain groups of elements could help make a random layout appear polished and structured.

DIFFERENT KINDS OF ALIGNMENT

There are two main ways to align elements on a page: edge alignment and center alignment. Edge alignment occurs when elements are aligned along a composition's edge and can be aligned to the top, bottom, left, or right edges, as seen in figure 2.15.

Center alignment occurs when elements are horizontally or vertically aligned down a central axis. Horizontal alignment occurs when the items are aligned through the center of their horizontal axes, and vertical alignment occurs where the items are aligned through the center of their vertical axes, as shown in figure 2.16.

Edge alignment and center alignment don't just apply to the groups of elements on a page; alignment values can also be set on text to help define that invisible line when all elements are aligned to the same thing. Text alignment can be done a few different ways on the web, just as in print. The different types of text alignment are left, right,

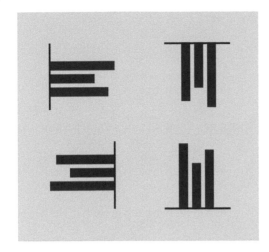

Figure 2.15 The different types of edge alignment. From top left to right: left alignment, top alignment, right alignment, bottom alignment.

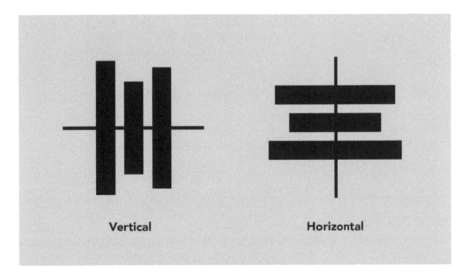

Vertical   **Horizontal**

Figure 2.16 Vertical and horizontal centers are shown in relation to their center axis.

center, and justified, as shown in figure 2.17. While left, right, and center text alignments mirror the edge alignment concepts mentioned previously, justified is a type of alignment in which the spacing between words is either increased or decreased to align both the left and right sides of the block of text. The main problem to look out for with justified text, as the example in figure 2.17 shows, is large gaps between words, which can form and thus decrease readability, as we'll discuss in chapter 7.

MIXING ALIGNMENT

While text alignment is a separate value to consider when aligning different elements, it is still a large part of a page's layout and helps establish order and a clear hierarchy.

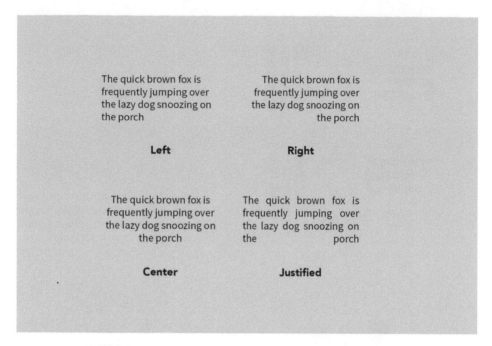

Figure 2.17   The different types of text alignment you can apply in design

In some instances, multiple elements, including a block of text, can all be aligned to an edge. However, the alignment may look mixed due to how the text, not its bounding box, is centered.

Mixing the alignment of items on a page can create a more unique and interesting layout, but it should focus more on the bigger content groups than on the individual pieces that comprise a group. Let's look at figure 2.18 as an example.

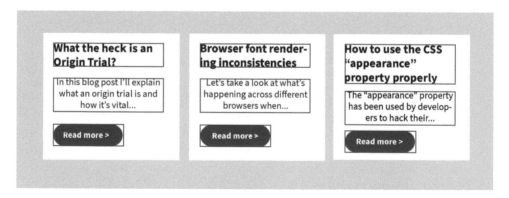

Figure 2.18   The bounding boxes of content are outlined to show that while elements can be aligned in one way, all our `<div>` elements—for example, mixing text alignment within those `<div>` elements—can have a noticeable effect on how cohesive a component feels.

We have a set of links to blog posts. Each blog link component consists of a headline and a snippet of the article, followed by a Read More button. In our example in figure 2.18, the blog title, the article snippet, and the button are all left aligned, as we can see by their bounding boxes. However, the article snippet's text is center aligned. Let's look at the components without the bounding box in figure 2.19.

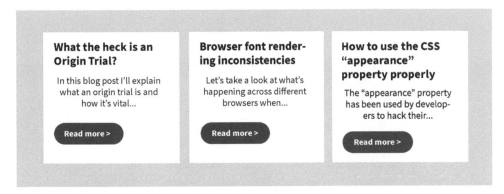

Figure 2.19 The text snippet in the middle is centered, unlike the headline and button.

We no longer have the invisible bounding boxes outlined, so we can see that even though the blog snippet's bounding box remains left aligned, visually, the text is center aligned. This design looks a bit off because the sharp edge created when all the elements are aligned to the left is disrupted by the middle text, which is center aligned. There isn't a clean invisible line along the left side linking the content. When we change the alignment of the text to be left aligned in figure 2.20, the shift in having a more cohesive component is noticeable.

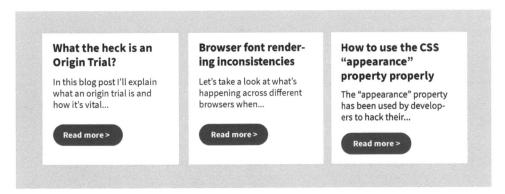

Figure 2.20 All components are left aligned and appear more cohesive.

This discussion isn't meant to advise you against mixing the alignment of items when thinking through a web page's layout. Mixing the alignment of elements can create a much more interesting layout, so focus on the alignment choices for components as a whole within sections on a web page.

When I was designing the website for the linting tool webhint, the site went through many different rounds of design updates. I recall playing with different alignment options for some of the individual content components. I tried to mix left-aligned text with content that was overall centered, and it felt unpolished. Instead, I focused on each section or band of content and alternating alignment methods to help reinforce the different sections of content (figure 2.21).

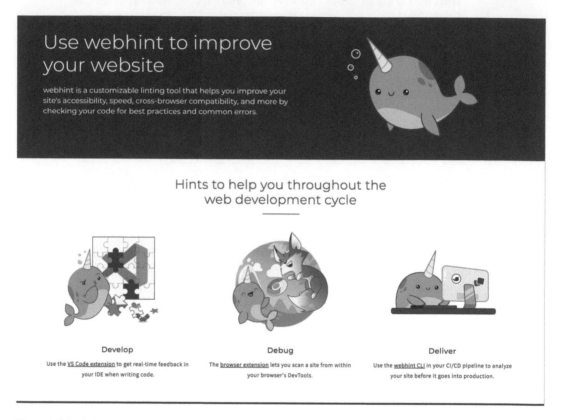

Figure 2.21   This example shows alternating alignment between sections, which helps differentiate the content on the page to draw the eye.

As you can see in figure 2.21, the first band of content is aligned left, and the second band has a few more groups of content accompanied by an image. Because the illustrations here do not have a hard rectangular shape like an image would, I opted to align the content of each group down the center. But the main goal of center aligning the content in this section was to help differentiate it from the section above.

Let's look at what this section would look like if the content was all aligned left in figure 2.22.

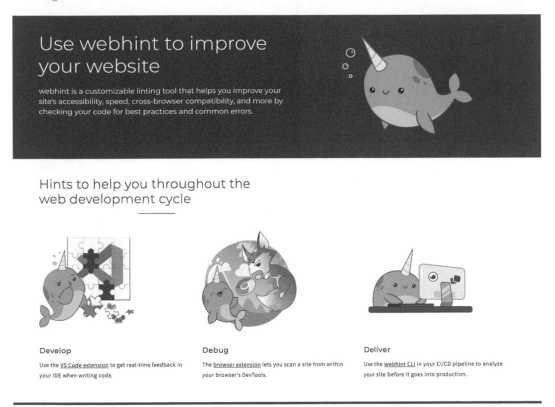

Figure 2.22   The second section of the website is aligned left like the top and bottom sections.

Even though the white band differentiates this as a new section, when we align everything to the left, it blends in with the rest of the page. The added center alignment helps drive home that differentiation between sections and reduces cognitive load when scanning a website's content.

Good alignment helps create invisible lines that guide the eye around the page and establish a sense of order rather than disarray. In figure 2.23, on a hotel website, we've listed a few hotels, and although they're aligned at the top, the different content lengths push the content in the right column down further than the other two. The names of the hotels are also center aligned, unlike the other component. That disrupts the invisible line that's formed on the left side by the different components that are perfectly lined up, except for that hotel title.

Figure 2.23   In this example, our hotel names are center aligned, and although they're all aligned to the same point on the top, the page feels disjointed and out of alignment.

In figure 2.24, we adjust the layout by aligning the hotel names to the left and moving them down below the images. The images are all the same size, which creates a sense of order. Even though the hotel name on the right still spans two lines, because we've

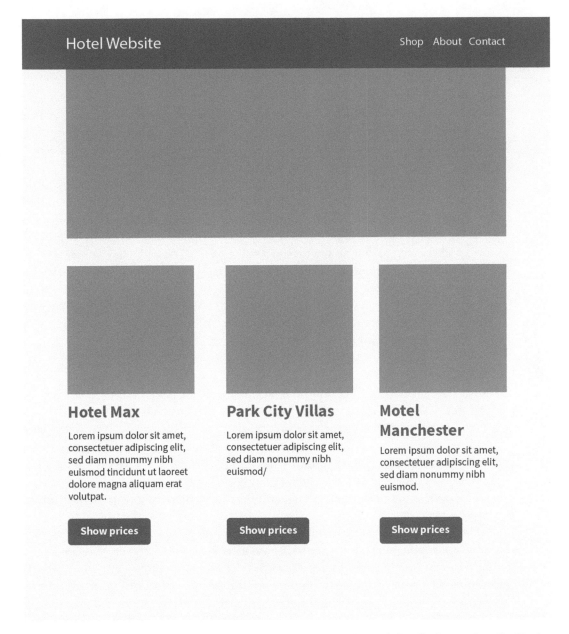

Figure 2.24 Aligning all the content to the left and moving the hotel name below the image gives the illusion that each component is a rectangle and establishes a more orderly feeling on the page.

also aligned the buttons at the bottom, each component is now the same size. The middle content doesn't necessarily have to align perfectly because the top and bottom components do, which creates the same-sized shape in each column.

The second example is much more orderly due to the invisible lines created by having all our content aligned to the left, across the top and bottom. Sometimes our content won't fit perfectly onto one line, but ensuring our top component and bottom components are aligned means that the middle content doesn't need to be the same size.

ALIGNMENT: THE KEY TO ESTABLISHING ORDER

We want our content on the web to be easily scannable and consumable. Establish a strong line and use that to align elements on the page. This alignment will establish a visible connection between pieces of content on the site and further help users understand the relationship between elements.

Don't be afraid to choose different alignments on your website, but look at those decisions on a larger scale instead of mixing the alignment of different pieces of the same smaller component. Mixing the alignment between sections can help distinguish sections on a website more effectively and keep the user engaged by creating a more dynamic layout that moves their eye through the content.

Good use of alignment on a website will establish a clear structure, even with more abstract layouts or more creative use of a grid layout. Understanding how to establish that structure with alignment from a component level to the overall page layout will help you create clarity on a page when exploring more creative layout solutions with more advanced grid layouts, which we'll explore in chapter 6.

2.1.3   *Repetition*

The design principle of repetition is the principle of consistency. Reuse the same styles and design elements, such as shapes, throughout a piece of work to create a unified and cohesive feeling and establish patterns.

Repetition has two aspects that fit into web design. The repetition of visual elements, like shapes or other graphics, can be used throughout a website to tie a brand together. On the more practical side, creating and reusing components and styles can help users on a website identify patterns in the actions certain groups of user interface components perform.

This principle is also extremely important to web design and writing web code. As a developer, imagine you were working on a large website project, and the designer created every single page differently and did not reuse components or styles. That would be a frustrating project to tackle, and the amount of unique code would probably affect the website's performance. Designing reusable components that can be used across multiple pages not only creates a cohesive look and feel across the website, but it's also extremely practical from a code standpoint because it has great scalability. If new pages are added later in a project, you have a library of components and styles to pull from, and that can help reduce the amount of code that gets shipped, which is great for site performance (in terms of reduced load time).

REPETITION: CREATING A CONSISTENT EXPERIENCE

From a design standpoint, repetition is the key to creating a unified brand experience across the web and print. Especially on the web, when we want to reduce the cognitive load of users coming to our website, repetition of elements and components is vital. We want our users to have a consistent experience across our site, so we reuse colors, fonts, and other visual styles to help drive that connection home and even help orient our users, depending on what section of our website they're on.

Repetition establishes relationships between content and helps the user quickly identify those repeated elements. If we look back at our simple blog post list in figure 2.25, we're reusing the same font styles for the headline and body snippet. With this example, we've established that the bolded items in this list are the titles, and the regular type right below the bolded items are the blog snippets. If we encounter this pattern of grouped content with these same styles elsewhere on the site, we could most likely assume that it is the same type of content: a list of blog posts or articles.

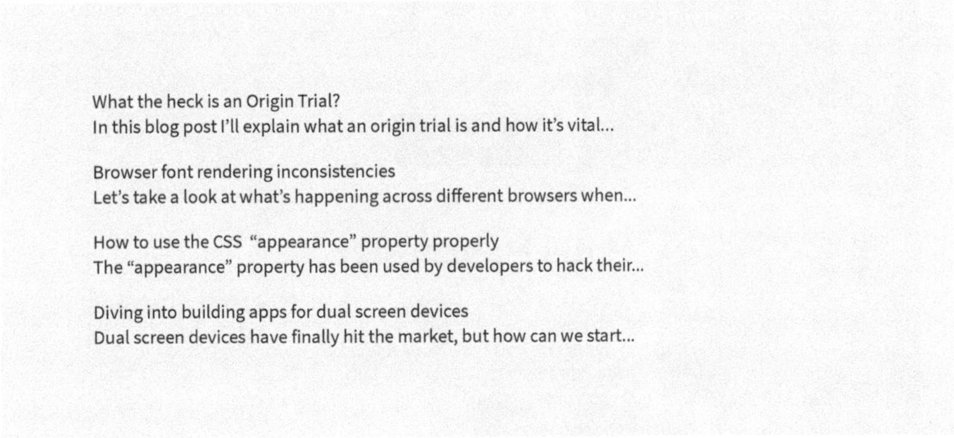

What the heck is an Origin Trial?
In this blog post I'll explain what an origin trial is and how it's vital...

Browser font rendering inconsistencies
Let's take a look at what's happening across different browsers when...

How to use the CSS "appearance" property properly
The "appearance" property has been used by developers to hack their...

Diving into building apps for dual screen devices
Dual screen devices have finally hit the market, but how can we start...

Figure 2.25   We've reused the same font styles for the headline and body copy to establish a pattern.

Repetition of patterns and styles across elements and components not only helps your users know what to expect when they traverse your website, but it can also help bring order to the experience. Let's look at figure 2.26, which shows part of a user interface of a hotel website where repetition isn't applied.

In this example, the images are of different widths and heights, and the hotels' titles are different sizes, as are the hotels' ratings. There's no clear indication why these things would be different sizes or colors. Each hotel listing has the same information, so there's no reason for any of these to have different styles, and it just ends up looking disjointed and sloppy.

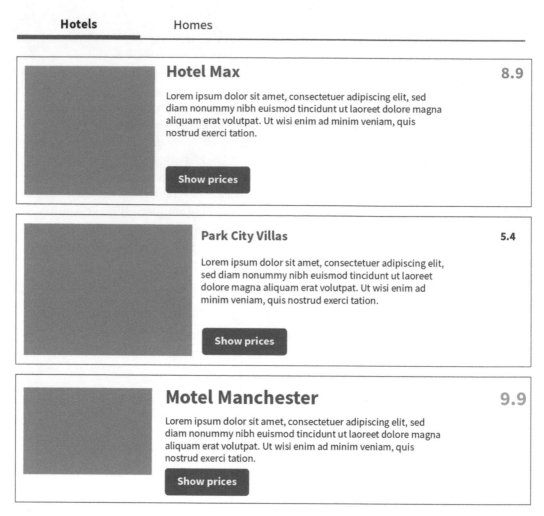

Figure 2.26   In this example, only the size of the text description and the buttons are the same, but this isn't enough to keep the elements tied together, so the page looks messy.

The pieces that are the same throughout each listing aren't enough to create an easily identifiable pattern. Let's look at a cleaned-up version of this example with the same style of elements repeating throughout each listing in figure 2.27.

The repetition of styled elements in figure 2.27 cleans up the page and makes it more readable. We're also better able to identify each of these items as a hotel listing and find its rating; we don't have to wonder what the different colors or different-sized text stands for. Users can expect to see this pattern throughout the site, understand that the content is a hotel listing, and recognize where to look for the information they're after. You want your users to quickly identify what they're looking at and where they are on your site: repetition establishes those patterns.

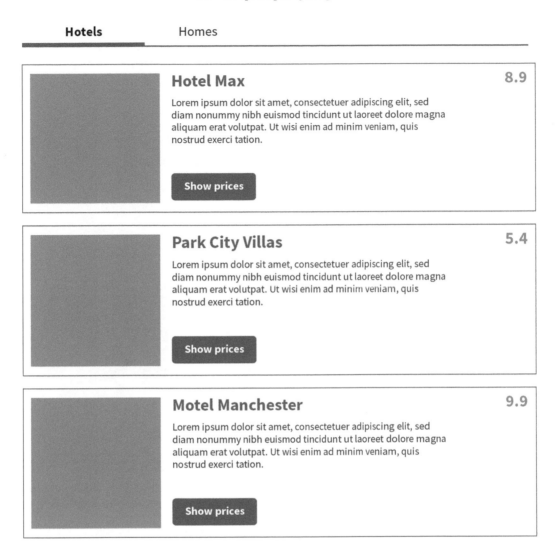

Figure 2.27   The page instantly feels more readable and scannable when styles and components are repeated in the same manner for each hotel listing.

The use of repetition creates a sense of cohesiveness that can span beyond the web to a brand if physical products come into play. Take the ipsa website in figure 2.28. The brand uses a distinct yellow as its primary brand color and a unique block-like typeface that is justified across each line. The typeface and the color extend to the product packaging that ipsa showcases on the website, and it immediately feels as though the physical products are a part of the same brand. They fit in with the site's aesthetic, creating a cohesive brand look.

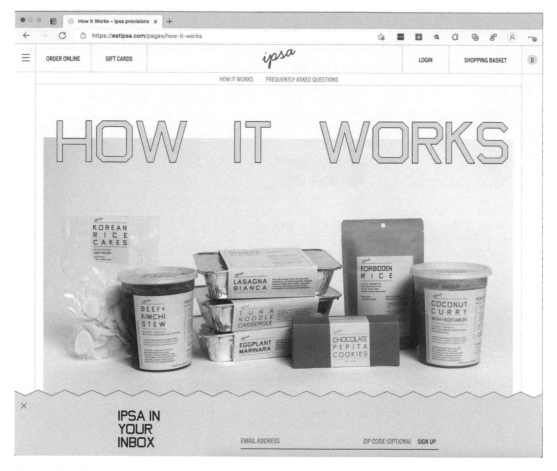

Figure 2.28   The ipsa brand uses a repetition of color and type treatment that extends from their website to their physical products to tie the brand and the site together. (Courtesy of Alright Studios, Brooklyn, New York)

REPETITION IN LAYOUT: KEEPING USERS ORIENTED ON A WEBSITE

Even the repetition of layouts on secondary pages and below is important. Usually, your home page will have a distinct layout that should catch the user's eye and provide information quickly but in short chunks. The pages that branch off from the home page should share layouts depending on the type of content presented. If you have three secondary landing pages, those should all share a template. Suppose you went a level further and added product pages under those landing pages; those pages should also share a template because they all serve the same function and purpose—to provide product information.

If you had to design and build out a set of documentation pages for your users, you wouldn't design different layouts for each page. As a user, I'd be extremely confused if I was reading through a page and clicked on a link to go to the next documentation article and was presented with a layout that didn't look like the page I had just come from. I might think there was a technical bug or the link was incorrect. I might even get a bit frustrated as my thought process has now been interrupted by a change I wasn't expecting, and I have to reorient myself on the page to ensure I'm where I want to be.

REPETITION OF UI COMPONENTS TO INDICATE FUNCTION

Along with using the same layout to orient a user, repetition can be used with user interface components across a website to indicate a component's function. For example, let's look at a set of buttons that are in a similar style to the ones I found on the LEGO website (https://lego.com) while writing this book (figure 2.29). LEGO used orange for its Add to Bag buttons across the website.

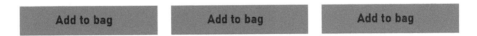

Figure 2.29   Orange buttons indicate the ability to add an item to the cart on the website. The use of color here immediately makes the desired action clear: we want your focus to be on the Add to Bag button.

Scanning the site, when we see orange, we identify that color as the user interface piece that performs the action of adding something to our bag. We expect this pattern because it's consistent. But after further exploring the LEGO website, I noticed that the button pattern started to change, with a mix of colors on the product group listing pages, as shown in figure 2.30.

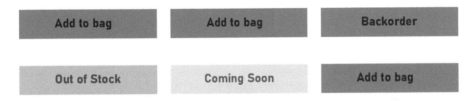

Figure 2.30   Coming Soon and Out of Stock use a fake button and different colors to indicate stock status.

Buttons indicate the stock status of an item throughout a page. Some buttons in the same orange as the Add to Bag buttons now say Backorder. If you can add a back-ordered item to your bag, why change the button text from Add to Bag and instead use a separate label that calls out the stock state?

Arguably, there's an additional cognitive load here with the three differently colored components that are visually, but not functionally, the same. Multiple colors are used to indicate that a product cannot be added to the bag. If we were to follow the pattern of having an item's button color indicate its stock status, the Backorder button should be a different color. One solution would be to design a component like a badge that indicates the stock status for items that aren't in stock, coming soon, or on back order and to grey out the buttons for items that can't be added to the bag. It would reduce the business of multiple colored buttons (some of which aren't even buttons!) and make that call to action to add to your bag so much stronger.

We want people to be able to quickly establish patterns to complete whatever task they've set out to do on your website. Reducing cognitive load is key to doing that. Using repetition helps, but we need to ensure we're using it in a way that won't confuse our end users.

REPETITION: ESTABLISHING RELATIONSHIPS AND ORIENTING USERS

Repetition is another principle that helps establish relationships between groups of content on the web by using similar visual elements or layouts of components and pages that share the same type of content or function. How we apply the principle of repetition across our web experiences needs to be done with care, as it can cause confusion if an established pattern for a certain task is applied across the website to other elements that may not share the same function. Ultimately, repetition allows us to tie an experience together across web pages and even into other design collateral, like print material, to tell a cohesive brand story.

2.1.4 *Contrast*

Contrast is the design principle that can most effectively bring visual interest to your website or application if used correctly—which is to say, strongly. With contrast, our intent is to draw users' eyes to a certain area of the page. As with all of our other principles, it is a way to establish hierarchy and indicate order on the page. Contrast is the most effective way to focus and guide users around the page. In figure 2.31, our eyes are immediately drawn to the shape that is unlike the others. It stands out. When using contrast to differentiate elements, the goal should be to make them extremely different if they're not the same.

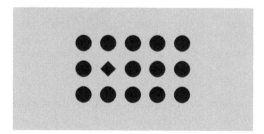

Figure 2.31 The eye is immediately drawn to the diamond that is surrounded by circles.

We like things that grab our attention, and on the web, that's vital when you're trying to get users to stay on your website. If they land on the home page and the content is all too similar, with no particular spot that draws their attention and gives them a place to start, they may abandon the site. Users want to be able to easily scan a page and identify where they need to go next. Using contrast effectively is how you can do that.

COLOR CONTRAST

Contrast can be used in multiple ways, and color may be the first idea to come to mind, as color contrast is critical on the web for accessibility purposes. Good color contrast on your website, especially in typography and form elements, is vital for readability and helps elements stand out.

Poor use of color contrast on a website can cause huge readability problems for your users, and that alone can cause them to abandon your site. One example I see frequently is text over a big hero image on a website. This pattern is common. But often, no treatment is applied to the image, and white text is placed on top, like in figure 2.32.

Figure 2.32 Some white text over an image that doesn't have enough contrast for the text to stand out

The white text over the photo, which has quite a bit of white in it, isn't the most readable. Font choice is also important. Another common choice I see is picking a very thin-weight font to put over a photo that isn't dark enough. Your users do not want to strain their eyes trying to read your website, so ensure you're overlaying text onto an image that is dark enough, like in figure 2.33, or there is some sort of treatment behind the text.

But images are not the only thing to be wary of when it comes to color contrast. A lot of websites, especially lifestyle blog–focused websites, tend to gravitate toward paler color palettes, which can be fine unless the colors used don't create enough contrast.

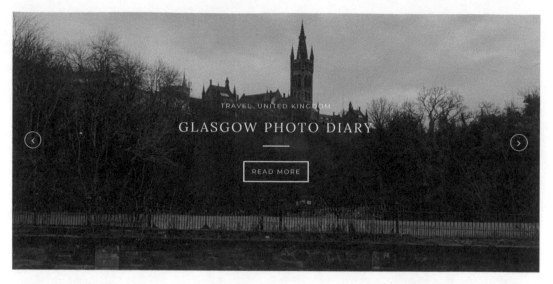

Figure 2.33   The photo chosen here has a much less busy background and is dark enough that the white text is brighter and more readable.

Figure 2.34 shows a recreation of a website footer I came across in an online shop. The owner used pale pink and put white text on top of the pink throughout the website. While it may look somewhat readable in this example, on a digital screen, it certainly is not.

Figure 2.34   White text on top of pale colors is a color-contrast nightmare and unreadable for most, if not all, of your website's users.

For the best contrast, you'll want to use high-contrasting colors for text on your site to ensure readability, but high-contrasting colors can also have other design purposes. High-contrasting colors—opposite each other on the color wheel, like green and red—can be used to create a very intense focus area. But we don't want to overwhelm your website's users, so contrast should be used to focus on bringing attention to the most important parts of your website. Too much contrasting color can lead to a design that is overwhelming and hard to scan, which is the opposite of what we want.

A great example of minimalist use of color to draw the eye is the website for a platform called Toast (https://toast.resn.co.nz/) in figure 2.35. Neutral tones are used, but one bold blue circle captures our focus immediately, even before the main headline of the site. Then, once we've scanned that focus area, we'll move to the next area with the highest contrast, the main headline, before continuing on through the rest of the page. The use of color here is minimal but extremely effective in directing focus.

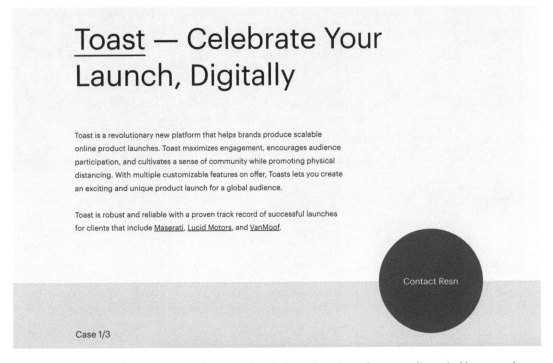

Figure 2.35 Focus is drawn immediately to the blue circle as the other colors are quite muted in comparison. (Courtesy of Toast!, https://toast.resn.co.nz/)

Another example of bold contrast is the site in figure 2.36. This site uses starkly different shades of blue, and we're immediately focused on the main title of the website, not just because of the color but also because of the size of the type. Clearly, our focus is meant to be drawn to this headline before noticing the paragraph to the left and then looking down the page to where it says Scroll. The contrast isn't overwhelming as only a few elements are in the viewport, so nothing else is competing with the headline. It effectively draws our eye through the page and onto the next section.

We'll explore color theory, the different types of color palettes, and how to apply color in greater depth later in the book so you can effectively use color to create contrast without it becoming overwhelming. But color isn't the only way to create contrast; you can also use size, shape, and typography to create contrast on the page.

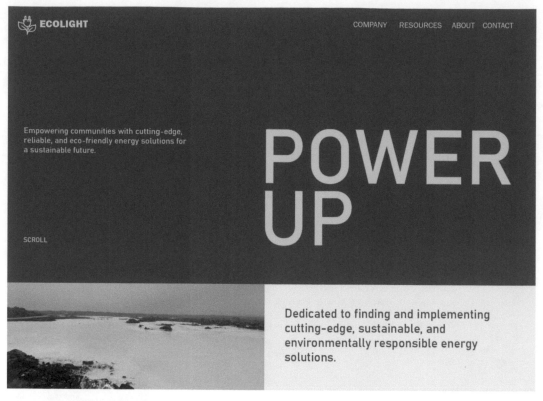

Figure 2.36   Contrast is created through large text and the bright blue text color on a dark background. The large font immediately draws our eyes to the right, then to the text on the left, and then down.

USING SIZE TO CREATE CONTRAST

Using different sizes is another way to establish contrast on the page. The larger the element, the more it will draw focus compared to the smaller items on the page. Figure 2.37 is an example of how size can be used to draw the eye. You are immediately met with text that fills the whole page, but it's not a lot of text, so it isn't overwhelming.

In figure 2.37, The European Review of Books website uses large text to draw emphasis. The page doesn't have any color drawing our attention, but the big, bold text across the page stands out compared to the paragraphs in smaller font.

Contrast is about making elements on the page extremely different to help draw focus. If too many elements are sized the same, the page can become cluttered and difficult to scan. Don't be afraid to play with whitespace here, either. Adjusting the size of the column width and increasing whitespace in the margins can contribute to contrast. The block of text on the right side of the page, while contrasted with the bold page title, also has a large chunk of whitespace to the left of it. This whitespace helps focus attention on the paragraph once we've moved on from scanning the title.

Using different sizes to establish hierarchy is an important part of building out a type system for your website. When scanning for content, we can infer from the different font sizes what role that particular piece of text plays on the website. The main title of

The European Review of Books   About   Read

The EUROPEAN REVIEW of Books

A magazine of culture and commentary

A new magazine of culture and commentary: the best essays, from many Europes and many languages. Online every week, book-length print issues three times a year. On books and everything else.

Good reading needs good writers; good writers need good readers. A good magazine needs support. This website is a start: an exploration, an *opuscule.* We invite you to imagine the ERB with us, beginning with a non-rhetorical question:

"Do we need a European Review of Books?"

(Our answer is yes.)

Sign up for updates	Subscribe

Figure 2.37   The use of extra-large black text on this website immediately draws focus. (Courtesy of European Review of Books, **https://europeanreviewofbooks.com/**)

a page should not be the same as a subtitle on the same page. When we scan the page, we're looking for similarities to piece together related content, so we want those styles to be vastly different.

Effectively using size to differentiate elements will create contrast on the web page and direct your users' focus to the most important information. We don't want to confuse our users, so use size to drive hierarchy and keep the page's design visually interesting while easy to scan.

USING SHAPES TO CREATE CONTRAST

Using different shapes can also create contrast in your design. There are two types of shapes: organic and geometric (see figure 2.38). Organic shapes are looser, often inspired by nature, and not rigid. Geometric shapes are things like rectangles, triangles, and circles and have a rigid shape.

Using shapes can dial up the intensity of contrast on a page when those shapes are the main focus. You can use a combination of multiple geometric shapes and one organic shape to draw focus to the organic shape.

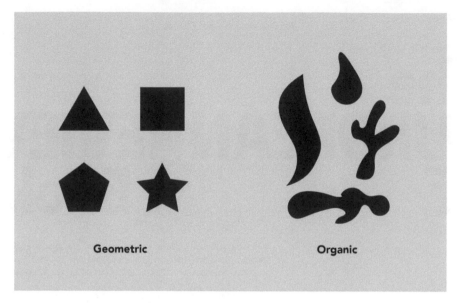

Figure 2.38   Geometric shapes vs. organic shapes

Shapes can also be used to enhance the design of a website by adding a more whimsical feel that aligns with the site's theme. In figure 2.39, the Calgee website uses organic shapes that align with what the website is selling. It's a shop that sells Omega-3

Figure 2.39   Calgee's website effectively uses organic shapes to align with the overall aquatic design theme.

supplements, which come from fish. The website has an aquatic theme, and the use of organic shapes similar to coral reef shapes brings a lot of character to the design.

You can combine size, shape, and color to really emphasize the focal point of your website. This effect is strongest on the home page, where you want to grab your user's attention immediately and then keep them engaged. On the web, we don't want all our home page's content to look the same. The home page is the chance to make a quick impression on users who land on the site, where they'll scan the page to assess whether they can complete a task or get the information they need quickly. Contrast helps differentiate items on the page and is useful in establishing hierarchy and creating an interesting composition that grabs attention.

2.1.5   *Balance*

Balance is the design principle that measures a composition's so-called *weight of visual elements*. It is vital to creating a design that feels complete and cohesive. An unbalanced design will look unproportioned and generally be overwhelmed by elements that feel heavier and aren't well-distributed. You may keep coming back to the same focal point if a design isn't well-balanced; a well-balanced design will move a person's eye throughout the design. This movement of focus is essential for our website's users. A well-balanced site will allow them to move quickly through the site and digest the different pieces of content.

Balance on the web starts with the website's layout and then adding additional weight to elements, either by using color, where darker colors are more heavily weighted than light ones, or by factors like the size of elements, the kind of photos used, and typography styles. These all contribute to the balance of a page and can throw that balance off when not distributed properly throughout the page's layout. Balance on the web has two main types: symmetrical and asymmetrical. Balance can be achieved with both types, but one is more predictable and a bit boring, while one is more interesting and perhaps more common on the web.

SYMMETRICAL BALANCE

Symmetrical balance is the more repetitive of the two. This type of balance is achieved by having the same visual weight on each side of a layout. The more precise definition of symmetry means that corresponding elements are arranged on opposite sides of an axis. If you took one half of a shape, repeated it, and flipped it to the other side of the axis, like in figure 2.40, it would line up against the axis perfectly and reflect the shape on the other side.

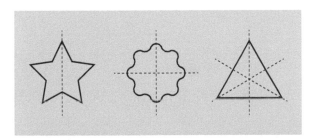

Figure 2.40   These shapes are symmetrical, and some are symmetrical along more than one axis.

On the web, you probably won't find a perfectly symmetrical design due to the difference in content length. However, you can build a symmetrical layout that at least distributes the visual of your elements equally and repetitively. The ENSEMBL website's landing page is a good example of a symmetrical layout (figures 2.41 and 2.42). A very clear and distinct line is drawn down the middle, making the grid layout quite clear. Balance is brought to the layout further down the page with the alternation of an image on the left and text on the right. Then, that composition is alternated below it so that the white space that the text lives in isn't all on one side. If the images were all on one side, the website would feel off-balance because those elements are heavier than the text.

Figure 2.41   This page is split into two equal-width sections, and while the right-hand side has more text, the white space helps counter the full image on the left. (Courtesy of ENSEMBL, **https://getensembl.com/**)

Familiar Products Reimagined

The things we own should serve us well – they should fit into our lives and enhance our experiences.

Find out more →

LIFE

Maggie Spicer teaches us how to stock a pantry

Figure 2.42 In this example, symmetry exists even though the layouts alternate each row, keeping items on the page balanced. (Courtesy of ENSEMBL, **https://getensembl.com/**)

ASYMMETRICAL BALANCE

Asymmetrical balance occurs when unequal weight is applied to elements, but they still balance the composition as a whole. Asymmetry is defined as simply having a lack of symmetry. Let's look at our example in figure 2.43, where we've taken the symmetry of our original examples in figure 2.40 and made them asymmetrical.

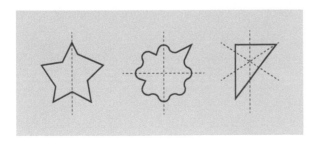

Figure 2.43 These shapes are not symmetrical. Compared to the same axes of the symmetrical shapes, the balance is not the same and is uneven.

This type of balance creates more interesting layouts and is especially good at creating movement when applied properly. Again, on the web, that's what we want our users to experience. We don't want their eyes to get stuck on one focal point; we want them to be able to scan and move their eyes through the different pieces of content on the website.

Creating an asymmetrical layout depends on the type of grid structure you use for your site's layout. We'll explore creating grid layouts and more advanced grid layouts in chapter 6. For now, let's look at the home page of the Whitehead Institute for an example of a well-balanced asymmetrical website in figures 2.44 and 2.45.

When you first land on the Whitehead Institute's home page, you're met with a block of white text in the bottom left corner and a cropped, larger version of the logo that fills the right-hand side of the page. If we took away the cropped blue logo shape on the right and just left the block of white text, this page would feel unbalanced with all that space. The use of color here is strong enough that this part of the page doesn't need anything else to bring much interest to it. It's already very bold. The white text on blue creates quite a bit of contrast, and the larger and darker blue shape offsets that and fills the space to bring balance.

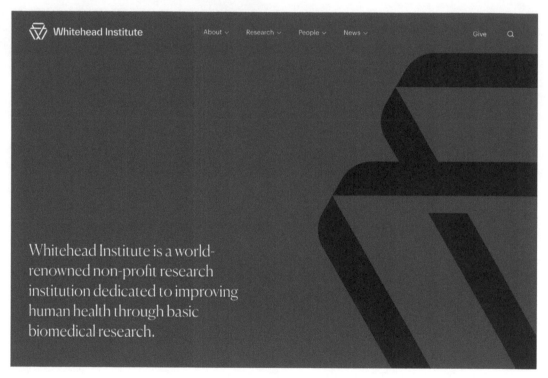

Figure 2.44   The Whitehead Institute's landing page is asymmetrical, but the two primary elements capture our focus and create a sense of balance. (Courtesy of Whitehead Institute, **https://wi.mit.edu/**)

When we scroll down to look at the next part of the page, in figure 2.45, this section continues to share the asymmetrical balance of the landing design, although the grid is

Recent News Read All News >

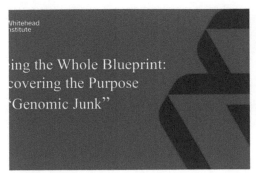

Cells are known by the
company they keep

TECHNOLOGY AND METHODS
MARCH 02, 2021

*Researchers conducted CRISPR
screens in traditional cell culture
media versus a physiologic medium
that more closely mimics human
blood, and found that the relative
essentiality of many genes could vary
with these different conditions. This
work further demonstrates the value
of studying cultured human cells in a
medium with greater relevance to
human physiology.*

Whitehead Institute
mourns the loss of James
Scheuer

AWARDS + ANNOUNCEMENTS
MARCH 11, 2021

Whitehead Institute and
MIT Biology seek
applicants for two tenure
track faculty positions

AWARDS + ANNOUNCEMENTS
OCTOBER 01, 2020

Ruth Lehmann talks to
STAT about the the
importance of basic
science and research
during the pandemic

AWARDS + ANNOUNCEMENTS
MARCH 05, 2021

Seeing the Whole Blueprint: Uncovering the Purpose of "Genomic Junk"

SATELLITE DNA
GENETICS + GENOMICS   MARCH 29, 2021

In this webinar, Yukiko Yamashita will highlight ways in which
fundamental research brings novel biological processes to light. And
she will introduce her lab's latest discoveries on the function of
satellite DNA, which has long been regarded as "genomic junk."

Figure 2.45   **The asymmetry of this section is caused by the size of the first column, which consumes 50% of the page width. However, the page is balanced by the next two columns, each taking 25% of the page width. (Courtesy of Whitehead Institute, https://wi.mit.edu/)**

much more defined here with the three columns of text. The asymmetry of this section comes from having two smaller columns that equal the width of the first column. Notice the natural flow through each column. Our eyes are immediately drawn to the largest blue image; we scan through the text and then come back up to the second column with the next image. Then we naturally continue through that text and onto the third column. The asymmetry creates movement and even helps establish hierarchy, with the largest column being the main focal point and the two smaller columns being less significant than the main column.

Often with asymmetry, one larger element will be balanced by several smaller elements. However, as we saw in figure 2.44, this isn't always the case; asymmetry can still be achieved with minimal use of elements. If we look at figure 2.46, just the skeleton of our website here looks off-balance.

To offset the imbalance here, we would want to look for imagery that could fill the hero area with our call to action, but that wouldn't be enough because the area below would still feel out of balance. We need to either adjust the layout of our stacked components, so they fit side by side to fill the space, or perhaps add a different component in that space that highlights some other piece of content. The goal is to make your

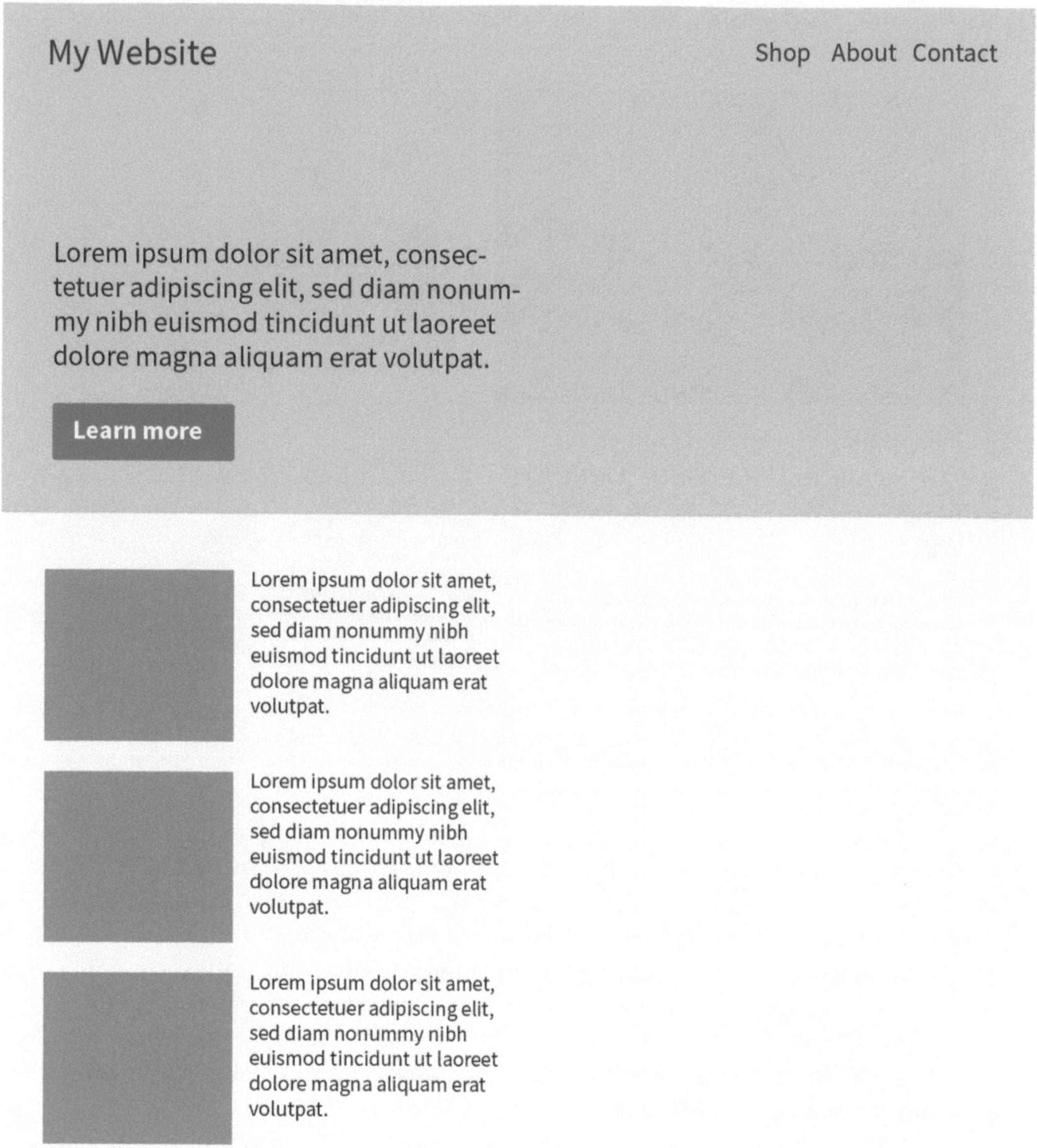

My Website   Shop   About   Contact

Lorem ipsum dolor sit amet, consectetuer adipiscing elit, sed diam nonummy nibh euismod tincidunt ut laoreet
dolore magna aliquam erat volutpat.

Learn more

Lorem ipsum dolor sit amet,
consectetuer adipiscing elit,
sed diam nonummy nibh
euismod tincidunt ut laoreet
dolore magna aliquam erat
volutpat.

Lorem ipsum dolor sit amet,
consectetuer adipiscing elit,
sed diam nonummy nibh
euismod tincidunt ut laoreet
dolore magna aliquam erat
volutpat.

Lorem ipsum dolor sit amet,
consectetuer adipiscing elit,
sed diam nonummy nibh
euismod tincidunt ut laoreet
dolore magna aliquam erat
volutpat.

Figure 2.46   The asymmetry of our website here is imbalanced and heavily weighted to the left side, and there's too much white space on the right.

website feel like the visual weight is even. In our example, it feels heavy on one side and looks a bit lopsided. It also looks incomplete because of all that white space. So, we want to utilize the white space to make the site feel whole and more cohesive, thus providing a pleasant experience for users.

2.2 Design fundamentals for user experience and beyond

The design principles we just covered all set the foundation for applying and building out the visuals for a website. Even before that, they'll help with initially creating wireframes. Wireframes are blueprints for your website layout; they can be sketches or a little bit higher fidelity and created in software.

These principles, some more than others, are essential in establishing the hierarchy and flow of a website. They will help you establish relationships between content pieces as you build out your initial wireframes, which we'll explore in the next few chapters. We'll first touch on the user experience process, and the different roles within, before diving into specific areas of visual design, such as typography and color. After these chapters, we'll go through a step-by-step exercise and design a web page to see how it all fits together.

Summary

- Visual design fundamentals are the building blocks of a well-designed website. Understanding how to use them to create hierarchy and basic alignment of elements on the page, although seemingly small details, differentiates a mediocre design from one that is well-designed.
- The fundamentals of proximity, alignment, repetition, contrast, and balance are the basis for any piece of a good design. They are the key to making a website easy for users to scan and quickly establish relationships between the content pieces. They lay the foundation for a website's visual design, and understanding them can help with the wireframing and planning phases.
- Proximity is the rule of relationships and is fundamental to organizing information. The closer items are grouped together, the more likely they are to be related, and the further apart, the less likely.
- Alignment is the principle that establishes structure within a design. When applied, it creates an invisible line between elements and brings a feeling of order. It also makes connections between elements via that invisible line.
- Repetition establishes consistency and, on the web, can help orient users. Repetition of elements and styles creates a unified experience that can extend beyond the website and tie a brand together.

- Contrast is the most effective way to bring visual interest to a web page and is the easiest way to establish hierarchy. We want to draw our user's attention immediately, so contrast should be used boldly. It can be created via shape, color, or size.
- Balance is the fundamental that measures the weight of visual elements and helps make a piece feel complete or evenly weighted. Balance on the web can be achieved through symmetrical or asymmetrical layouts. A well-balanced design will draw the user's eye throughout the layout; otherwise, a user may get stuck on a focal point.
- These fundamentals rarely get used alone, so mix and match to create a well-defined hierarchy and layout and more visually interesting web designs.

Part 2

User experience

This part of the book delves into the user experience portion of a project. It's essential to understand the user experience before starting the visual design phase. This phase covers more than just the user experience design phase and involves researching competitors, conducting user research and interviews, establishing who your audience is, and deciding what content should be prioritized when organizing content on a page.

Chapter 3 gives a high-level overview of what user experience encompasses, including the different roles specific to the user experience you could find in a larger company. In smaller companies, these roles are frequently combined into one or two positions but generally reflect the different parts of the user experience phase.

Chapter 4 is about the different types of user research that can happen in a project that shape the direction of a product or experience. The list of research activities is by no means exhaustive but covers some of the most common types that scale if you're working alone or with a small team.

Chapter 5 is where visuals start to come into play. This chapter addresses the design part of the user experience. You're figuring out content structures, how content should be laid out on the page, and the way users will move through your website or web app. The loose structure of your website design starts here, but you will not include precise details. You'll use the design principles from chapter 2 to begin establishing relationships between content and groups of content. These chapters lay the foundation for the next part of the book: applying visual design elements on top of your structure.

User experience basics

This chapter covers

- What user experience encompasses and how it integrates into a project lifecycle
- The different career specialties that exist in user experience
- User experience versus user interface
- Different frameworks for user experience that can aid in creating a plan to tackle a project

When I worked at a public relations agency on the creative team, it was clear we were the minority when it came to the type of work we handled. We were our own creative agency within another agency, and there were very few of us, so it wasn't uncommon to fill the role of multiple creative job titles per project. I became extremely accustomed to this experience as we moved beyond providing marketing and print and static digital materials and into building digital experiences.

Most of my team came from a background in branding or package material design. Because I was the one with some basic frontend code skills, I started to take on web design projects. This point was when I finally started to dive deeper into building for the web and when I fell in love with code. In my deep dive, I was also

59

learning about the breadth of roles within the web. It wasn't just taking my visual design skills and learning how to build my designs out—that is, how to become a frontend developer. I went in the other direction as well: I was learning about everything that needed to come before the wireframes and visual design. I was responsible for doing research, pulling together competitive analyses, and developing an information architecture. I had to build not just wireframe sketches but clickable wireframe prototypes before I could move into the visual design phase of a project.

The title I held when I moved into this role was Experience Designer. That always struck me because I wasn't given the title of User Experience Designer, which I felt was the industry equivalent at the time. However, looking back, I was responsible for the entire lifecycle of a project—from research to information architecture to visual design and development and even quality assurance. My task was to deliver the entire digital experience. The title User Experience Designer would have boxed me into certain roles later in my career, and I think my manager knew that. I was more than a user experience designer; I was filling all the roles of a team that worked on digital experiences. And, ultimately, I believe it was my combined knowledge of design and code that helped me land a job at Microsoft.

Now, when I think of the title User Experience Designer and how I thought it would box me into certain roles later, I consider it an oxymoron because of how wide a field user experience is. At the time, I thought of user experience as being just about design. What I failed to realize in my junior years was that user experience is a vast, all-encompassing field that goes beyond just visual design.

And, sure, part of the user experience process and the roles that companies or agencies commonly hire for revolve around planning for the features and the visual design of a product, application, or website. However, user experience doesn't stop with the visual design phase, nor does it necessarily start with the research phase.

3.1   *User experience transcends visual design*

Every part of a project lifecycle, from business or marketing goals through technical development, not only affects the user experience; it is also a part of it (figure 3.1). More often than not, developers are not included in those early phases of planning and research or even the visual design. This siloed approach to roles can have negative consequences when different teams don't work together from the beginning, especially when developers are not involved from the beginning.

When a design is handed off to a developer, they are the one responsible for bringing that application or website to life. They are creating the functioning experience for customers—the

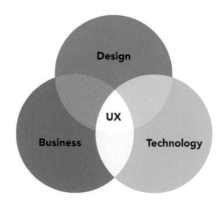

Figure 3.1   User experience isn't just about design; different departments all have an effect on the final user experience of a product or an experience.

end result! Excluding them from the planning or design phases runs the risk of causing delays in the development phase if a particular feature or design aspect either isn't possible to create or negatively affects the site—for example, slow page loading caused by too many superfluous animations.

Some career paths are labeled "user experience focused," which we'll explore briefly in the next section to clarify these roles and responsibilities. However, the main point I want to drive home is that user experience as a whole is not limited to these roles. Each person on a team—from marketing to research, design, development, and even quality assurance—directly affects the final user experience for customers.

You may not be a part of a larger team where different individuals fill each role, or you may be a freelancer who owns your own business and wants to take on more of this work yourself. In either case, understanding the different roles and responsibilities outside of design and development will help you identify work that may be unnecessary for you to complete in your projects so that you can work more swiftly by focusing on the crucial parts of a project's plan.

The other important thing to note here is that there is no one "right way" to work user experience practices into your workflow. The workflow or user experience activities that a team at a Fortune 100 company does will not be the same as those done by a smaller creative agency. Nor will they be the same as what a freelance designer or developer does. This overview of the roles and responsibilities helps set the stage for discussing the different frameworks for carrying out a project, which we'll address later in this chapter, before diving into the essentials of each user experience phase in the next few chapters.

3.2 What is user experience?

Before we can examine user experience roles and the different tasks those roles are responsible for, we need to define user experience. User experience refers to the interaction someone has with your product or service, including how that interaction makes the person feel while using the product.

Using a microwave and manually setting the time on the keypad is an interaction with a product. The different features and buttons on the keypad have all been designed for the microwave. Depending on the order or location of specific feature buttons, like the Add 30 Seconds button, a user may or may not be frustrated by the keypad design and the arrangement of the buttons. When my parents updated the microwave in their kitchen and I went to visit, I had a confusing and unpleasant experience with their new microwave because it used a dial to set and start the cooking time. I had never encountered this setup before and found it unintuitive and clunky. This confusion affected my experience with microwaves: I decided I wouldn't buy a microwave with this dial feature.

When someone interacts with your product, be it physical or digital, a few questions come to mind to help form their opinion of the experience. Is it usable? Does it provide value? Does it work well? The latter question is especially important in digital spaces because a buggy or slow experience can negatively affect a user's perception of your website or application. These questions all contribute to the overall view of the user experience. Peter Morville, an influential figure in information architecture and user experience, created the User Experience Honeycomb (figure 3.2), which represents the different aspects of a product that are required to create a valuable and meaningful user experience.

Figure 3.2 Peter Morville's User Experience Honeycomb defines seven facets of user experience.

User experience goes beyond just the usability of a product or, in our case, a website or application. Morville's honeycomb helps define the following areas to ensure we deliver a meaningful experience to our customers:

- *Useful*—Does our site fulfill a need and do so successfully?
- *Usable*—Is the site easy to use?
- *Findable*—Is it easy to find things and navigate through the site?
- *Valuable*—Does the site bring value to those funding it? Does it create profit or fulfill a mission?
- *Desirable*—Is it well-designed? Does it use branding, imagery, and other elements to create a visually pleasing experience?
- *Credible*—Can users trust the content and its source?
- *Accessible*—Is the website accessible to users with disabilities who use assistive technology to access the internet?

These different facets provide a high-level overview of a project's different areas. They can be referenced throughout a project's process to ensure that new features or content is aligned correctly. They're a north star to ensure that when we're designing and building a project, we're providing value and fulfilling a need, ultimately creating a meaningful experience for our customers.

3.3 *User experience roles*

As I mentioned at the start of this chapter, although every role outside of design influences the user experience, when we talk about careers in user experience, we usually end up focusing on the design phase. User experience design then gets broken down into a few more niche areas that don't necessarily always focus on visual design, which can be a bit confusing when we use the phrase "user experience design."

The areas under the umbrella of user experience design are research, design, prototyping, testing, and measurement. Some roles may have responsibilities that overlap these different areas. This overlap is a good example of how nonlinear or iterative a project's process can be. The following sections provide a brief overview of the different roles and areas, which we will explore in depth in the next few chapters.

3.3.1 User research

User research should be the foundation of any project, whether working with a team or as a freelancer taking on web projects independently. The research phase is important in identifying the target audience for your project and using different research methods to begin to understand their needs and behavior. Using this research is key to making informed decisions about how to design your website or application instead of just guessing what your users may need from your product.

Depending on the project, the research phase isn't always a single phase; numerous iterations may be necessary, especially when testing designs or prototypes before development begins. But even after a website or new feature on a website is launched, the work isn't done. Research still falls into the category of measuring things, such as whether the website or new feature is gaining traction or being abandoned or even how quickly users are landing on your page and then leaving. These sorts of metrics are vital for making decisions about what the next iteration of a project should entail.

3.3.2 User experience design

The actual design phase is where the site planning, layout, and visual design start to take shape. This phase encompasses work such as information architecture, wireframing, user interface design, static visual design (noninteractive design mock-ups), and interactive prototypes. The landscape of user experience design is constantly changing, and the responsibilities assigned to user experience (UX) designers can vary drastically across companies. Some UX designers are responsible for wireframing and the static mock-ups of a website but then hand off that work to someone who focuses on creating interactive prototypes. Others are responsible for the research, wireframing, and some level of prototyping before handing the project off to a visual designer and a web developer.

Often in smaller companies or startup environments, a UX designer is responsible for every part of the design process (similar to the role I discussed at the beginning of the chapter). At larger companies, these responsibilities are broken down into individual roles. For example, I worked with a user research team whose main responsibilities were to conduct user interviews and surveys and aggregate the findings into a report.

In the more traditional terms of design, UX designers can fill the roles with titles such as interaction designer, product designer, and UI/UX designer. In some instances, like those positions at smaller companies, a UI/UX designer is responsible for the entire visual design of a website, including illustrations or other graphics.

NOTE As previously mentioned, a UI/UX designer is a common job title I'll see on career sites. However, it's important to make a distinction between the two because while there can be and often is some overlap, UI and UX are very different in the sorts of tasks that would fall underneath each role if they were separate.

3.3.3   *User experience writers*

A good user experience isn't only about the features and functionality of a website or application; the other critical component is the copy that goes with the visuals. While visual design elements will draw a user's eye through the page (using some of the visual design fundamentals discussed in chapter 2), it's the copy's job to tell the user what they're looking at and do so thoughtfully.

A user experience writer is more than just the wordsmith for the marketing team. While the role will most likely involve working with the marketing team, there's an additional level of detail and thought that goes into the copy content. Just as there should be deliberate decisions around the use of colors, buttons, and animations on a website, there should be deliberate decisions about the words that are chosen. The role of UX writer goes beyond just being a marketing copywriter. For example, UX writers use research and user personas to craft copy for all pieces of the user interface that customers may come into contact with. They ensure the content is useful or helpful while being mindful of the overall brand voice.

A UX writer doesn't necessarily have to have a background in copywriting. I've worked on projects in conjunction with a writer who was focused on the main chunks of copy for a website that had a marketing focus, whereas I was responsible for the smaller bits, sometimes called *microcopy*, that directly tied into the user interface components. I've also worked with writers who fall under the category of technical writers, which is very different from a UX writer or marketing copywriter. Technical writers focus on content that is more instruction or documentation focused, like a how-to guide. Depending on the amount of technical content, an entire project may be built around the user experience of that section of a website, as the target audience may change depending on what kind of technical content you're sharing.

I've frequently filled this role of a UX writer in many of the positions throughout my career. Perhaps the most memorable example of a thoughtful experience, which I mentioned in chapter 1, is when I designed for the initial launch of the webhint.io (originally named Sonar) website. I crafted the design for the scanner queue page that users were sometimes shown due to the technical limitations of the backend database. I took the knowledge of our primary target audience and created a design (figure 3.3) that paired an illustration of a stressed-out narwhal with the main headline "Nellie's working overtime." That was followed by some smaller copy detailing the reason for the wait and providing a link to the scan results, which the developer could reference later.

Eventually, the infrastructure for the website improved, and that message was no longer necessary. Nonetheless, it was one of the key moments in my career that highlighted the importance of knowing your audience and tailoring the experience, including the copy, to them. This example also highlights how an experience is more than just the visuals provided. Without the written copy, this design may have created a negative user experience. Without that extra information about the reason for the wait, I'm confident that many users would have abandoned the tool and not returned, thus negatively affecting the project's future.

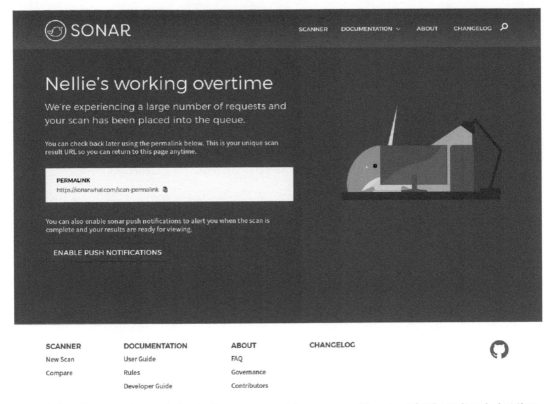

Figure 3.3 This concept page design for the scan queue informs users of the reason for the wait and what they can do in the meantime.

3.4 *User experience methodologies*

Just as web development and software engineering use certain methodologies, such as Agile and Waterfall, user experience can also use methodologies. Often these UX processes are combined with something like Agile over the course of a project's whole process, especially at large companies building an application or software that is in a constant state of iteration. Smaller projects may only go through one initial project phase and not require major, iterative changes. The frameworks we will review provide a general overview of what the user experience and design process before the code is written look like from start to finish.

These processes aren't set in stone. You may find a methodology that works well for the type of work you do. Or you may find that *most* of one works for you, and you remove the irrelevant bits. These processes are flexible and meant to provide an example of how things *could* be done, but not necessarily how they need to be done. Especially if you're a developer working as a team of one, some of these phases may be reduced greatly in the tasks you take on compared to if you are working on a larger team. You'll also start to see how the different phases tie into different roles and how role overlap can easily occur between user research, UX design, UX writing, and visual design.

There are many methodologies out there, and often larger companies, like Google, will create their own user experience and design methodology for internal work. But we'll focus on two of the most common ones: user-centered design and the double diamond process. These frameworks help you frame the progression of a project as a whole, from research to development. They can also be useful on a more granular level when focusing on specific parts of a product, website, or application. That is, these processes can be applied to an entire website project or building a new feature or part of a website that has already been launched.

3.4.1 *User-centered design*

User-centered design keeps the user at the center of every part of a project's process, focusing on creating an extremely usable product or experience. From ensuring the business needs align with user requirements to getting feedback from users and making iterative changes based on those cycles of feedback, the user is a constant priority in this process.

This particular way of thinking can be incorporated into how you already work. For example, if you're part of a team using Agile, Waterfall, or other methods, you can apply the user-centered design approach to these methods. Usability.gov outlines four general phases for user-centered design, although the tasks and phases will depend on how you work or where you are in a project:

- *Specify the context of use*—Identify who the primary target audience is, why they're using the product, what their requirements are, and under what circumstance they'll use it.
- *Specify requirements*—What business requirements or user goals need to be achieved for the product to be successful?
- *Create design solutions*—The different phases of wireframing, visual mock-ups, prototyping, and actual development happen here.
- *Evaluate designs*—Test your designs and prototypes, ideally with actual users, to gather feedback and begin the iterative process of incorporating that feedback into the designs.

These four general phases of this iterative process are displayed in figure 3.4. Depending on the type of project you're working on, gathering feedback and incorporating changes into the project may be continuous.

If you work at a company that builds software, for example, you may gather feedback continuously from your users and ask for feedback on specific features, which can then be applied to help improve users' experience of those features. Feedback can also provide insight into new user needs, which would kick off a new cycle of research, design, testing, and development. For smaller projects like websites or applications with limited use, this feedback process can be applied to the whole site or

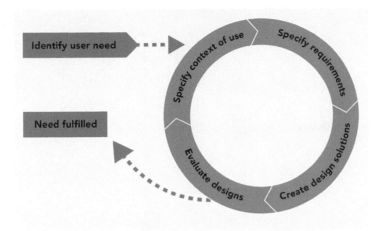

Figure 3.4 The user-centered design process starts with identifying a user need you are trying to solve and then moves on to how users are going to utilize what you provide, identifying the requirements needed to solve the use case, building a design solution, and evaluating whether the design fulfills the user's need. If the process does not satisfy the user's need, it restarts.

application. Ultimately, it depends on the project and its goals, but user-centered design processes should be applied when you want to make the end product the most usable for and satisfying to your users.

3.4.2 Double diamond process

The double diamond process combines divergent thinking, exploring a problem widely, convergent thinking, and taking focused action. Unlike the user-centered design approach, the double diamond process focuses on identifying a problem, defining the problem, and creating solutions for that problem. That's not to say users aren't important or can't be involved in this process. However, whereas user-centered design focuses on creating designs based on user requirements, the double diamond process centers on creating designs to solve a specific problem.

The British Design Council developed the creative process roadmap for the double diamond process in 2005 after studying and analyzing the different methods companies used to solve creative problems. Those working on this study began to identify common patterns among the different processes and laid those patterns out to create the double diamond process. It gets its name from the way divergent and convergent thinking are visually represented in the process diagram (figure 3.5).

As figure 3.5 shows, we start with the problem on the left. Divergent thinking comes into play as we next explore and research the problem. We then converge in the center to define the problem.

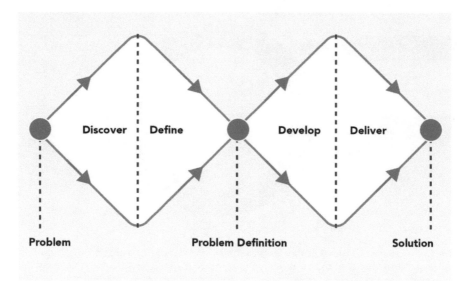

Figure 3.5   The double diamond process starts with a problem, exploring it widely and then scoping down the definition before widely exploring solutions and then scoping them down to one solution.

In the next phase, we again head into divergent territory as we develop many possible solutions for our problem before converging on one solution. Like user-centered design, we can break this process down into four phases:

- *Discover*—Data is gathered through research to gain insight into the problem.
- *Define*—Research is filtered through to focus on and define the problem to solve.
- *Develop*—Multiple solutions are explored and tested.
- *Deliver*—Solutions are honed down to the most successful one, which is then delivered.

Although this process seems linear, it doesn't have to be and probably won't be. Perhaps you define the problem to solve and build out some solutions to test but find that none of them resonate with users. You would then assess your feedback from users and go back to the second phase of the process to work on redefining the problem. These frameworks are just that: a framework that can be adapted and altered to fit your needs for a project.

The user-centered and double diamond approaches are two common design methodologies. Countless more exist, some developed by tech companies and others by design agencies. One process may work for a specific type of project and timeline, and another may not. You may decide to define your own. For example, you may want to start including users earlier or later in the process compared to what these frameworks lay out. These frameworks help define the stages and how a project process evolves. Try one out, see what works and what doesn't, and then go from there to figure out how these frameworks can fit into the way you work.

3.5 *Exploring user experience practices in depth*

I've provided a high-level overview of the different parts of a project's process and the common roles in a user experience career outside of and including design. Now we know what the general project process is and its different phases. Next, we'll start to dive deep into the work involved in those phases and roles. We'll explore topics like different research and testing methods and information architecture so you can start to decide which tasks in those areas are the most essential for the types of projects you work on.

Summary

The user experience phase of a project covers more than user experience design, where you would design wireframes that lay out the website's content. It also encompasses the research and testing phases of a project. Developers and team members focused more on business roles, such as sales or client relations, also affect the user experience, whether through code choices or by bringing client requirements to the research phase:

- User experience is defined as the interaction someone has with your product and the way they feel about it.
- There are seven facets of user experience, as defined by Peter Morville, that can help guide us to ensure we're providing a meaningful and valuable experience for users. Is an experience useful, usable, findable, valuable, desirable, credible, and accessible?
- Although several different roles exist in user experience, the tasks someone is responsible for often overlap with areas like research and design.
- User-centered design focuses on solving user requirements and needs first and foremost. It involves the user in nearly all, if not all, aspects of the process.
- The double diamond method focuses on a problem and finding solutions for that problem through divergent and convergent thinking.
- Although many different design methodologies exist, none are set in stone, and all should, at the most basic level, provide the different phases of a project. The tasks within each phase are ultimately up to you.

User research 4

At their developer conference in the spring of 2012, Google publicly announced a new product called Google Glass. It was a pair of smart glasses; the most publicized feature was its camera and video recording capabilities. Other features included a touchpad and a display that wearers could use to look up information quickly. It was a shiny new piece of technology and surely innovative at a time when wearable technology was just starting to gain traction. But due to the nature of this piece of wearable technology and the focus on its camera and recording capabilities, privacy and security concerns were abundant.

However, those concerns weren't only focused on the privacy of the people a wearer could encounter and record on the street. Las Vegas and a few other states with casinos banned Google Glass while gambling, and The Motion Picture

Association of America banned them from movie theaters. There were also safety considerations if someone was wearing the device while driving, which could reasonably cause them to be distracted. Many states in America now have distracted driving laws in place that will get you ticketed if you're caught on your phone. A wearable headset with display would be no different.

While Google Glass was presented to the world as a new cutting-edge piece of wearable technology, it flopped with the general consumer, although there were use cases for it in the enterprise sector. Initially, the focus was on the medical field, but use cases for Google Glass have grown in certain workplaces beyond the medical industry. This piece of technology has evolved since its introduction in 2012, but its target audience is scoped down. It is available to enterprises and isn't inclusive of the average consumer.

The flop among consumers with Google Glass can be reduced down to the fact that it provided a solution to a nonexistent problem or user need. From the consumer angle, the focus seemed to be heavily on the camera and video recording features and providing that via glasses. But what benefit was provided to users? One thought that a Google spokesperson put forward was that this product would be great for a parent recording their child, as many parents have (mine included, but with a VHS tape recorder) to capture childhood moments. But what average parent would spend $1,500, the cost of Google Glass at the time, on a pair of glasses to complete this task?

At that price, someone could purchase a very nice camera by 2012 standards rather than a new, experimental piece of technology you had to wear to use. In addition to privacy and security concerns, the design of the glasses was an additional point that probably deterred consumers from getting on board. A camera was clearly attached to the frames. I imagine most people would feel uncomfortable encountering someone who had a recording device blatantly attached to their frames and available to start recording at the press of a button. At least with a smartphone, there's a general pattern of how people hold their phones when they're recording, so most of the time, it's somewhat obvious. Right away, the product had a creep factor.

Based on the amount of security and privacy concerns, coupled with a mediocre response and lack of adoption from the general public, we can make some hypotheses about the lack of user research that went into the initial prototype design for Google Glass. This brings us back to providing a solution for a nonexistent problem. People didn't need such a unique and separate piece of technology for their photo and video capturing. The features of Google Glass didn't provide users any more benefit than what was already out there.

If more research had been done with users, the Google Glass team probably wouldn't have focused so heavily on the photography aspects of the product; it would have further identified enhancements the smart glasses could bring to their target audience. At the end of the day, the consumer flop of Google Glass is due to a lack of user and market research, providing a solution for an unvalidated problem, and making assumptions about what users wanted or needed, which resulted in a product that didn't bring any additional benefit to the average consumer's life.

4.1   Introduction to user research

User research is always required to build successful products that fulfill a need and are useful to the end user. Whether you think you know what users want or not, assumptions are not data. User research provides the data to make informed decisions and ensure you're building the right solution for your end users.

Often in my career, I've encountered someone who says, "Well, I have this problem, so others like me must also have the same problem. So, we need to solve it, and here's a solution." This is a perfectly fine starting point for an idea as it provides a rough hypothesis of a potential problem. However, it's important to remember that both the problem and solution are shaped by your biases, and it's vital to avoid assuming you understand your user and what they actually want to help prevent failure. Your solution may not be the most beneficial to your users, and if you're trying to sell a product or get people to use your website or application, you can't be the only one using your solution for success.

Whether a physical product or a digital experience, user research is critical to discovering what your users want. You can then apply the research results to your product to provide an updated experience, which can be retested to ensure you are on the right path to offering some benefit to your users.

4.1.1   User research seems costly, but failure is costlier

The iterative process of guessing what your users need and want, conducting research to validate these hypotheses, creating a prototype, and testing it with users to ensure their needs are being met can seem daunting and a lot of work. If you're working freelance, building in that extra time and cost to conduct research can feel burdensome. Or perhaps a client doesn't see the value of taking the time to do research. However, in the long run, research can reduce the number of changes you need to make by ensuring you're aligned with what your users want. It can even help prevent going over budget or extending a project timeline.

For example, let's say you are building a web application for a client. You skipped the user research part, and your client didn't provide any research. Instead, you go straight into designing the UI and building out the application with whatever technology stack you choose, still omitting any user research between the design and development phases. You get the backend technology wired up and connected to the user interface. Then, after you do all this work, you put the application in front of users for the first time just before getting ready to launch. You then conduct interviews and walk through the application while having your users in the research session provide their thoughts and feedback.

In this scenario, the feedback from the research session contradicts what you assumed your users wanted or needed from the application. You also uncover other problems with how easy it is to navigate and use the site. You were expecting your users to validate that you had built the right solution. However, due to the nature of the feedback, you find yourself going back and making extensive revisions to the site design and architecture. This rework delays the launch of the application, which is costly because you can't get your product out so that people can start using it. Going back to redesign and rebuild parts of the application takes more time, and if you're building something on behalf of a client, it may cost them more money that they weren't expecting to spend and could lead to a strained client relationship.

In another scenario, let's say that no research was conducted at any point in the process, and you launched the website for your client. But after the launch, the bounce rate is high. People aren't spending enough time on the application, or they're not upgrading to the "pro" version of the application during the checkout process. Your client is now actively losing money and needs to figure out why. They'll want to solve this problem quickly so they stop losing money, and you're now working in a rushed state to try to get it solved. It will cost more time and money that may not have been accounted for in the original project plan. Ultimately, it costs both you and your client time and money. In addition, having to rearchitect entire parts of an application to fit in with the code you've already written can be frustrating.

Both of these scenarios could have been avoided if some form of user research had occurred before the development process. Even if you're working on a smaller project with a smaller budget, user research doesn't have to be expensive. Many different research methods are available to choose from and can be applied to your project. There are also a few different items that you can work on defining and validating with users to ensure you're at least on the right path before you start the design and development work. This preparation can save unnecessary revision cycles that can take time to complete. Let's look at what you should work on defining when you first start a project.

4.1.2 Initial data gathering

If you're starting a project from scratch and don't have any good data about your potential target audience, you'll want to run some sort of research study. Research can include, for example, individual interviews, focus groups, and surveys. You want to concretely define your target audience and figure out what they need and want. In this phase, you should focus on gathering as much data as possible to build a base of information and data that will help you define things like user personas and identify potential user needs.

If you don't have anything to show your initial set of users or you're building a completely new product, focus on your competitors. Ask questions about what they provide or don't provide that would be beneficial to your users. This information about your potential users is available for you to tap into before you start designing. We'll look at some of the different research methods you can use in the beginning research phase to start to gather information and form hypotheses around what you want to provide your users or what problem you're looking to solve.

4.1.3 User personas

User personas are an important tool in helping define your target audience for your website or application. A persona is a realistic but fictional description of someone who may be a user of your product. It helps build empathy while putting a face on the user you are building for. Empathizing with your user is key to building a successful user experience, and user personas can help put you in the user's shoes so you can somewhat understand their mindset when they interact with your website or application.

As I'll frequently reiterate throughout the different project phases, validated data and observations are required to ensure your user personas are accurate representations of your target audience. User personas should be based on some of the data and observations you made in your initial data-gathering phase.

In the event you don't have the budget or time to conduct the initial data-gathering phase to talk to real users, you can still make some personas based on what you do already know about the user. You can look at existing support forums for similar websites or applications to help define a persona. The World Wide Web is a vast source of knowledge and can provide some answers when time and resourcing are scarce. If going this route, take care not to let your own bias skew the personas toward the goals or user needs you think you understand without research.

The information in a user persona can vary greatly. Some are more in-depth and have a lot of information, and some can be briefer. Let's look at what a completed user persona can look like in figure 4.1.

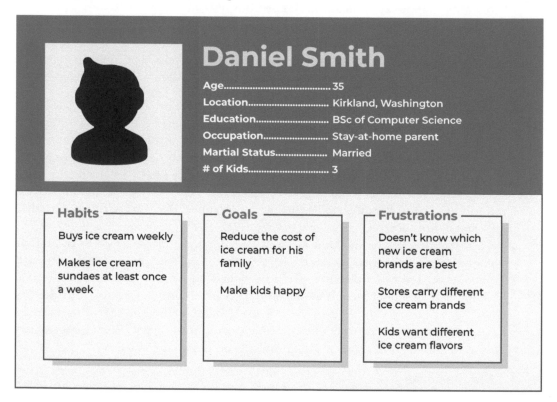

Figure 4.1   An example of a user persona card detailing one of our target users

As we can see in this example, the user persona details our fictional target user's age, occupation, marital status, number of kids, goals, and frustrations. These details are again important to help build empathy for the target users. These tools should be referenced throughout a project's lifecycle to ensure you're keeping the user at the center of your decision-making, even in the development phase.

Keeping a user-centered focus is an important reason for developers who are part of larger teams to be involved from the start of a project. Our end users don't necessarily care about the technical details of our chosen technology stack for a project. However, if our development choices somehow create a negative user experience and contribute to a persona's frustrations, that's an important piece of information that should be considered before development starts.

4.1.4 User needs

After we have our user personas, we need to define our user needs for our project. We want to determine what problem our website or application will solve. User needs, also called problem statements, are vital to establish before you begin more in-depth research and before you begin building your website or application.

The Norman Nielson Group defines a user need statement as the following:

A user need statement is an actionable problem statement used to summarize who a particular user is, the user's need, and why the need is important to that user. It defines what you want to solve before you move on to generating potential solutions, in order to 1) condense your perspective on the problem, and 2) provide a metric for success to be used throughout the design thinking process.

—Nielson Norman Group
(https://www.nngroup.com/articles/user-need-statements/)

User needs give us the problem we're trying to solve and set a blueprint for our application or website that focuses on that problem. Larger projects or applications that have multiple functions will have more than one user need, which could change depending on the page your user is on. There can be a hierarchy of user needs with one main overarching goal with smaller goals grouped by section of the website.

You may start a project having not spoken to any of your users or potential users, but you have a few different user need statements defined already. Similar to our user personas that can be created without talking to users, these statements should be validated before taking them any further. These are hypothesis statements and should be treated as such. They need validation and research to confirm that they reflect the actual needs of your users. Interviewing customers is the key to finding out what your users need, and we'll talk about how to conduct these interviews and alternative methods to gather this data later in the chapter.

4.1.5   *Defining site objectives: Aligning user goals and business goals*

When establishing the goals for a website or application, there are two aspects to consider: business goals and user goals. Business goals may come from the marketing team and will normally focus on, for example, driving sales and increasing market share, which can affect the business. User goals are what your users are coming to your site to accomplish. They can also be described as tasks your users are coming to your site to accomplish.

As a designer, you typically won't be responsible for identifying business goals, but it will be your job to ensure that end-user goals align with and contribute to the business goals. If you're working with a larger team, your product manager will be responsible for bringing the business goals to the table. If you're working on your own as both developer and designer, you may be asked to do research to identify the project's user goals. It will vary from project to project and team to team, but defining goals is an important step in the overall process. Let's look at an example of how the components and content on a page, as shown in figures 4.2 and 4.3, can help contribute to a business goal.

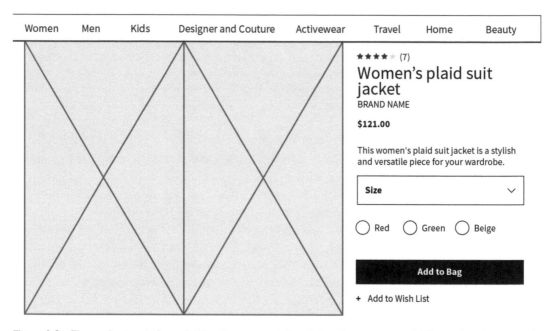

Figure 4.2   The product page for a clothing item on a retail website where you can add the product to your cart

A high-end retailer has an online and physical store. Let's define a somewhat generic business goal that is measurable and two user goals for their online store:

- *Business goal*—Increase the number of items added to the cart to increase online sales by 10%.

- *User goal*—I want to find a specific clothing item online and need to determine its availability, sizing, and price.
- *User goal*—I want to purchase this item of clothing.

The website design that we end up with should satisfy all these goals, business and user. If we look at figure 4.2, we see a wireframe for a product page. We'll look at wireframes in greater depth in chapter 5, but a wireframe acts as a layout and content blueprint before we start designing. The page we have here provides us information about the item, like the color, sizes, reviews, and a description. The two boxes on the left side are placeholders for product images. Figure 4.2 solves both of our user goals, but how can we increase online sales to meet our business goal with just one product page?

In figure 4.3, we would use a wireframe to propose a set of components that act like style boards. These would contain various products that would "complete the look" with the main product we're looking at.

From the business side, we want users to add not only the item they originally came to the website for but also additional items. Suppose a user scrolls down to read reviews or other information on the product. They're met with multiple ways to style the product and may be inspired to add some of these items to complete the look, helping to meet the business goal of increasing items added to the cart and increasing sales.

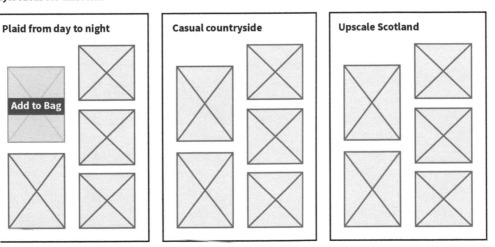

Figure 4.3   This set of components would be full of different products that pair well with the product we're looking at and could help meet the business goal we defined.

4.1.6   *Creating S.M.A.R.T. goals*

The important thing about defining user goals (and even business goals) is to make sure they aren't general and vague. Goals should be measurable and specific, which helps keep the main problem you are solving for users at the front of everyone's mind. This also prevents scope creep by ensuring that you're not building in excessive features that don't meet users' needs or achieve the user goals you set out.

In our hypothetical business goal for our retailer product page, the goal we established was increasing the number of items added to the cart and increasing sales by 10%. This goal is measurable and something we can track with the Style Ideas component to determine whether or not users are adding additional items to their carts. We can make a direct correlation between that specific piece of the web page and whether or not it is successfully contributing to the business goal. If our analytics show that it's not being successful, then we can continue to run user research studies, ask questions, or conduct surveys to find out how we could make that part of the page more useful to users and reach our business goal.

When writing our user goals, a good framework to use to ensure that your goals are effective, specific, and measurable is the S.M.A.R.T. framework. The original definition of each letter was

1 *Specific*—The goal is clearly and succinctly defined.
2 *Measurable*—The goal is measurable with data and analytics.
3 *Assignable*—Who will own the goal?
4 *Realistic*—This goal isn't a moonshot or overly ambitious.
5 *Time-related*—Within what time frame can this goal be achieved?

But some modifications and alternatives have been provided to help make this framework more applicable across other areas. In a 2011 article from *Smashing Magazine* (http://mng.bz/MBM8), author Dickinson Fong used some of those alternatives to create a technique for defining user goals:

1 *Specific*—What is the user trying to accomplish?
2 *Measurable*—What can we measure to ensure that users are being successful?
3 *Actionable*—We should be able to create and execute specific design and development tasks to reach the goal.
4 *Relevant*—We want to ensure that the features we add to the page meet the user's needs and don't make completing their task too difficult.
5 *Trackable*—Tracking the success or failure of our designs over a specific amount of time is critical to continuing to improve the experience provided to users.

Let's look at our combined user goals again for the product page and see if they fit the S.M.A.R.T framework:

- *User goal*—I want to find a specific clothing item online and need to determine its availability, sizing, and price.
- *User goal*—I want to purchase this item of clothing.

For the sake of this exercise, we'll combine the first goal with the second. While on its own, it is fairly general; it's still an important user need for our page:

1 *Specific*—The product page provides all the information the user is looking for as well as an easy way to purchase the item.

2 *Measurable*—We can track the number of times Add to Cart is clicked and checkout is completed.

3 *Actionable*—We can build a prominent Add to Cart button and provide size information, availability, and price front and center for our users.

4 *Relevant*—We don't want to add unnecessary information that hogs page space and takes our user's attention away from their main task. For example, if the product is available in a store for pickup, we don't want to clutter the page with the store's contact information and location.

5 *Trackable*—We can track the page abandonment statistics to see how long users are staying on a page without hitting Add to Cart and conduct additional research over time to find out if they aren't finding the information they need or what is stopping them from hitting Add to Cart.

Our user goals for the product page successfully pass the S.M.A.R.T. goal test. Data and research are key to improving user experience over time. This framework sets you up to ensure your user goals are reachable and effective so progress and improvement can be tracked. It also ensures you're defining the right goals for the specific parts of your website and not getting hung up on features or functionality that have no benefit to your users. Focusing on solving the needs and wants of your users is the key to creating a successful user experience on your website or application.

4.2   User research strategies

There are so many different methods of conducting user research, and we'll touch on some of the more common ones in a few sections. To help sort out all the different methods, we can categorize them across two axes: qualitative and quantitative on one axis and attitude and behavior across another (figure 4.4).

Depending on the project you are working on, you may have some access to user research or none at all. For example, if you're starting a brand-new project, you most likely won't have any quantitative data or a way to acquire it at the beginning of the project. However, you are able to acquire qualitative data by talking to potential target users, with plans to gather more data to test your designs after launch.

In a different project scenario, you may be asked to solve a new problem for an existing website or application for which plenty of quantitative data is available that indicates a problem needs to be solved. But you'll need to conduct more qualitative-focused studies to answer some of the questions that quantitative data doesn't address. Both types of research are important, and each has its place in the project cycle. Each axis can provide the other with insights and should validate the results of the other. If they don't, and you find, for example, that your qualitative results contradict your

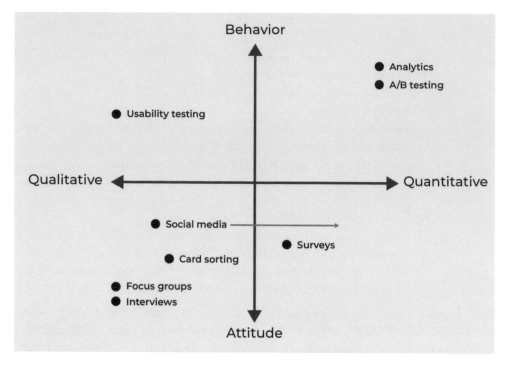

Figure 4.4   **A range of user research methods and where they fall on the spectrum of qualitative vs. quantitative and behavior vs. attitude focused**

quantitative results, it is important to dig into this and find out what disconnect is happening for your users.

4.2.1   *Qualitative vs. quantitative*

Qualitative research focuses on gathering nonnumerical and free-form data or, simply, words. Qualitative data is gathered through methods like interviewing, focus groups, and observing and talking to users first-hand. It gives us insight into our users' attitudes and behaviors and provides a way forward to start designing for what our users tell us they want or need. However, to ensure our designs are working as intended, we should use quantitative data to validate what users said they wanted.

Quantitative research is the numerical counterpart to qualitative research and is different because it is gathered indirectly from users by methods like surveys or analytics tools. It focuses on numbers and statistics. An example of quantitative data is the page clicks overview in Google Analytics shown in figure 4.5.

This data gives insight into what users are clicking on. If they aren't clicking on the items we expect them to, we want to tap into our qualitative research methods to find out why. For a more complete picture of research results, these two research methods should be used together to validate and support each other, thus allowing us to form a more supportive base for design decisions later in the project cycle.

Figure 4.5 Google Analytics dashboard that details page clicks and average time spent on the page. This data is quantitative because we only have the numbers; we don't have the *why* behind the numbers.

4.2.2 User attitude vs. user behavior

The second axis from figure 4.5 is a range of user attitude versus user behavior. Attitude focuses on measuring how users feel about something, their opinions and judgments. Behavior focuses on what users actually do. Sometimes these things don't align. Users may express a certain point of view, but when their actions are studied, their behavior contradicts what they had expressed earlier.

For example, you may have data from an analytics tool that tracks what buttons are clicked on your website. Your analytics could show that most users aren't clicking the main call-to-action button you want them to, or they're spending more time than you would expect on the page before clicking it or not clicking it at all. This data may be interpreted to mean that users aren't easily finding the way to this call to action, so their behavior is saying there's a problem. But when you interview your users and ask them how easy it is to find the call to action, they say it's easy and have no trouble with it. There's a mismatch between what the users are saying and what their behavior is demonstrating. You would then want to use your interview to demystify this discrepancy between the recorded behavior and recorded attitude. This data can help you find and solve your design problem, leading to more clicks on the main call-to-action button.

Like qualitative and quantitative data, both user attitude and behavior can provide helpful insights into how we build our products. Different kinds of user behavior studies can help us identify usability problems or whether different designs perform more effectively and give us better results than others. On the other hand, user attitude studies can help us identify missing features or functionality that users expect in a product and that we normally wouldn't be able to identify through observing behavior alone.

The qualitative/quantitative and quantitative/qualitative research methods axes create the four quadrants in figure 4.4 and show the vast range of methods available that can be used together to make informed decisions about the design of a website or application. The research gathered also helps us center our focus on the user and what they need rather than what we think they need or like. In my experience, presenting design decisions based on user research data is also much more effective than presenting decisions based on assumptions. The data should provide an answer to the question of why you're building specific features. If you or your stakeholders start to add excessive information or functionality that hasn't been validated by users, user experience can suffer. Your additions may not be as beneficial and could even frustrate your users, leading them to abandon and not return to your website or application. And losing customers affects a business's bottom line.

4.2.3 *User research methods*

We've identified the two larger axes of user research; now let's look at some of the more relevant individual user research methods you can use when building a website or application. Of the methods available, we'll only investigate a handful that are easier to adapt and use if you're working on your own.

CARD SORTING

Card sorting is extremely useful in establishing the information architecture of your website or application and, compared to some other methods, is relatively cheap when it comes to cost. At a high level, card sorting is a way to establish the organization of a website's content. Another way to think of card sorting is developing your website's navigation menu. You are asking users to group pages and content how they would expect to find them in your website's menu.

To run a card sorting exercise, start by writing out the main topics of content that will live on your website on individual cards or sticky notes or, if you're working with virtual participants, by using one of the tools available online. You could even use the design program Figma (https://www.figma.com/), set up with artboards, as a low-cost way to run this exercise. If you have titles for the sections of content, you can use those. Then, choose one of the two card sorting methods: open or closed.

In an open card sort, you ask users to group the content according to how they think it should be grouped and then provide a label or name for that group of content. This label or name would help define your main site navigation menu items. Do this with three or more users and note where content gets grouped and what labels are applied to identify similarities.

In a closed card sort, you ask users to group content into predefined categories as opposed to having them name each group. Again, pay attention to what gets grouped where to identify similarities or differences. At the end of either of these exercises, you should have a good idea of the site's content structure based on how your users would generally expect the site to be organized.

COMPETITIVE ANALYSIS

Competitive analysis is just what it sounds like: a chance to analyze and compare your competitors with a list of criteria. This list of criteria can assess a multitude of things:

- Visual design
- Content
- User flows to perform the same or similar tasks on your website
- Functionality
- Navigation
- Usability
- Tone

Document what you think competitors do well and what you think they do poorly. Identifying their flaws can be an important consideration when you start the design process so you don't make the same mistakes.

When conducting a competitive analysis, identify your top three to five competitors so you don't get caught up in an endless list of comparisons. By the end of the analysis, you should be able to identify areas where your product or experience outshines your competitors, providing things they lack; areas where your product or experience is lacking compared to competitors; areas where your competitors are lacking that you can use for your benefit; and, finally, areas where competitors excel.

The tools you use for a competitive analysis are up to you. You can use a spreadsheet program like Microsoft Excel, or for a more visual approach, you can build out competitor artboards in Adobe Illustrator or Figma. Don't be afraid to take a lot of notes, as well as screenshots for visual reference.

Building out a competitive analysis will also make use of qualitative and quantitative data. Qualitative data is documented as opinions on the design or functionality, and quantitative data assesses whether or not a certain feature or functionality exists in each competitor's product or site.

A competitive analysis should provide insight into commonalities between competitors that users will probably expect on your site and inform you about experiences to avoid and what experiences inspire you. However, don't get caught up in copying a competitor. Ensuring that you've reviewed a number of competitors means you can draw inspiration from multiple sources. Your product or website should stand out on its own and highlight its strengths, not be a copy of a competitor.

FOCUS GROUPS

Focus groups are a form of qualitative research conducted as discussion groups of 5 to 10 people. Focus groups are qualitative because they focus on the participants sharing their opinions, attitudes, and beliefs about a topic. They also allow deeper exploration compared to other forms of research, such as a survey, because the participants are present with you while you conduct the session. You're able to ask more questions about the answers being given, and you can control the discussion by asking specific questions that get you the information you want.

Focus groups can be used at any point in the research process. They can be used at the beginning when you're trying to get an understanding of how users perceive a product. Even if you don't have a design developed yet, you can base your questions on your competitors or a generalized product with no competitor names attached. The responses you receive can give you valuable insight into your users' likes and dislikes, allowing you to improve in the areas they found problematic.

When conducting a focus group session, select your participants with care. You want people who have an understanding of the topic to be discussed. The group should have a mix of people who have used a similar product and people who are prospective users. The purpose of a focus group is discussion, so if your participants don't have any knowledge of the product or product area, they can't participate in a discussion that will provide you with insightful answers.

Also, in addition to having someone take notes, record the session so that you can review participants' responses to ensure they were captured correctly. You can also catch anything that may have been missed in the initial note-taking.

When writing your questions, ensure they're open-ended, or if they're yes/no questions, provide follow-up questions to keep the discussion going. Start with some introductory questions to get a feel for the group and how much they know about the topic before getting into more in-depth questions. Let's look at a few examples of introductory questions you could ask if you were running a focus group on ice cream:

- How do you feel about ice cream?
- How often do you buy ice cream?
- What words or phrases come to mind when you think of ice cream?
- What things do you consider when buying ice cream?
- What brands do you associate with ice cream?
- What do you not like about current ice cream products on the market now?

These questions should open the floor for discussion and allow you to ask more in-depth or clarifying questions about the topic.

Focus groups are a great way to interact with your users first-hand and gain valuable insight into their perceptions and opinions about a specific product or product area. The additional interaction among focus group members helps fuel the discussion and provides insights you otherwise wouldn't have gained in a one-on-one interview.

INTERVIEWS

Interviews are another common research method conducted in one-on-one sessions. Like a focus group, the person conducting the interview asks open-ended questions to learn about user behavior, attitudes, and beliefs. Because the setting is one on one, user interviews can be conducted in person or over video or voice conference. Interviews can also be conducted at any point in the project cycle to confirm you're building the correct solution. You want to conduct interviews with a minimum of 10 people to identify common themes that reoccur between users and can influence your product.

Interviews should have a specific goal defined that you want to achieve. What specifically do you want to learn about your users regarding your product? Do you want to find out how they use it? How they feel about it as a whole, or how they feel about a specific feature or functionality? If we revisit the ice cream example, a specific goal we could set for our interviews could be something like "How do parents feel about building an ice cream sundae for their kids, and how could the process be improved?"

With this question, we want to discover how the interview participants feel about the process of making an ice cream sundae. We are asking participants to walk through the process of making an ice cream sundae. What's the hardest part of the process? Do they enjoy it? Is there a way to make it more enjoyable? Be sure to always follow up with the question "Why?" to get to the root of why participants feel a certain way. Ask open-ended questions, even with follow-up questions, such as "How did that make you feel?"

Use the same set of questions for each interview, and be sure to define the goal you're hoping to achieve by the end of the interview. Using the same set of questions allows you to identify common themes among participants, which could be things you may need to address in your product. When you prepare your list of questions, don't include leading questions because you want unbiased answers from your participants. If the question is phrased in such a way that they think you're looking for a specific answer, they may not answer truthfully.

Another important aspect of interviewing is making sure your participants feel comfortable and heard. Acknowledge when they answer a question by saying "I see" and don't interrupt or speak over them. One-on-one interviews are a great chance to practice empathy and can help you understand participants' points of view more clearly.

Interviews are another cheap research method to gather qualitative data. Because they are conducted one on one, you have a chance to really dive deep with each person and explore their thoughts and attitudes.

SURVEYS

Surveys are one of the cheapest and easiest ways to gather a mix of qualitative and quantitative data from your target audience. A multitude of free digital tools are available to conduct surveys. Your choice comes down to personal preference and the features you need to conduct your survey. Some tools offer functionality that will split a survey depending on how a participant answers and show them a different set of questions compared to someone who answered differently.

As with other research methods, establish what you want to learn from your target audience and draft questions that stay within the scope of your goal. If you're asking quantitative questions that require users to, for example, rate something, be sure you provide an opportunity to let them elaborate on why they rated something the way they did. When I was conducting surveys to get an idea of what web browser features resonated with web developers, I asked, "On a scale of 1 to 10, how useful would you find this feature?" However, I didn't provide a follow-up question to find out why they would or wouldn't find it useful. After realizing this, I made sure I included the option to elaborate on the reasoning behind an answer.

Keep surveys short and scoped to your goal. When I was conducting the browser feature surveys, I had a long list of features that I grouped into categories, such as CSS and JavaScript, and built the shorter surveys around these categories so that developers not interested in CSS features could ignore the survey.

As with any method that involves asking questions, make sure questions aren't leading survey participants to answer a particular way. Also, avoid asking questions that will only provide a favorable outcome for your goal. Such questions don't generate an accurate representation of what participants feel and can skew your results, which will have a negative effect later on once your website is launched.

Surveys also allow you to gather data from more people than you could interview. Services are available to set up a survey that will recruit participants, but more informal ways can also be used, like sharing on social media, which I'll discuss in depth in a few sections.

USABILITY TESTING

Usability testing is a task-based method of user research in which participants are observed using your product. This type of research can be done in a few different ways depending on where you are in the design process. Ideally, the testing will happen before you've started the web development process so you can identify potential design problems ahead of time and not have to rewrite any code.

In this case, you can use clickable wireframes or mock-ups. Many visual design and wireframe applications offer this interactive functionality so you can create these clickable experiences without having to do any coding. If you don't have access to these applications, you can get creative with an application like PowerPoint and import all the different screens of the user flow you want to test from your wireframes or mock-ups. The only difference here would be manually moving between slides instead of using an interactive mock-up. We'll explore prototyping and testing more in chapter 11.

Usability testing can also be done on an existing website to identify where the experience could be improved. Let's say your telemetry data shows that people are clicking into a certain tool in an application, but they're closing out of the tool within 10 seconds without going further. This quantitative data would provide a great starting point for a qualitative usability study. You would come up with a list of tasks and questions about the application in general and the tool specifically that people are abandoning rather quickly. Our quantitative metrics tell us it's being abandoned, but we don't know why. That's where observed usability studies become important. They provide a chance for participants and facilitators to interact in real time and for the facilitator to ask follow-up questions.

When running a usability study, whether moderated or unmoderated, ensure that the tasks are concise and clear so they don't leave room for questions or an interpretation other than what you set forth. If you're conducting the usability session on your own, record it so you can reference it afterward to ensure your note-taking is accurate.

Otherwise, if someone else observes with the sole duty of taking notes, that should suffice. After the session, you'll want to analyze the results, which should provide actionable outcomes for you. In other words, you should have some design changes to consider before moving on to implementation.

Unlike the other research methods we've looked at, usability studies can be costly. There are a few different areas that can be considered to reduce cost. However, between recruiting for the usability studies (which usually provide an incentive in exchange for a participant's time), constructing the study, analyzing and gathering results from the study, and where and how you conduct the study, it's going to be costly, whether that's in time or money. Be sure to establish clear goals for what information you want to gain from running usability studies so that you have action items to complete afterward. Although there's no such thing as a perfect experience, usability tests will tell you where you should strive to improve your design while also saving valuable developer hours by not having to rewrite features and functionality after they've been built.

INFORMAL METHODS

Finally, I want to look at informal methods of user research. The internet is a vast archive of user data that can be tapped into, whether it's social media or online forums and message boards. The web has both qualitative and quantitative data ready to be gleaned.

One of my favorite research methods for a quick and informal gut check on something is utilizing Twitter for both the qualitative and quantitative aspects by conducting a Twitter poll. If I have a few pieces of data and a hypothesis or want to get a signal from developers on whether something needs more formal research, Twitter is my go-to, but it is absolutely not my only tool. Your Twitter audience can be its own bubble and may skew more one way than another. For example, my following on the platform is comprised of not just tech-savvy people, but many who are interested in the cutting-edge of web development. They want to try out the next shiny tool or framework and usually aren't limited by what technology stack they can use.

This description isn't accurate for the whole developer community. If I conduct initial research on Twitter, I then follow up with a survey that isn't built into Twitter so that other participants can respond.

If you're on a low budget, use social media and other online platforms to broaden your reach for data. But following up with more formal research methods is vital to help validate the data you gathered and ensure your data is good and that you should act on it. These informal methods offer a quick and low-cost solution for some of that initial data gathering to get a project started.

4.2.4 *Research as a continuous phase*

From project start to finish, research should ideally be built into each phase. Conducting research through the development process guarantees you're constantly getting feedback from your target audience and prospective users. It also ensures that your users stay centered throughout the project cycle. Remember, you're building your website, application, or product for them first and foremost.

In chapter 11, we'll explore this cycle of iteration. We'll focus on different types of prototyping and some more hands-on testing methods for when you have a design or the minimal viable product of your website up and running.

Summary

- Starting a project off with research to ensure you're solving an actual business or user need or problem can help ensure you're not building something that won't be used.

- The initial research will ensure you have a solid direction for your product that will inform the design decisions from both user experience and visual design standpoints.

- Before you begin any design for a project, start with some form of research to inform your design decisions.

- Letting research inform your design decisions, especially for larger projects, can help prevent costly revisions later in the cycle that could affect the bottom line. Starting with research ensures you have a solid foundation to begin designing from and focuses your users' needs at the center of your design.

- Multiple research methods fall into categories that provide qualitative and quantitative data and that measure user behavior and user attitude. Picking a combination of these methods will ensure that you have data to back up each one.

- Numerical data like analytics should be verified by running qualitative studies or asking qualitative-focused questions to back up the numbers.

- User attitudes, opinions, and feedback should be measured with quantitative data to provide a base that supports those opinions. If your qualitative data isn't backed up by quantitative data, or vice versa, this discrepancy is worth exploring in depth as your users may be confused or unclear about what's being asked. This disconnect should be used as an opportunity to provide your users with greater clarity and a better product experience.

- Research isn't a one-and-done phase. While some methods are more appropriate for a particular project phase, others can be used throughout the entire cycle.

User experience design

5

This chapter covers

- Defining information architecture and its usefulness for website and content planning
- How to organize and structure website data and/or content
- How to build user flow diagrams to identify the paths a user can take to complete tasks on a website or application
- The visual cycle, beginning with wireframing, followed by visual design and prototyping

Before you can start building a house's structure, you must have your foundation in place. That is what your initial user research insights are—the foundation for the rest of your website or application. These insights equip you with a solid start to begin designing a solution focused on your users' needs.

As discussed in chapter 3, *user experience design* is a broad phrase because it can cover many different aspects that aren't necessarily considered design as you may think of it. In one of my roles, my title was Experience Designer, which encompasses the phase of work we'll discuss in this chapter.

This phase covers not only the visual look and feel of the site and the user interface but also building a website's scaffolding using information architecture and wireframes, as well as interaction and how a user flows through your website. It involves planning and building out the whole visual experience of the website before moving on to the development phase.

5.1   *Information architecture*

If you've ever been to a maze or labyrinth, you know it's intimidating when you start! When you enter, you have no idea which way to go to make your way to the end of it. If you don't have any clues, you end up wandering about, hoping that the way you picked doesn't lead you to a dead end from which you then must backtrack and pick a new path to attempt to get to your goal. When users land on your website or application, they are attempting to reach a goal and should have a clear idea of where to start their journey through your product. While your website may initially feel like a labyrinth to a user upon first reaching your page, they should be able to deduce where to click to find what they're looking for. This experience should continue through the website.

You don't want your users to feel like they're wandering through a labyrinth when they're on your website. If they hit dead ends and have to backtrack or are unsure of the next step to take, their frustration is bound to grow and, with it, their chance of abandoning your website before completing their task. Depending on the main goal of the website or application, user frustration can lead to a loss in revenue and sales. Thus, the information architecture of your website is critical to get right. This phase of the project is when your user research starts to come into play. If you conducted a card sorting exercise with users, those results can help inform how you structure the navigation and group content based on what your users would generally expect.

Information architecture on the web or for your app is about structuring and organizing data and content and labeling it, as well as establishing relationships between the different pages and pieces of content. It also informs the navigation and content strategy of the website. Successful information architecture helps orient users on your website by telling them exactly where they are, what they're looking at, and what may come next when they click through the website to complete whatever task they've come to accomplish. When done correctly, it keeps your users from feeling lost and can even be used as a baseline in the beginning to assess the usability of your website. For example, when you're labeling the different pages and content, you may realize it takes too many steps for a user to complete the main task of the website; therefore, you need to reduce how many steps it takes to get there. Having your information architecture materials planned out before you start to build wireframes will help identify these points if they exist and streamline the experience.

This preparation can prevent you from wasting time building out wireframes and mock-ups for pages or content you don't need. It can also help identify gaps in the user flow where you may need to add another page or more content.

This step in the project is all about laying a foundation before you begin to design to ensure that business and customer needs are being met by documenting the website structure and types of content found on each page. Usually, this phase is full of spreadsheets, text-focused documents, and charts. Having all this documentation in one place in an easy-to-read spreadsheet is especially useful when working with other team members like writers, content strategists, or business counterparts. It gives a plain view of what will be included on the website from a content perspective and can serve as a checklist for not just the design portion of the project but also for the content writing.

It's good to have all the website structure and content documented for any size website; however, it's especially important with larger, content-heavy websites that can have 50 or more pages of content, such as news or research-focused science websites. This documentation of the structure and content is vital to ensuring content not only gets grouped correctly but also gets tracked to prevent duplication of work when it comes to writing content. Let's look at some of the different ways to document the information architecture of your website or application.

5.1.1 Site mapping

A sitemap is exactly what it sounds like: a map of your website's structure and content. It provides a more visual look at a website's structure and is usually in some form of a chart that shows the hierarchy and relationships between the pages of content. Often the sitemap will also help inform the website's top-level navigation but isn't necessarily an exact copy of the navigation, depending on how in depth the sitemap details the content. In general, it is a breakdown of all the major landing pages and subpages. Let's look at a few examples of sitemaps, starting with figure 5.1.

CREATING A SITEMAP

Depending on how big the website or application you're building is, you may want to limit how much you document in your sitemap to save time. Sitemaps should provide a high-level overview of the type of content you'd expect to see on the page. You don't need to include every individual page of a larger, content-heavy website in the sitemap. For example, if you are working on an e-commerce website that has hundreds of product pages, there's no use in documenting every one of those pages in the sitemap—just how you can get to them.

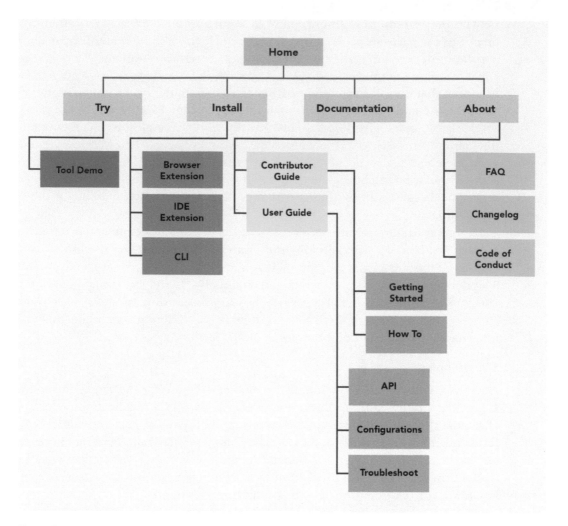

Figure 5.1   An example of how a sitemap may be laid out

Ultimately, your client's expectations and whether you're working with a design team should determine how detailed your sitemap will be. For example, the website map in figure 5.2 goes beyond just documenting the main landing points. Alternatively, you may choose to place this type of content in a spreadsheet that includes content inventory information.

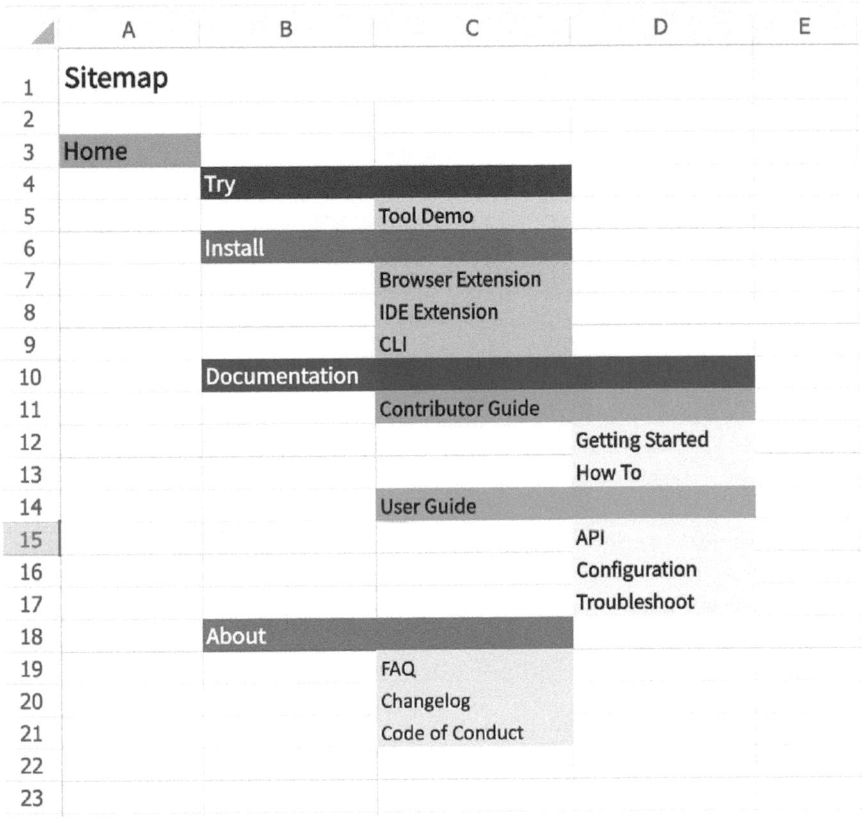

◢	A	B	C	D	E
1	**Sitemap**				
2					
3	**Home**				
4		**Try**			
5			Tool Demo		
6		**Install**			
7			Browser Extension		
8			IDE Extension		
9			CLI		
10		**Documentation**			
11			Contributor Guide		
12				Getting Started	
13				How To	
14			User Guide		
15				API	
16				Configuration	
17				Troubleshoot	
18		**About**			
19			FAQ		
20			Changelog		
21			Code of Conduct		
22					
23					

Figure 5.2   An example of a sitemap in a spreadsheet

Sitemaps also have a technical use once the website is live. The sitemap can be included in the footer, like in figure 5.3. Having a sitemap on the website gives users a clear view in one place of your site's main sections, which can be helpful if they're unsure of where they need to go.

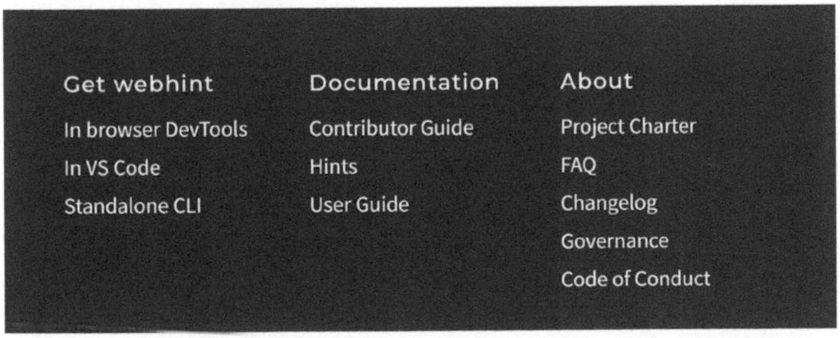

Get webhint	Documentation	About
In browser DevTools	Contributor Guide	Project Charter
In VS Code	Hints	FAQ
Standalone CLI	User Guide	Changelog
		Governance
		Code of Conduct

Figure 5.3   A sitemap displayed in the footer of a website that highlights the main landing points

Developers can also go a step further and create a sitemap in an XML document, either by hand or by using available tools to generate the file. This document provides browser search engines information about the website and adds an SEO benefit. A visual sitemap, developed early in the process, can later inform this XML document, created in the development phase, and speed up its creation if you're coding it by hand rather than by using an automated tool.

A sitemap can be built in a number of ways, but its ultimate purpose is to give a high-level overview of the website's structure, hierarchy of the pages, and, if applicable, how pages are linked. It can help inform later user flows, also called *journey maps*, which represent a user's journey through your website or application; we'll cover journey maps in more detail in the coming sections.

> TIP   Often, when building out a website, we and our clients may have opinions on what we think is the best way to group and display content. We think we know best because we're so close to the product. However, this type of thinking doesn't put the site's users at the forefront. How they'll approach your website and explore content typically will differ from that of you or your client. Thus, user research is vitally important, and at a minimum, a card sorting exercise should be completed. This research will provide insight into how your users expect the content on the website to be organized and grouped and will ensure the site organization starts in as strong a place as possible.

SITE NAVIGATION AND WAYFINDING

I often create sitemaps based on how I plan to build the website navigation. While the navigation structure is a part of the information architecture process, it is not the only consideration, as it doesn't account for the relationships between pages and content. The sitemap and content inventory should inform the main navigation menu on your website and can influence its design depending on how many levels deep the website or application goes.

Navigation is more than the main menu on a website; it also informs users where they are on your website. For example, say you have a website with a menu at the top and a dropdown that links to second-level landing pages, as in figure 5.4. Users who click into one of those pages may encounter even more navigation options, leading them three or four levels deep. Because they can't reach these pages from the main menu navigation, you should include a secondary navigation menu for sections at level 2 and deeper to provide breadcrumbs that orient users to exactly how they got to the page they're on.

So, while your sitemap can be representative of your main website menu for navigation, it's important to remember that it is not the only mode of navigation on the website. Often, main menus only highlight your site's top-level landing points. Thus, it's important to provide other navigation tools so users can find their way back to higher levels and know where they are in relation to the other pages and content.

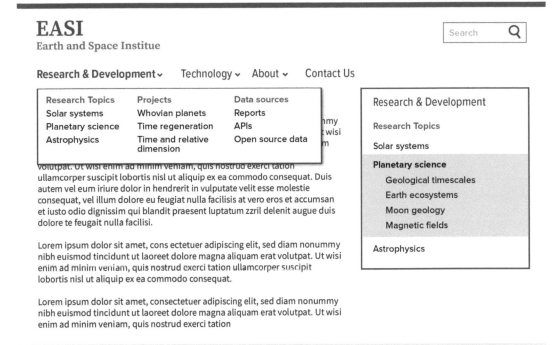

Figure 5.4   **The navigation on this website extends deeper, beyond what's available in the header navigation. The sidebar on the right serves as navigation to the site's deeper levels and as a wayfinding tool to let the user know where they clicked from.**

5.1.2   *Content inventory and audit*

You usually take a content inventory when you're working on redesigning a website or application that already exists and drop it all into a spreadsheet. However, when I work on new projects with no content, I find the spreadsheet approach beneficial to track the kind of content I need to be written for the website. The spreadsheet values might be a bit different than when performing an inventory of existing content, but they provide a straightforward outline of all the content needed, grouped by page or other factors. This list may be much shorter for new websites than existing ones, which may have had content, such as blog posts, created over several years before the inventory is taken. Using a spreadsheet is a low-cost way to track this work and can be kept on hand for a future content inventory or audit.

Generally, the content inventory spreadsheet will include, but is not limited to, the following information:

- Page the content lives on
- Page metadata
- Title of content or summary of what the piece of content is
- Author
- URL

- File format (image, article, piece of UI, downloadable file, etc.)
- Description of the content
- Date content was created (if available)

Countless examples exist of the type of data you can capture in a content inventory on the web, which can be adjusted to fit your needs. The spreadsheet will look something like figure 5.5.

	A	B	C	D	E	F
	Page	Title	Content	Summary	Author/Owner	URL
	Homepage					https://coolwebsite.com
		Hero image title	Hero image	Describes image + purpose	Design and marketing	https://coolwebsite.com
		Subsection title	Copy and image content	Describes content purpose	Marketing	https://coolwebsite.com
	Documentation					https://coolwebsite.com/docs
		Search documentation	Search input textbox and button	Searches documentation pages		
		User guide	Icon and text tile	Links to user guide		https://coolwebsite.com
		Contribution guide	Icon and text tile	Links to contributor guide		
	About					
		Changelog	Icon and text tile	Links to changelog		
		Code of Conduct	Icon and text tile			

Figure 5.5   An example of a simple content inventory spreadsheet

As mentioned previously, I've used a content inventory document to help plan content for new websites. Using a spreadsheet to track the type of content you need, whether or not you're working with a writer, is easy and straightforward and puts everything in one place. If you're working on a website redesign, a content inventory will give you a concise overview of what currently exists and how it fits into the redesign of the website. At this point, a content audit comes into play.

A content audit goes beyond just documenting content inventory on a website; you must now evaluate whether that content needs to be scrapped altogether and rewritten or whether it can be kept as is. Some key questions to ask when conducting the audit are as follows:

- Is the content meeting its goals?
- Is it providing value to your end users?
- Is it meeting user goals?
- Is it meeting business goals?
- Does it match the voice and tone of your brand?
- How is the content doing? (Is it getting views?)

Running a content audit will help inform a content strategy for the website going forward and should align with the user and business goals of the website or application. Content and writing are what drive users to your website or application; a website or application design is nothing without content. Performing an audit ensures that all team members continue to be aligned on the website's goals and can craft the appropriate experiences, whether an article or media, to meet those goals.

5.2   User flows and user journeys

Once you have the hierarchal structure of your website documented in a sitemap and the layout of your website developed from an information architecture perspective, you can start to define user flows and map out the user journey for your website. A user flow and a user journey map sound like the same thing, but they're different in the type of narrative they each provide. User flows focus on providing clarity about each step in the process that completes a task. A user journey map creates a narrative from a user persona's point of view. It maps out the experience of your main user persona and ties in an emotional element to identify what your user is thinking and feeling at each stage in their journey through your product. When building out a user journey, having solid user research data about your target users is vital to be sure you're not making assumptions about their point of view when interacting with your product.

5.2.1   User flows

User flows are the routes users take to complete a task on your website or application. These routes start at the entry point for a specific task and include the steps between that point and when the user completes their goal. User flows can simply be flow charts with labels for each interaction to complete a task, like in figure 5.6, or they can be more detailed visually in wireframes.

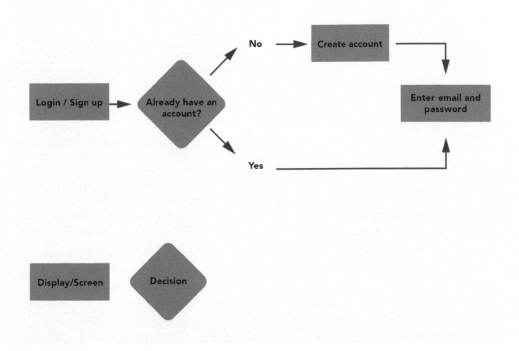

Figure 5.6   A simple user flow chart showing a login flow. Shapes can be used to represent different points a user may reach. Do they see a screen? Do they need to take an action?

The flow chart and the wireframe versions have their unique benefits. The flow chart, for example, gives an objective overview of each step along a path that a user may take to complete a task without focusing on layout or design as the wireframe version would provide. This approach is beneficial because when it comes to stakeholder review, the visual design and layout can be distracting and take the focus away from getting feedback on the steps to complete an action on the website or application you're designing.

Creating user flows before the wireframing and visual design phases is key to identifying points where the user experience can be optimized and reducing time spent creating wireframes that may be unnecessary. These user flows can aid in informing prototypes when you reach that stage in the project to ensure that nothing in the planned user interaction has been forgotten in the visual design phase. Once you have wireframes created, translating your flow chart into a wireframe user flow is helpful. The flow chart will identify the touchpoints that need to be emphasized in the visual design phase, directing users to where they need to click to complete a task.

User flows are versatile because they can either be scaled down to a specific task flow that a user may complete on one page of your website or application or scaled up to look at a bigger flow across multiple pages. They're useful tools for both a new website being built from scratch and a redesign of an existing website. In a redesign, they can help you assess the different paths objectively to identify where they can be improved or streamlined.

5.2.2   *User journeys*

User journeys look visually different from user flows and provide a much richer view of the user's path through interacting with your product. Although based on a user flow, user journeys add additional information and a few more layers for assessment, creating a narrative from a target user persona's point of view. They offer an emotional assessment of how your users may feel when they engage with your product and allow them to make suggestions to improve their experience based on those feelings. The added layers of a user journey map compared to a user flow make it extremely valuable, so let's define those steps or layers you'll want to add to your user journey map.

CREATING A USER JOURNEY MAP

First, we want to define our target user persona for the journey. This persona will take on the perspective we will be viewing the journey through. Focus on one persona and type of user as different audiences may take various actions and traverse your site differently. Next, decide the scenario or scope of the user journey. Who is this person, and what goal are they trying to achieve, or what task are they trying to complete? What are their expectations? You'll want to limit the scope of the task or goal and be specific for the best insights. Next, map the scenario steps to what the user may be thinking, doing, or feeling while completing each step. These steps can be positive or negative moments and are key in helping you analyze the user flow and make decisions from a place of empathy to provide the best user experience. Finally, from these moments, identify any opportunities for improvement. When put together, a user journey map can look something like the document in figure 5.7.

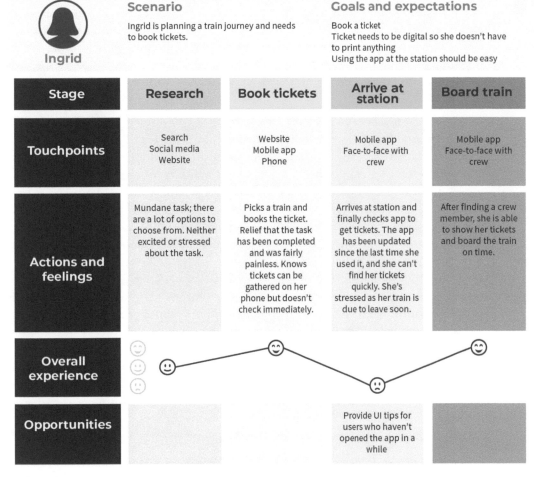

Stage	Research	Book tickets	Arrive at station	Board train
Touchpoints	Search Social media Website	Website Mobile app Phone	Mobile app Face-to-face with crew	Mobile app Face-to-face with crew
Actions and feelings	Mundane task; there are a lot of options to choose from. Neither excited or stressed about the task.	Picks a train and books the ticket. Relief that the task has been completed and was fairly painless. Knows tickets can be gathered on her phone but doesn't check immediately.	Arrives at station and finally checks app to get tickets. The app has been updated since the last time she used it, and she can't find her tickets quickly. She's stressed as her train is due to leave soon.	After finding a crew member, she is able to show her tickets and board the train on time.
Overall experience				
Opportunities			Provide UI tips for users who haven't opened the app in a while	

Figure 5.7   A simple user journey map that depicts the scenario of a user booking a train ticket and their experience with the app. User journey maps can be created with tools such as Figma, Illustrator, or even Microsoft Word.

Journey maps can transcend the digital space and extend into a physical space. These physical spaces are called *touchpoints*, and a user journey may be a mix of both. For example, say you're building a website or application for a client in the healthcare industry. Your users will most likely enter a digital space (your website) and a physical space (visiting a healthcare provider). The digital and physical touchpoints are connected, and both should be considered when applicable. Creating a journey map for these scenarios is vital for identifying gaps a user may encounter that negatively affect their physical experience, such as in a healthcare provider's office. It is a great way to identify the information you can provide on the site to help lessen a negative experience. You'll want to pinpoint those negative areas where the experience could even stop a user from making it to the physical space, ending their user journey early.

User journeys are a key tool that puts you in the shoes of your target users and helps you empathize with what they are feeling as they interact with your product. Negative and positive experiences are vital to identify, so it's important to consider the emotional or mental state your users may be in when using your website. What are they there to do? How might they be feeling? Use those scenarios to identify where you can make your user's journey even smoother so that they can complete their task without any obstacles.

CREATE A USER JOURNEY FOR THE USER UNDER STRESS

I once attended a talk given by Eric Meyer, known for his expertise in HTML, CSS, and web standards, at the conference An Event Apart, and it changed how I thought about building user experiences. When you're building journey maps for specific scenarios and users, consider creating one for the person who may be on your website while in a state of stress. For example, if you work on a banking application, this person under stress may be someone whose banking information was hacked, and they're watching transactions deplete their account in real time. Another example could be someone who needs to book an urgent flight because a loved one is ill or has died. Or someone's phone was stolen, and they didn't have a tracking app downloaded, so they need to report it and cancel their service. Your journey map would identify that these people are most likely feeling overwhelmed and not thinking clearly. The map would focus on reducing barriers for people who aren't able to process information as clearly as someone who isn't under stress.

I once worked on a website for a client whose main goal was to provide information for military veterans whose service was ending and who were looking at possible career paths into tech. This site needed to provide that information, and when I started to map out the user journey for the main sections of the website, I asked a few questions to try to put myself in their shoes:

- What might they be feeling upon first landing on this website?
- What's their state of mind?

I approached the user experience from a state of stress, putting myself in the shoes of someone who was experiencing a rather significant ending to an important period in their life. This person must start considering the next phase of their life, which can be a scary and stressful experience. I worked on making the website's information architecture as clear as possible and eliminated all dead ends. Assuming they may get to the end of a section and not find exactly what they were looking for, I made sure to link to other pages with information to help guide them.

After the website's launch, analytics showed that people were spending an average of 7 minutes on the site. In a world where people abandon websites in under a minute, or even less than 30 seconds, if they can't immediately find what they need, this time felt like a huge success. The client was extremely happy, and in my career history, I still view that as one of the most, if not the most, successful project I've ever led. I credit that success to thinking and designing from the point of view of someone under stress.

The wonderful thing about this approach is that if someone under stress can easily find the information they need and complete their task, so will the person who is not under stress. In the end, all your users, as well as your product, benefit from this user experience.

5.3 Designing your site and application

Once your research is completed, your information architecture created, and your user flow or journey defined, you can start building and applying visual design principles to lay out your website or application. The previous phases provide the blueprint for designing your website, but before you begin picking out fonts and color palettes, you'll want to build the foundation and skeletal structure of your website with wireframes. If you are building a house, you can't apply paint or hang blinds before putting up walls and installing windows.

The design phase is broken down into subphases and starts with wireframing, followed by static visual design and then interaction design. The static visual design and interaction design phases don't necessarily have an order in which they need to be completed. Interaction design could start after the wireframes are completed. You may choose to create clickable prototypes with the wireframes to get client approval and ensure the interaction and user flow holds up with the proposed site layout and content organization. Or, interaction design could start after the static visual design phase when you have the refined visual mock-ups of your site or application. You may decide to create high-fidelity prototypes with these mock-ups instead of wireframes. The order of these steps depends largely on you, how you prefer to work, and your client's expectations.

5.3.1 Wireframing

Whether you want to start with the interaction or static design phase, neither can nor should occur before you build wireframes. Wireframes are the initial exploratory visual outline of your website or application that focuses on giving life to the information architecture by translating it into a visual medium.

However, wireframes are devoid of any design aesthetic, like in figure 5.8, meaning there shouldn't be a focus on picking out typefaces, colors, or graphics in this phase. Wireframes should focus on establishing relationships between content on the different pages and creating a blueprint for the functionality expected on those pages.

I have been responsible for all phases of a website project, and my wireframes have always informed the final website layout in the visual design phase. Building wireframes should also be an iterative process, and because you aren't thinking about color or typography yet, they are low cost to iterate on. Therefore, they're easy to get in front of users and project stakeholders for feedback to ensure you're headed down the right path visually. Getting this approval and making these changes before things like color and typography are applied helps reduce overhead and cost on the design side. Spending time building out fully designed pages is time consuming, as is having to iterate on fully designed pages. You will consider more design factors when you

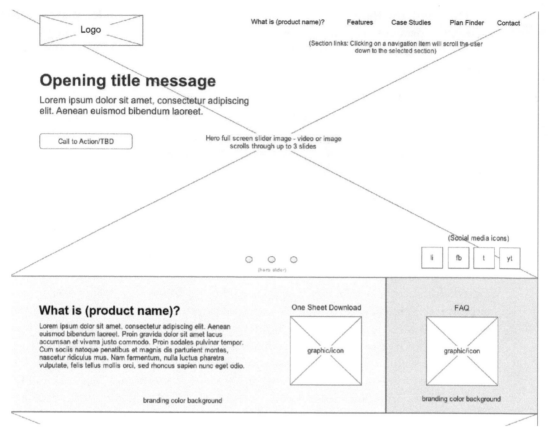

Figure 5.8   An example of the top part of a wireframe that defines a site's structure. This wireframe focuses on the hero section of a home page and the content immediately below it.

start reorganizing content on a fully designed page; wireframes provide a greyscale skeleton of the website.

You can also use different levels of fidelity—low, medium, and high—with your wireframes, depending on what you're trying to accomplish. Laying out medium- and high-fidelity wireframes can be time consuming, like the visual design phase (where you're choosing colors and typography). Thus, low-fidelity wireframes can be a good place to start to make sure you're headed in the right direction with stakeholders before investing a lot of time in building out wireframes with more details.

LOW-FIDELITY WIREFRAMES

Low-fidelity wireframes are an extremely rough version of the page's layout and have the lowest number of details possible. They tend to look like a lot of shapes on the page that represent where pictures and text will go, and the spacing of elements isn't remotely close to being accurate. These wireframes can be created digitally or with pen and paper for quick ideation. This type of wireframe is the cheapest to create and emphasizes the interaction and functionality of pages in the most basic way to get an idea across (figure 5.9).

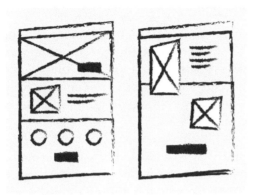

Figure 5.9   Low-fidelity wireframes have hardly any detail but convey a general idea.

Low-fidelity wireframes are a great tool when working with users during the research phases, especially at the beginning of a project when you want to get an idea of what works for your users before investing a lot of time into a layout from scratch. They can be very helpful when working on a broader team to be sure all members are aligned in the same basic direction as you start building out more refined wireframes.

If you're working on a large site or application with many different pages or screens, you may not have the time to create wireframes with a lot of detail. Low-fidelity wireframes can be created quickly so you can spend the time you need to add more detail to the pages that need them.

MEDIUM-FIDELITY WIREFRAMES

Medium-fidelity wireframes are more detailed than low-fidelity wireframes. They are created with a digital tool, such as Figma, Balsamiq, or Axure RP, which can provide better accuracy in spacing, layout, sizing, and component design but isn't pixel specific. Some basic elements of design may start to creep in when building out these wireframes, with different typographic weights applied to show hierarchy of the content. You can use the design principle of contrast in wireframes, even if they're in grayscale. Different shades of gray can also be used to bring attention to components that should stand out from other content on the page.

Images are still placeholder shapes, although some basic line drawings may be added to demonstrate the basic content of the image, and icons may be included if applicable. You may include some actual content for the main pieces, such as the navigation, headings, and calls to action, but subtitles and paragraph text will use Lorem Ipsum filler content. You can find free-to-use Lorem Ipsum generators online, or some wireframing software will generate it in the application.

HIGH-FIDELITY WIREFRAMES

High-fidelity wireframes are the most detailed of the wireframes and are pixel specific. They are the closest representation of what will be designed and built in the next stages of the project. They are still created in a greyscale color palette, although you may start to include color on certain components, such as buttons, to bring more attention to them. My personal preference is to avoid using color in the wireframing process. Often, the client or stakeholders focus too much on the color choice in their review when, at this stage, color hasn't been determined. Thus, color can distract from the main purpose of the wireframes, which is to bring clarity around features, functionality, and content organization.

You should have as much content as possible when building out high-fidelity wireframes; placeholder text should be limited. You can include imagery if you have it, but use it in grayscale. Otherwise, you can still use placeholder rectangles for the components with images, rather than two lines forming an X through this shape. You may also choose to use an icon that represents an image.

High-fidelity wireframes are the most time consuming of the three different levels and should be completed after low- or medium-fidelity wireframes are done. This phase is not the time for experimentation or when you need to iterate quickly. A high level of detail should be included only when concepts have been locked into place.

MIX AND MATCH YOUR WIREFRAME APPROACH

When building out wireframes, you don't have to create all three types in your project for all the pages on the site or application. Low-fidelity wireframes are key to quickly iterating and establishing a direction to build medium-fidelity wireframes. You may decide that only a handful of pages need to be high fidelity before moving onto the mock-up phase of design where you start to apply color and typography. Your medium-fidelity wireframes also may be enough before you start diving into the design phase, and you may not need to spend time on high-fidelity versions. In the end, it's largely up to you to determine how much time and how large a budget you have available, as well as what your client wants to see in the process, before you start designing and coding.

5.3.2   *User interface design and full-color mock-ups*

Whether you move into the user interface design phase from a medium- or high-fidelity wireframe, you'll have already started to think about some visual design elements when building out those wireframes, such as space, layout, and the relationships between different pieces of content (the principle of proximity). User interface design refers to both the visual and interactive elements of the website. It considers how they work together to guide your users through their tasks on your website or application. In the coming chapters, we'll go over skills related to color, space, and typography. How to establish a grid, pair typefaces, and choose and apply a color palette are all part of visual design but are considered in different parts of the design process, from wireframes to creating full-color mock-ups of the website interface that focus on the aesthetics of the website or application.

Once you create your wireframes, you should have established a general layout and grid structure and have figured out the content's organization. The next phase is to turn your wireframes into full-color mock-ups. In this phase, we will focus on the website's aesthetics, which are just as important as the information architecture and structure.

Before anyone who lands on your website starts to read or explore the content in depth, they first see the site's visual design. They see your color choices, use of space, and the readability of the typography. Based on this first impression, they choose whether to continue interacting with your website. They have an emotional reaction to the choices you've made. So, your visual design choices should be strategic and have meaning. Your decisions, from the colors to the typefaces, convey an image of the brand and create the first impression anyone has before they start to get to know your website's content on a deeper level.

Full-color mock-ups should be created after wireframing and when concepts are locked into place. These wireframes are the costliest to make in terms of time. While this phase is not where experimentation with content organization happens (wireframing), there is still room to explore many different options for the look and feel of the website or application. Clarify with your client how many options they would like to see and start with one or two pages of the website to iterate on. I've personally had clients who want to see as many variations in image treatment, color, and typography as possible, and one time I showed as many as 15 options. This request doesn't come that often, but it can. Others may only want to see three variations. From these variations, the client typically chooses a direction before you start to design the rest of the pages.

Depending on the number of pages on the website, you should focus on creating only a handful of these mock-ups, especially if pages share layouts and design. For example, if you have a site with multiple landing pages that share a layout, there's no need to create a mock-up for each one unless your client asks for it. Focus on the pages that have unique layouts, and optimize your time by only creating one mock-up for pages that share layouts.

Full-color mock-ups are the final piece before starting to build a functioning product, whether that's a prototype for user testing or building the final website. The mock-ups provide the look and feel of the website in a static form, meaning not interactive, although they can be made to be interactive. This phase is important to ensure buy-in from your client or stakeholders before starting to code to avoid drastic design changes in the development phase, which can be costly to the project.

5.3.3 Prototyping

Whether presented as wireframes or clickable, interactive versions built from refined user interface mock-ups, testing your concepts is part of the iterative process of working with your users. You want to ensure you're building the right website or application before you start the development process. The goal of testing your designs and concepts early with users is to avoid rewriting all your code due to a major redesign instituted based on user research and feedback gathered late in the process.

Prototyping tests the usability of your designs. Like wireframing, different types of prototypes of varying levels of fidelity can be created depending on your project's goals. Whether you're working with a high- or low-fidelity prototype, you're trying to learn how your users would interact with your design and are focused on getting that usability feedback, but each level of fidelity has its uses.

LOW-FIDELITY PROTOTYPES

Low-fidelity prototypes can be created early on with pen and paper or by using some low-fidelity wireframes you created for the early stages of the project. Low-fidelity prototypes should have some level of walking through the prototype with the user you are interviewing since the interactivity will be limited; that is, they can't click through the components, especially if they're viewing a sketched prototype. Sketched prototypes are very helpful in early sessions because you can respond to user feedback at that moment and propose new concepts then and there.

Low-fidelity prototypes are cheap and fast to create, so you can quickly get them in front of users. This type of prototype is key to ensuring that your user experience flows as it should. It can be used for quick iterations when you're still trying to bring clarity to a concept or the functionality of your pages.

HIGH-FIDELITY PROTOTYPES

High-fidelity prototypes are much more detailed, similar to high-fidelity wireframes. However, in this instance, you can use those wireframes or your user interface mockups if you have them. These prototypes will have some level of interactivity, whether fully clickable with components linked to the correct pages or fake interactivity if limited by your budget.

If you're trying to test a specific scenario with one route a user can take, you can use PowerPoint and lay out a different screen on each slide to represent a step forward in the scenario. You want to ask users questions in any prototyping session; however, if you take the route of faking interactivity using a slideshow, communicate with your user to determine whether the steps in the scenario flow align with what they are expecting. PowerPoint can also be used with low-fidelity wireframes.

High-fidelity prototypes, especially fully clickable ones, can be extremely time consuming to create, although some wireframing applications like Axure have this functionality built in so you can easily create clickable wireframe prototypes. High-fidelity prototypes should be used when you're trying to identify any lingering usability problems that did not get addressed in the early stages of design before you start the development phase.

PROTOTYPING AS ITERATIVE RESEARCH

In the last chapter, I talked about research being an iterative process that should be done continually throughout the project before reaching the development phase because making big design changes then can be costly. Prototyping is just another tool to help reduce those types of changes. If you don't prototype at all, but go straight to development, build your site or application, and launch it, you're still testing a prototype. The only difference is that this prototype is now live. If your users run into usability problems, it can affect the website in the long term if users don't return to the site or aren't able to complete their tasks, which, if your site or application is selling something, affects revenue. To retain users coming to your website, test early and often before going live to ensure you're delivering the best experience. In chapter 11, we'll discuss additional testing that comes after prototyping has been completed that can be done to improve your website or application after launch.

In the next chapter, we'll discuss common layout patterns you can use, applying a grid, and overall refining the structure to be pixel perfect.

Summary

- The user experience design phase lays the foundation for your website. It focuses on the content organization from the site map, how users get from point A to point B, and the general layout of the website through wireframing.
- Information architecture is the backbone of your website's structure and organization and informs the content strategy. This work should be done before any wireframe or visual design is built.
- Good information architecture will inform the site navigation but does not necessarily reflect how the navigation should be labeled. Rely on user research to ensure pages and content are labeled appropriately.
- User flows are flow charts that map out how a user would complete a task on the website or application and can be used to identify points where the experience may be optimized.
- User journeys add an emotional element and focus on one target user persona of someone who would use your website. Developing user journeys is a good practice in empathy and putting yourself in your user's shoes to identify both negative and positive points in their journey in interacting with your product. These points should provide opportunities to improve or enhance the experience on your website.
- Wireframes are the first step in translating your user research and information architecture into something visually representative of the experience someone will have in interacting with your website. They are the visual skeleton of the site, focused on organizing and grouping content.
- User interface design combines the interactive elements of the website and the overall aesthetic using visual design principles. The user interface offers users their first impression when they land on your website and can often be the deciding factor in whether they stay to continue to explore the website or leave.
- Prototyping is vital to both clarifying usability expectations from users early in the design process and identifying usability problems once a design has been refined. Prototyping is part of the cycle of testing and iterating that takes place before the development phase to catch any large problems since making changes later in the process can be time consuming and costly.

Part 3

Visual design elements

Part 3 discusses visual design language basics. These elements bring your website to life! We will cover the fundamentals of layout, common layout patterns, and how to use animation to enhance your layout. Then we will get into typography and color before applying what you've learned in this part of the book.

Chapter 6 picks up right after chapter 5 and goes into more depth about defining a website's structure and how you can lay content out. You can stick to some common patterns before getting too experimental with the layout. This chapter also covers responsive design and the different form factors to think about when adapting your layout to be responsive.

Chapter 7 brings in some elements of fun by using animation to enhance your layout and overall design. Animation can be used in several ways to make an experience memorable or serve a functional purpose. We will review some scenarios you could use, how to plan for animations, and technical considerations of animation-heavy designs.

Chapter 8 gives a high-level overview of typography on the web. Typography is a key visual element, as whatever type you choose can change the entire undertone of a design. We will discuss how to pair typefaces and establish a type ramp and vertical rhythm, which can immediately make a web page feel more polished.

Chapter 9 covers the most common design problem developers face: using color. We will consider color relationships, the meaning of colors, terminology, and how to pick and apply a color palette step by step.

Chapter 10 puts together everything we covered that touches on visuals from chapters 5 through 9. We will walk through building a website with the requirements defined by a client. We layer on each design element discussed in the book until we have a designed web page.

By the end of this part, you should feel equipped with the tools to use the principles in chapter 2 and the elements in chapters 5 through 9 to make your websites feel more polished and structured.

Web layout
and composition

This chapter covers

- The basic layout fundamentals of creating a website's structure
- How to create and use grids to create consistency and familiarity
- How to apply visual design principles when laying out sections and place components to create hierarchy and rhythm
- Different user reading patterns that can affect a page's layout

Until the mid 2010s, the web technology available to developers to easily create unique and interesting layouts using only HTML and CSS was limited. If you did any sort of web development that involved building the structure of a website in the early 2000s, you probably had your CSS utility classes for specific layout fixes like clearing floats and vertically aligning items. CSS was fine for building website layouts until our devices became portable; as we started viewing the web on phones, screens got smaller, and sizing became more irregular.

111

With the introduction of responsive web design and the advent of smartphones, creating fluid layouts that smoothly collapsed from a desktop screen to a phone screen became a vital part of a website's strategy. You wanted your users to have a cohesive experience across both mediums. This phase of the web brought the beginnings of code libraries such as Bootstrap that made the responsive web much easier to build for, especially as rapid iteration and deployment became a part of project lifecycles.

The drawback to using libraries like Bootstrap, especially for layout, is that all developers started to design websites within the confines of these libraries, and many sites started to look the same: a big hero section at the top, which typically consumed the entire top of the layout and told people what your site was about, followed by a band below it that was split into three columns, like in figure 6.1. Each column contained a subheading, a blurb of text, and sometimes a call to action.

Figure 6.1   A big hero image followed by three columns is a frequently used layout on the web.

Across the web, designs became homogenized as the same layouts started to appear repeatedly. The benefit of using a framework like Bootstrap is the ability to get started rapidly. The downside of using that same framework is that its popularity and ease of use meant many websites started to look the same, which can be bad for your brand. Additional knowledge of design fundamentals can help make a website stand out even if you're using a standard library to quickly get a usable and nicely designed website up and running. If you don't have design knowledge, you'll probably look to other websites for design inspiration and copy techniques to create something similar. However, you want your website to be memorable so your users return to it.

The other downside to using a framework is that you're using someone else's code and trying to fit your design into their framework. You may have to modify the code somewhat heavily to get what you want. But we're no longer in an era where we need to rely on using frameworks to build grid layouts easily. An overview of the advantages and disadvantages of frameworks is highlighted in table 6.1. The standardization of Flexbox and CSS Grid means we can still create beautifully responsive layouts like what Bootstrap gives us, but we now have much more control over the elements in our layouts.

Table 6.1 Advantages and disadvantages of using a framework

Advantages	Disadvantages
Ready-to-use code, get started quickly	Confined by the design framework, only so many layout combinations are available
Little design knowledge needed to produce a website that looks professional	If you want to customize your site design heavily using a framework, you're using someone else's code, and that can get a bit messy to manage as opposed to writing code from scratch.
Easy to use codebase out of the box	Depending on the framework, lots of extra code and components you may not even use come bundled with it, causing larger code file sizes.

For example, we're able to define a four-column layout with CSS Grid and have our heading span all four columns. Using a few lines of code in our CSS Grid, we can then have a second row of content that spans the same four columns as the heading, two groups that span two columns each, or four groups, each taking up one column. From a layout perspective, CSS Grid allows us to use less code to get what we want without using a plug-and-play–type framework. With CSS Grid, we can create designs that fluidly adapt to whatever screen we're on without writing a lot of code or hacking around someone else's code.

Even if you're using a framework to build your website, it's important to remember that the design of your website goes beyond the main structure you build. The main structure of the site should organize and group your content. You want it to be solid, which you get with something like Bootstrap, which, again, is quick to implement. But how you use typography, color, whitespace, and animation is where your design can flourish and stand out from the rest. Start with a solid structure before you paint the walls and put up drapes, but be thinking about paint color and types of drapes as you build the structure.

6.1 Establishing your website structure

When you move into the design phase to plan your website structure for wireframing, you should already have your website's goals and purpose in mind and an outline of the types of content on each page from your site-mapping phase. Now, we want to start translating this visually, so let's figure out what we need to put on the page.

First, we need to establish the most basic sections of our website—how we will split up our page. If we think of our finished website as a main dish of food—for example, pasta carbonara—we first must know what each ingredient is before we can begin cooking. We must also follow a particular order of adding ingredients to make the final dish. The sections of our site are our ingredients, and we need to know what those ingredients are before putting them together.

All websites generally have three sections: a header, the main content, and a footer. The header contains the website navigation and a logo or the website name; it can also include other items, like a search bar and social media links. The header tells the user where they are on the web. The main content is the largest part of the page and should provide value to the user by including what they are looking for. The footer at the bottom of the page contains copyright and contact information; it can also include a high-level sitemap or other information that may be relevant or important to link to, such as privacy policies and terms of use. A footer isn't always necessary, depending on the type of page. Twitter, for example, doesn't have a footer.

A sidebar can be used as another section of content, depending on the website's or page's requirements. If you're designing a website whose primary function is as a blog or daily news, it may make sense to include a sidebar on the homepage. The sidebar includes any less important information not displayed in the main content section; it contains secondary content. It can also be used for a secondary set of navigation. For example, on websites with many pages and subpages that go a few layers deep, it's helpful to include all those links in a sidebar rather than in the main site navigation. Once a user clicks into a certain section of the site, those additional subpages may surface through a table of contents in the sidebar, keeping the main site navigation clutter-free and easy to scan.

Once we have our basic high-level sections, we'll want to break down exactly what the main content section should contain. This decision will again depend on your website's goals, but you can continue to chunk out the main section into subsections based on the content, which could look like the following:

- Image of product at the top of the page with a call to action
- Product description
- Product highlights with links to product information pages
- Testimonials
- Product returns and exchange information

Once we have this information, we can start to figure out how we want to lay out the information and start making our initial design decisions for the webpage.

6.2   Using a grid

Before you choose how you want to organize your content, you'll want to establish a grid structure for your website. You can use a grid to organize and place content on the page.

6.2.1   Defining the grid

The grid comprises columns, rows, and the gaps between each. When using a grid, you'll focus largely on the columns for placing content and how items line up vertically, as this alignment will create an invisible, hard edge down the page that will give the page a sense of organization, like in the example in figure 6.2.

With rows, you won't always necessarily have a hard edge horizontally. It will depend on the content and the length of the text. For example, you may have two columns side by side, one with an image and one with text. The text won't necessarily be

Figure 6.2   An invisible line is formed on the left side from the logo down past the first headline and to the subheading.

flush with the bottom of the image, and you'll want to center it vertically, like in figure 6.3. This placement will create balance within the row without the sharp lines that columns provide to give a sense of organization.

Creating a grid system for your website ensures that even the pages that don't share the same layout have the dimensions and ratios of the columns. Whether your content is one or three columns wide, the dimensions can scale up or down, and the site has a sense of balance even as the layout changes between devices.

If you're exploring more experimental layouts, the grid is another way to ensure your website still feels like it's organized and structured, even if elements aren't always

Flowers that bloom in
late summer

Lorem ipsum dolor sit amet, consectetuer
adipiscing elit, sed diam nonummy nibh euismod

Figure 6.3   Centering text creates balance and organization when a headline
and image aren't stacked.

lined up precisely. Even if elements appear to be placed randomly or asymmetrically,
they're still utilizing the grid as an organizational tool.

6.2.2   Grid dimensions

The more columns you have, the more flexible your grid is. If your grid only has two
columns, you only can place content in those two lines. One thing to remember when
creating your grid is that the column widths should not be defined by how many columns of content you want in your layout, which we'll look at in the next section. You
may have content that spans three columns of your grid to create one column of content. Figure 6.4 gives an example of how your grid columns can make up larger columns of content.

Where to stop

Lorem ipsum dolor sit amet,
consectetuer adipiscing elit, sed diam
nonummy nibh euismod

Ancient sites

Lorem ipsum dolor sit amet,
consectetuer adipiscing elit, sed diam
nonummy nibh euismod

Castles

Lorem ipsum dolor sit amet,
consectetuer adipiscing elit, sed diam
nonummy nibh euismod

Figure 6.4   Four columns in the grid make up each component width, which gives greater flexibility
in a design.

When you define your grid, you'll first want to decide the maximum width of the website's container. This box will define the outermost edge of both sides of your content.
No content will go beyond this container (figure 6.5), which will create that invisible
line on the left edge of the site when content is placed.

Figure 6.5 No content goes beyond the maximum width of the container and grid.

The most common widths for desktop screens are 960 and 1200 pixels. Multiple tools are available online to help you quickly build out a grid system, which I've listed in the appendix.

Grid templates will help generate the columns for your grid system and give you the dimensions you need for your high-fidelity wireframes or website mockups. The number and width of the columns are up to you, but often, the number of columns is 12 for desktops, 8 for tablets, and 4 for mobile phones. You'll also need to define the margin between each column. Let's look at an example of a grid with a max-width of 1200 pixels and eight columns in figure 6.6.

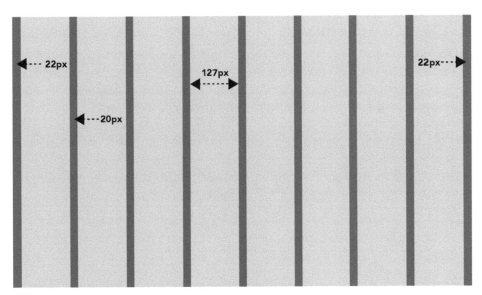

Figure 6.6 This grid has a maximum width of 1200 pixels with a margin of 22 pixels on the left and right; columns are 127 pixels wide, and the remaining grid gaps between columns are 20 pixels.

Rarely in the design phase will you define rows for your grid. If you're using CSS Grid to build your layout, your content length will typically define your grid rows. If you have a layout that strictly adheres to the CSS grid—similar to something like a masonry layout, which we'll look at in a moment—then you may want to define your rows more strictly. Once you've defined your grid, you now have your most basic organizational system in place for your website and can start thinking about how you want to lay out your content.

6.3 *Choosing a layout*

Different pages on your website or application will have unique content and goals. While elements of your layout structure should be the same throughout the website, like the header and footer, the main content section's structure and design will most likely differ on the home page versus the subpages. Picking your layout structure will depend on your page's goals and what is most likely to keep your users engaged. You want them to stay on the page, and by combining the principles of design and research on how users typically read through a page, you can understand how to draw a user's eye through your page. Let's start by deciding how to structure your content and the different columned layouts.

Once you have your list of content, you need to decide what kind of layout you want your website to have that you'll build on top of your grid. At the most basic level, you must decide how many columns your layout will have. Most websites utilize one to three columns for the desktop layout, which will scale down to one column on mobile phones for readability reasons.

6.3.1 *Using one-column patterns*

One-column patterns on websites built for desktops are most frequently used for purposes such as articles and blog posts—pages with a lot of text content. A one-column pattern is simple to define. Once your grid structure is defined, you'll want to decide how many columns will make up your maximum content width. Let's look at a visual example in figure 6.7.

In figure 6.7, we have a 12-column grid across 1200 pixels with the columns set to 81 pixels; the gutter, the space between columns, is set to 20 pixels; and the margin on the left and right sides is set to 0 pixels. We want to pick an even number of columns for our content to span so that we have an even amount space on the right and left.

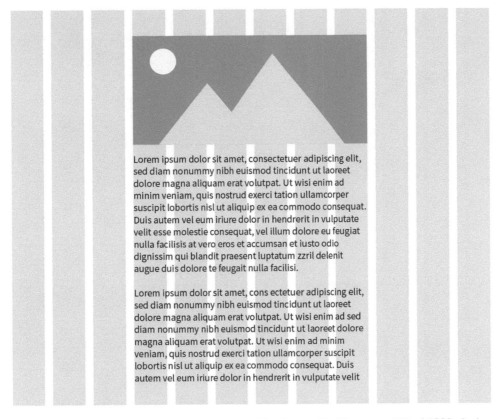

Lorem ipsum dolor sit amet, consectetuer adipiscing elit, sed diam nonummy nibh euismod tincidunt ut laoreet dolore magna aliquam erat volutpat. Ut wisi enim ad minim veniam, quis nostrud exerci tation ullamcorper suscipit lobortis nisl ut aliquip ex ea commodo consequat. Duis autem vel eum iriure dolor in hendrerit in vulputate velit esse molestie consequat, vel illum dolore eu feugiat nulla facilisis at vero eros et accumsan et iusto odio dignissim qui blandit praesent luptatum zzril delenit augue duis dolore te feugait nulla facilisi.

Lorem ipsum dolor sit amet, cons ectetuer adipiscing elit, sed diam nonummy nibh euismod tincidunt ut laoreet dolore magna aliquam erat volutpat. Ut wisi enim ad sed diam nonummy nibh euismod tincidunt ut laoreet dolore magna aliquam erat volutpat. Ut wisi enim ad minim veniam, quis nostrud exerci tation ullamcorper suscipit lobortis nisl ut aliquip ex ea commodo consequat. Duis autem vel eum iriure dolor in hendrerit in vulputate velit

Figure 6.7   A one-column design pattern across a 12 column grid with a max-width of 1200 pixels

Because we have so many columns, though, we can play around with our text container width so that it's smaller than our images, like in figure 6.8. A one-column layout can be varied by playing with the widths of certain elements and exaggerating the ones we want to emphasize.

Figure 6.8   The 12 columns of the grid offer the flexibility to explore different sizes of the main column that contains content. An image can span more columns than the text, which can nicely break up the flow of the page.

6.3.2   *Common multi-columned patterns*

Before the introduction of better layout capabilities with CSS Grid and Flexbox, creating responsive multicolumn layouts was a bit more complicated, and building a layout that contained a different number of columns in each row wasn't easy. We used our CSS Floats followed by our hacky clearfix to make our content sit the way it was supposed to on the page, but once we reduced the viewport size of those layouts, it took more code to make them cleanly adapt to a smaller screen. Even the simple pattern in figure 6.9 gave me a headache in my early days of coding when I was just trying to get it to resize and flow properly on smaller screens.

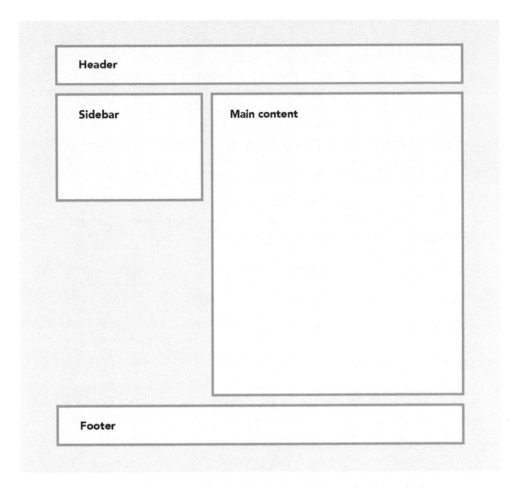

Figure 6.9 **A common web pattern with a header, footer, sidebar, and main content**

Creating responsive websites in the early days of smartphones with a web browser was a bit more cumbersome. It was possible but not nearly as fluid as it is today with the availability of CSS Grid and Flexbox. Personally, when I worked in an agency and turn-around time on projects needed to be quick, these problems affected how I designed. Using tools like CSS Floats, I wasn't nearly as adventurous as I am today about mixing the number of columns in each section on my home page. So, when you're deciding how to lay out the content on your website, especially your home page, take advantage of the currently available web technology to mix and match how you lay out sections. These tools also make scaling down to smaller screens much easier, with less additional code needed.

CHOOSING YOUR COLUMNED LAYOUT FOR THE HOME PAGE

On our home page, mixing how many columns each section of content has is much more common than on subpages. Each section of content on a home page is meant to be a snippet and provide a preview of what the site has to offer before diving into longer-form content on the subpages. Using a different number of columns for each content section is also a natural way to divide up sections and establish a relationship between content. Figure 6.10 shows two columns of content stacked on top of three columns of content without any other sort of design to create separation. Yet, we can tell they're separate because each row is different.

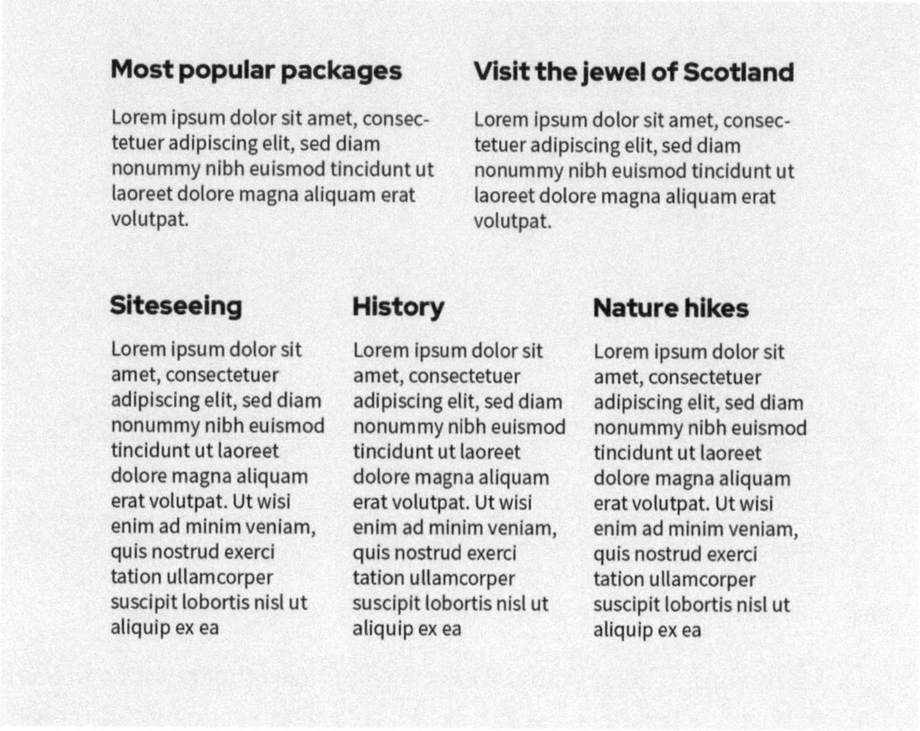

Figure 6.10 Using different content widths from row to row helps break up content and establish a natural relationship based on similarity—in this case, content width.

Let's take the list of pieces of content from section 6.1.1 for a home page for a specific line of products and look at the different columned configurations we could consider for it in a wireframe format in figures 6.11 and 6.12.

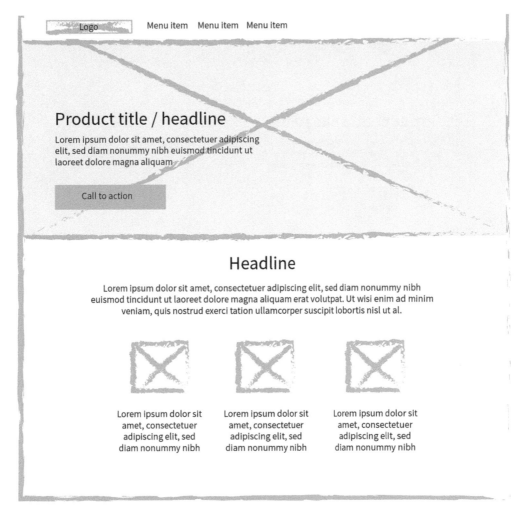

Figure 6.11   One example of a homepage design utilizing a common layout with an image, a call to action, and a description followed by another section with highlights

CHOOSING A MULTICOLUMN LAYOUT FOR SUBPAGES
The subpages of your website will contain more in-depth content than your home page. When deciding on the layout of your subpages, mixing the number of columns on a subpage should be done with thought and attention to detail, especially on content-heavy pages. On a documentation page, for example, your main content section will be text heavy and may have several images throughout the text. You can break outside the container your main text content is in to make the page more visually interesting with things like images and pullout quotes.

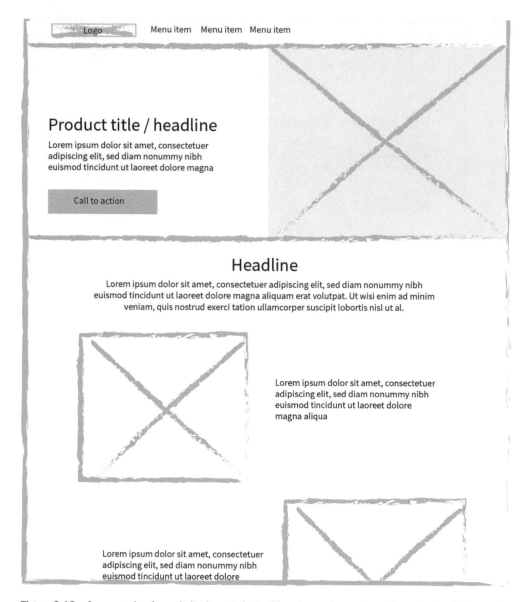

Figure 6.12   An example of a website layout that utilizes two columns to split content and shares the same content from figure 6.11

However, when it comes to the main body of text, maintain the same column choice for consistency throughout the page. Let's look at a couple of examples in figures 6.13 and 6.14 to see how to effectively mix columned layouts on subpages in a way that doesn't disrupt the page's main content.

Explore by Classification

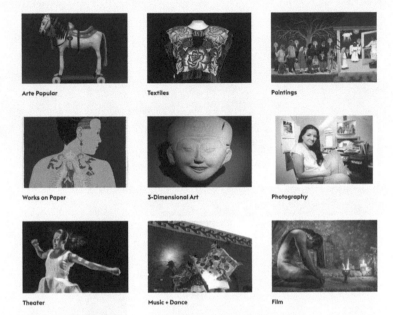

Arte Popular · Textiles · Paintings

Works on Paper · 3-Dimensional Art · Photography

Theater · Music + Dance · Film

Carlos Cortéz
1923–2005

Carlos Cortéz was a Chicago-based artist, poet, illustrator, muralist, and activist. Regarded as a political artist, both in practice and belief, he is best known for his prints and illustrations that address labor rights, union organizing, identity and culture. As a longstanding Chicago community activist, Cortéz was integral to the Museum's founding and mission. The NMMA frequently exhibits his prints, and is the exclusive repository of the Carlos Cortéz Archive. When you visit the National Museum of Mexican Art, you'll find the artist's printing press and personal effects on display in the exhibition Nuestras Historias: Stories of Mexican Identity from the Permanent Collection.

Carlos Cortéz >

Exhibiting Artists

○ Visual
Carlos Almaraz
1941–1989

○ Visual
Josefina Aguilar
b. 1945

○ Visual
Alfonso M. Castillo Orta
1944–2009

○ Visual
Olga Costa
1928–1993

Figure 6.13 The National Museum of Mexican Art's website goes from rows of three columns to a row of two and a row of four. (Photo courtesy of National Museum of Mexican Art; https://nationalmuseumofmexicanart.org/)

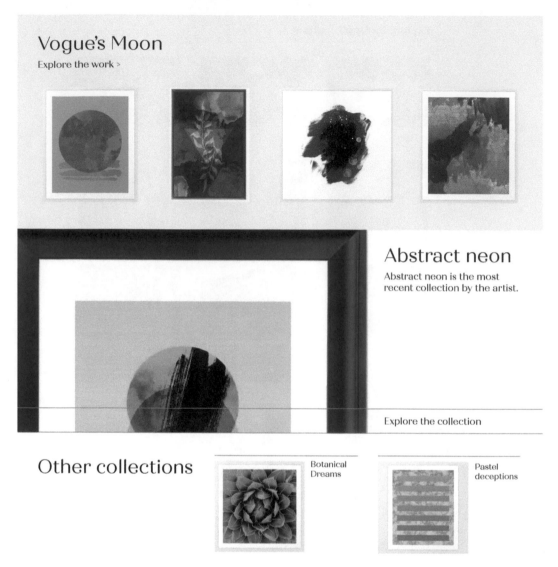

Figure 6.14   This example has three rows with three different column layouts—four columns in the top row, an asymmetrical two-column row in the middle, and a three-column row in the bottom row.

With subpages, you may have a few different types of layouts to define depending on the page's purpose, but for each one, you'll want to keep the main structure the same and create a template to use throughout. For example, if you have product pages, those should have the same layout and design. If you're going to break away from that layout for a reason, ensure that it is different enough that it stands out on its own so that your users aren't confused by the different experience between pages.

Your website header and footer should be consistent across the site, acting as an anchor and bringing some form of consistency to each page, even if the body of the home page is laid out differently from your subpages. Regardless of the type of layout your main content has between pages, the header and footer should be consistent.

Next, let's look at a few common patterns for multicolumn layouts that are heavily grid based and can be used in sections of a website or as the main layout for a page.

MODULAR AND MASONRY GRID LAYOUTS

Modular and masonry grid layouts are similar in concept but behave differently. If you've ever been on the Pinterest website, you've seen a masonry grid layout in action. A masonry grid layout has multiple columns and rows, but the rows are not a fixed height. Unlike a modular grid, with strict row and height sizes, a masonry layout fills up the vertical space between each block of content no matter its height (figure 6.15).

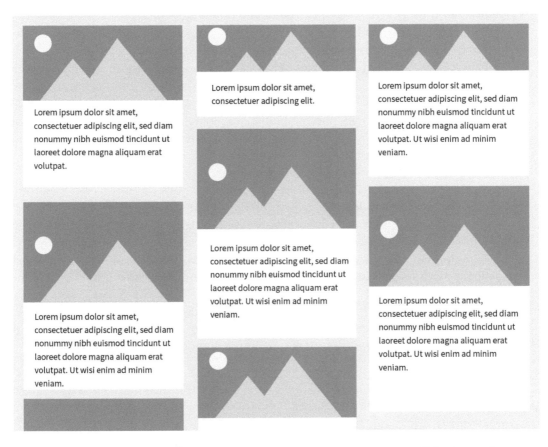

Figure 6.15 A masonry grid layout has no extra space between content items, even if they're not the same height.

This type of layout can be used to display content like images or cards (like a list of blog posts), which is more visual than a normal list. If you look at a real-life example, like Pinterest, which is probably the most famous site with a masonry layout, you can see how many different sizes of content can flow together. Different lengths of headlines of each post can make cards a bit different in size, creating visual interest on the page as opposed to a list of content with the same type of treatment just stacked on top of each other.

Deciding on what type of layout you want for each page is the first step in figuring out your site's skeleton structure and how content will be laid out. Another factor that can influence your page layout choice is user reading patterns.

6.3.3   *Reading patterns*

Reading patterns are identified by research groups using eye-tracking studies to determine how users read or scan a page. Some of the most well-documented research on eye-tracking and reading patterns has been done by the Nielsen Norman Group (NNG) and is well documented on their website. Although not a way to lay out your page per se, reading patterns can help you make design decisions based on how users typically scan a page. This information can help you group content more effectively and figure out where it can be placed to benefit your users.

It should be noted that the two patterns we'll look at in the next sections are based on reading patterns from groups who read left to right. Cultures whose languages are read from right to left or top to bottom are going to have different directional patterns for scanning content. If your website is going to be translated into one of these languages, it's important to think about how your layout should change to accommodate the directional difference. You should identify at the beginning of the project whether you'll have to accommodate both a left-to-right and right-to-right or top-to-bottom language. It shouldn't be an afterthought while designing or in the development phase, as this delay in consideration can lead to task churn and trying to fit the requirement into the layout after the fact as opposed to building it with the requirement in mind.

There are also a handful of other types of reading patterns, but I'll focus on the two most common, the Z-pattern and the F-pattern. I provide references for more in-depth information about this subject in the appendix.

THE Z-PATTERN

The Z-pattern is how a user scans a page with minimal text content. It's the path the user's eyes follow between key elements and forms an actual Z shape, as we see in figure 6.16.

Many sites use this pattern already (figure 6.17). This pattern guides the user very clearly through the page. When we apply design principles to our components and content, we're able to create a flow that will keep the user reading through the page instead of getting stuck and fixated on one point on the page.

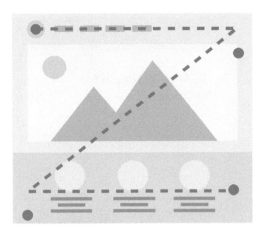

Figure 6.16 The Z-pattern is how a user typically scans a page: from left to right, and then back down to the left and right.

r/d studio   work   brands   press   about   create with us

We are a design & technology studio building **transformative** experiences for brands.

Work

Illuminated
Immersive fashion experience

Figure 6.17 The headline at the top is the first piece of content you read. Next, your eye is drawn to the Work headline and then the graphic.

This pattern acts as a blueprint and can be very helpful if you're struggling to figure out how to define the hierarchy of the page on a website. Using this pattern, ask yourself, "What's the most important content?" and "What's the page's primary purpose?" Overlay a Z shape onto your wireframe or sketch—that's where you should place your most important content. This reading pattern will be commonly used for home pages or landing pages—again, those pages that aren't dense with text.

This pattern can also be used repeatedly throughout the page (figure 6.18). It can also act as your guide if you're just learning how to use layout and want to figure out how to effectively place components and content on your home page and subpages that aren't heavy on content.

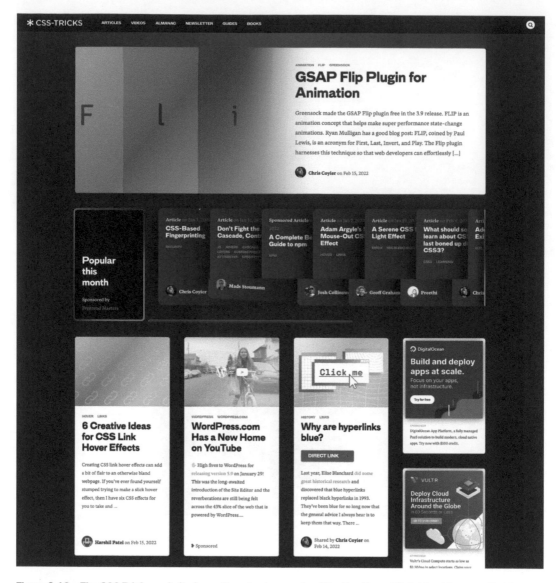

Figure 6.18   The CSS Tricks website is another good example of the Z-pattern. It's laid out in a way that keeps our eye moving through each row. (Courtesy of CSS Tricks; https://css-tricks.com/)

THE F-PATTERN

Unlike the Z-pattern, which can be helpful when deciding where to place content on your page, the F-pattern, as shown in figure 6.19, is useful for determining how you can lay out your page so that it benefits users the most.

According to NNG, the F-pattern is the most common reading pattern observed in studies, and it applies to how people scan the main body content of the page, especially

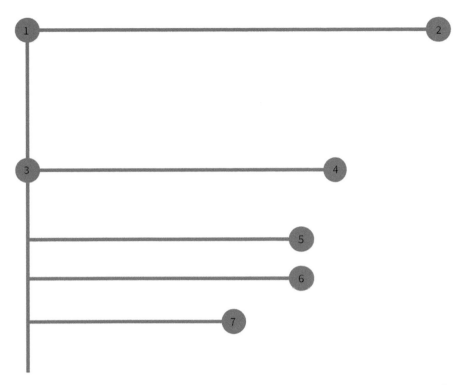

Figure 6.19   The F-pattern is a common reading pattern and works well when working with a large page of content like a news article.

text-heavy pages. On a site that reads left to right, users start in the left corner and read across that line and then move down on the left side and again scan across from left to right. Finally, they scan back to focus on the left side. They don't generally span a whole other row, although sometimes this does happen. The F-pattern visualizes how people initially scan a page. It can also indicate that your page layout has problems, especially if it's text heavy.

NNG found that the F-pattern of scanning is commonly used on pages with the same three criteria present. First, it's used on pages or sections of pages that are text heavy without any additional visual treatments to break up the wall of text. For example, text isn't broken up into subsections with subheadings, it's not bolded, and pull-out quotes or bullets are absent. It's just a wall of text. Second, NNG found that users scan in this manner when they want to be the most efficient. Finally, users scan in an F-pattern when they aren't completely engaged in the page to the point that they want to read every word.

If users are scanning in this pattern on the page, they're trying to figure out what the content is about and find the most important bits by scanning those first few lines before jumping to the next section. If some of your pages are content heavy, the F-pattern can act as a good guide to assess whether your content is broken up into consumable chunks.

Are there places you can add links? Does it make sense to bold anything or break it out into a list? Can you break things out into subsections?

Despite being the most common way people scan content on the page, the F-pattern isn't a pattern you want people to follow on the page. You'll want to counteract it with a few of the previously mentioned tips to make your page easily scannable and ensure your users can break out of reading in that pattern.

6.4   Using space

The number of times I've worked with someone who is not a designer on a project and been provided with feedback that there's "too much whitespace" makes it feel almost stereotypical. I frequently would get frustrated with this feedback. Whitespace in a design is not something to be feared and is key to making the content on a page more consumable and user friendly.

Using whitespace or negative space is vital to creating clear focal points and defining relationships between content on a page through the design fundamental of proximity and keeps your user interface clutter free. When a design has room to breathe, it feels much less overwhelming to the user. It directs them where to look and leads them through the page.

Let's look at an example where whitespace isn't used very effectively in figure 6.20. This example is based on websites from the late 1990s when developers had little control over layout. It has no space between columns, and spacing between sections and rows is tight.

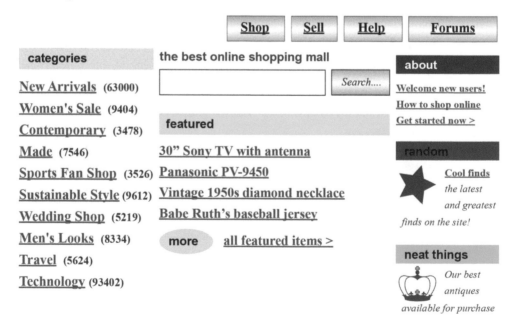

Figure 6.20   Early websites didn't use space effectively, making the page look crammed together.

Everything is squished together in the example in figure 6.20. Each section has the same heading size, so there's no clear indication of where to look. Even though the middle Featured section is bigger than the left and right columns, the content above it creates clutter. There's nothing to direct the eye to where to look first.

Let's look at an example of good use of negative space with a personal website by Henry Desroches in figure 6.21. As you scroll down the page, the eye is drawn to the section heading, which clearly tells us where we are. We know what we are supposed to look at, and there's nothing to distract us from it.

Figure 6.21 The use of negative space creates a focal point for each section heading before scrolling into the section content.

The use of negative space on this website also creates a feeling of elegance. Negative space is commonly used on high-end brand websites to create that feeling of luxury that's prevalent in physical stores. In a high-end store, items of clothing and accessories aren't crammed onto the rack but rather highlighted to showcase each piece. If clothing is hung on a rack, the number of items is limited and strategically spaced to give each piece room to breathe.

Let's look at a before-and-after example. Figure 6.22 shows several text components with a link to Read More in a simple grid format with three columns. In this graphic, the components are all placed tightly together. This creates the illusion of one big block of content as if it's all the same component, which doesn't make it easily scannable. It feels cluttered.

This is a headline
Lorem ipsum dolor sit amet, consectetuer adipiscing elit, sed diam nonummy nibh euismod tincidunt ut laoreet dolore magna aliquam erat
Read more

This is another
Lorem ipsum dolor sit amet, consectetuer adipiscing elit, sed diam nonummy nibh euismod tincidunt ut laoreet dolore magna aliquam erat
Read more

Another headline
Lorem ipsum dolor sit amet, consectetuer adipiscing elit, sed diam nonummy nibh euismod tincidunt ut laoreet dolore magna aliquam erat
Read more

This is a headline
Lorem ipsum dolor sit amet, consectetuer adipiscing elit, sed diam nonummy nibh euismod tincidunt ut laoreet dolore magna aliquam erat
Read more

This is another
Lorem ipsum dolor sit amet, consectetuer adipiscing elit, sed diam nonummy nibh euismod tincidunt ut laoreet dolore magna aliquam erat
Read more

Another headline
Lorem ipsum dolor sit amet, consectetuer adipiscing elit, sed diam nonummy nibh euismod tincidunt ut laoreet dolore magna aliquam erat
Read more

Figure 6.22   Even though different pieces of content are included on the page, they are placed too close together. There isn't much visually that makes each one distinct. If you blur your vision and look at the components, it all looks like one block of content.

If we add space between each component in figure 6.23 and make our Read More buttons more visually distinct, we get a better sense of each individual component on the page. We can more easily scan through and distinguish each unique piece of content. We know where each one starts and stops because more breathing room is included, and the added visual treatment to the Read More buttons helps further distinguish each block.

This is a headline
Lorem ipsum dolor sit amet, consectetuer adipiscing elit, sed diam nonummy nibh euismod tincidunt ut laoreet dolore magna aliquam erat

[**Read more**]

This is another
Lorem ipsum dolor sit amet, consectetuer adipiscing elit, sed diam nonummy nibh euismod tincidunt ut laoreet dolore magna aliquam erat

[**Read more**]

Another headline
Lorem ipsum dolor sit amet, consectetuer adipiscing elit, sed diam nonummy nibh euismod tincidunt ut laoreet dolore magna aliquam erat

[**Read more**]

This is a headline
Lorem ipsum dolor sit amet, consectetuer adipiscing elit, sed diam nonummy nibh euismod tincidunt ut laoreet dolore magna aliquam erat

[**Read more**]

This is another
Lorem ipsum dolor sit amet, consectetuer adipiscing elit, sed diam nonummy nibh euismod tincidunt ut laoreet dolore magna aliquam erat

[**Read more**]

Another headline
Lorem ipsum dolor sit amet, consectetuer adipiscing elit, sed diam nonummy nibh euismod tincidunt ut laoreet dolore magna aliquam erat

[**Read more**]

Figure 6.23   Adding space and making the Read More button more prominent help define each component as its own, making the page easier to scan.

Whether it was a printed flyer or a web page, I've often received the feedback "Make it bigger; there's too much whitespace" in my career. It's important to be mindful of the perspective and experience of your stakeholders when you encounter this feedback. Sometimes stakeholders don't have an eye for design. If they're asking you to fill the whitespace—we'll use a logo as an example—they may not understand that the purpose of the whitespace is to make the interface look less cluttered and busy. Every choice you make in design has a reason, so try to communicate the purpose of the whitespace—what it brings to the design and how its absence, in the case of a larger logo, will negatively affect the design.

This conversation can be applied to any piece of the interface design. If the stakeholders don't like a color, ask why. Explain why you're using the colors you're using. This sort of questioning helps get to the bottom of why they don't like something in a design and can lead to a more fruitful discussion on how to solve it. Don't leave their feedback at "I don't like this," which can cause tension in the professional relationship.

6.5 Responsive design considerations

In the modern world, we have access to the entire web on a screen that fits in our pocket. Browsing the web now happens more often on mobile devices than on a desktop. In the early days of the mobile web, many sites were just a scaled-down version of the desktop site, which was a terrible experience for users. You had to zoom in on the page to read anything, and forget about clickable targets for buttons or links when you weren't zoomed in. Just navigating through the page in that environment was frustrating. Responsive design practices have come a long way since the advent of mobile phones, as has the web technology to build designs that easily respond to the device they're on.

6.5.1 Designing for mobile

Just because we're working with limited screen space doesn't mean our design and functionality need to suffer. It's vital to understand the needs of your users when they interact with the mobile version of your website or application. Their goals may be slightly different from your desktop users. Use data and research to inform the design decisions for your mobile experience. Let's look at the key things to consider when thinking about how to adapt your website or application for smaller screens.

KEEPING CONTENT MINIMAL AND FOCUSED

We want to keep the interface of a mobile version of a website as decluttered as possible. It's not uncommon to hide certain elements or create a slightly different way to serve up information displayed by default on a desktop. This content includes things like the main navigation or components that might have a lot of information in a list format. We don't want to clutter the space by showing the full navigation. Instead, create it as an overlay that can be opened from a menu button like in figure 6.24, rather than trying to display all the navigation at once in figure 6.25.

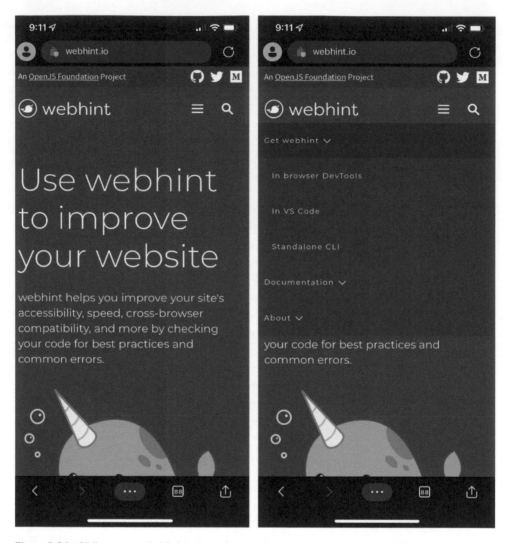

Figure 6.24   Hiding menus behind an icon the user has to open keeps the interface clutter free.

For example, a travel website with a list of hotels should only show the most vital information in that interface component, like the name, price, rating, and location or neighborhood. More information can be provided on a secondary page that a user can click into.

Figure 6.25   **Listing each menu item at the top of the page creates a lot of clutter, and it's not inherently clear whether the navigation has a hierarchy. It's just a block of links that blends in with the rest of the copy below it.**

Or you can even create an accordion menu experience that keeps the user on the list page and expands the component with information typically hidden on the smaller screen, like in figure 6.26. Focus on serving up the most important information that's easily scannable and then provide an option to show even more information through an interactive interface.

Additionally, think about what additional pieces of media you may have on your desktop site that could negatively affect how long your website or application takes to download on a phone. If you have an embedded video on the home page that doesn't contain information vital to the experience, can you replace that with a more easily consumable piece of media like an image? Are there unnecessary images or videos elsewhere on the website that you can remove that won't affect the overall experience? Focus on what your users need to see and are trying to accomplish when they're on their phone and your website and streamline your content and experience for those primary tasks.

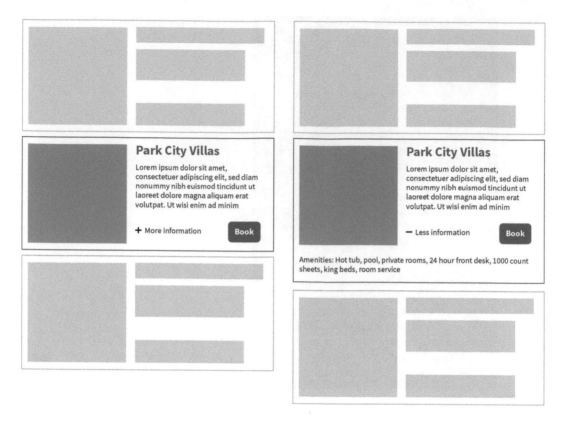

Figure 6.26   To reduce information overload and visual clutter, show only the most vital information and allow users to click in to find more information if they want it.

DESIGNING FOR TOUCH

The next factor to consider when adapting your design for smaller screened devices is designing for touch. The primary way users interact with their mobile phones is through a touch screen, which means our interactive elements need to become bigger and have better touch targets. Items like buttons should be larger on the screen, and you should also consider how people hold their phones and interact with the screen if using just one hand.

Figure 6.27 shows thumb zones for a right-handed person. We want our interactive elements to end up in the green zone labeled Natural. However, we should also consider whether it makes sense to put some sort of navigation or toolbar with common actions for our users in that space so they don't have to stretch to the top of the screen to access them. Again, it depends on your website's and your users' goals. Maybe it doesn't make sense to have the navigation at the bottom of the screen constantly but rather to provide a Back to Top button that is easily reachable in that area.

When considering touch targets, also make sure there's plenty of space between user interface elements like buttons, whether they're side by side or stacked on top of

Figure 6.27 Thumb zones for people holding a phone in their right hand. Consider how your users interact with your design and keep things in the Natural zone as much as possible.

each other. They need to be big enough with enough space between each so that users don't accidentally hit one button instead of the other, which can cause frustration and confusion.

UTILIZING CONTENT CHUNKING TO CREATE MORE MANAGEABLE TASK FLOWS

For items in long forms, especially payment and shipping addresses, use content chunking to create a more manageable task flow and make it clear where the user is in that task. For example, you can visually represent the steps they need to complete. Instead of serving up an entire page of inputs for payment and a shipping address, we've broken out the form into steps—the payment method (figure 6.28), the shipping address, and shipping options, all on their own screens with very clear buttons to go back and forward in the process.

This sort of content chunking makes the task more manageable and doesn't overwhelm the user. It's also easier to fix problems like errors from user input, such as a missing credit card number, when each step in the task is broken out. The user can focus on fixing the error with the credit card as opposed to fixing multiple errors on a page with all the form inputs for addresses and payments. This streamlines and focuses the experience when your user is trying to complete a task.

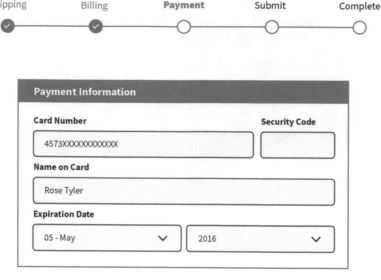

Figure 6.28   Break up larger task flows into individual pages when possible and indicate where users are in the flow to keep the task manageable.

KEEPING VISUAL STYLES AND ELEMENTS CONSISTENT ACROSS ALL EXPERIENCES

Finally, keep the visual styles and elements of your mobile experience the same as your website, adapting things like sizing and reducing content clutter. However, don't use a different set of colors and typography or change the visual treatment of illustrations or photographs on your mobile website. These items create brand consistency and familiarity so users don't get confused when moving between your desktop and mobile experiences. Your mobile website should look like the desktop website, just adapted for better usability on smaller screens.

6.5.2   *Designing for multiscreen and foldable devices*

A new class of devices emerged on the market in 2019 after years of different prototypes since the early 2000s: multiscreen foldable devices. These devices fold open and closed like a book, and depending on the device type, either have two screens divided by a physical fold, which can obscure content on the web, or one screen that folds in half, which does not obscure the screen.

A few companies continue to invest in the production of this new class of devices. Designing for these types of devices might feel daunting. But multiscreen foldable devices are the next step in responsive design and provide a unique opportunity to offer users an enhanced experience that uses both screens. For example, in figure 6.29, a recipe website could be adapted to display the ingredients on one screen and the recipe's steps on the other screen. So, the ingredients and their amounts are always available when scrolling through the recipe steps.

Pasta Carbonara

Yield: 4 servings

Time: 25 minutes

Ingredients

2 tbsp salt

4 oz. guaniciale, pancetta, or bacon

1 oz grated pecorino Romano

1 oz grated Parmesan

4 large egg yolks

2 large eggs

Freshly ground black pepper (coarse)

2 tbsp. extra-virgin olive oil

1 lb. spaghetti, bucatini, or rigatoni

Preparation

Step 1

Heat 6 quarts of water in a large pot and add 2 tbsp salt when water starts to boil.

Step 2

Remove guaniciale, pancetta or bacon from packaging and cut into strips that are 1/4 inch thick

Figure 6.29   With dual-screen devices, web layouts can now be split across two screens.

At the time of this writing, the APIs for creating layouts for dual screens are experimental and not yet available in all browsers. However, they provide a look into what the future holds for multiscreen devices and an opportunity to design enhanced experiences that delight users.

From a coding perspective, APIs for JavaScript and CSS were written with familiar coding concepts like media queries and environmental variables. As a result, developers won't need to learn new concepts to write code adapted for the device and can spend more time focusing on how to use two screens for a more functional and interesting experience design for users.

Summary

- Before applying any visual elements, such as typography and color, you want to establish and refine the website structure by creating a blueprint. Define each section of content that will be on a page, like your header, footer, and main content, and then define how your main content section will be divided up.
- Define the grid you want to use to organize the content within the sections that you have listed out. This grid becomes your system for organizing and placing content on the page. The grid comprises columns, rows, and gaps between each. The most common number of columns used is 12 for desktops, 8 for tablets, and 4 for mobile phones. Many free tools are available online to help you define your grid easily.

- When choosing a layout for your website, consider the type of content that will be displayed on the page. Not all pages have to share the same type of layout, although pages that offer similar content should have the same page structure. For example, all your product pages should share a layout so as not to cause confusion, but your product pages will not share the same layout with the home page.

- Reading patterns, as identified by research groups, reflect how users scan a page. While these patterns shouldn't necessarily inform how you lay out the entire page, they can affect where you place some pieces of content.

- Whitespace should be embraced and utilized in a design to create a cleaner and less cluttered user interface. Every pixel on the page does not need to be filled by imagery or a component. Spacing between components and blocks of content is vital for defining relationships between items on the page, making it easier to scan and consume.

- When designing for mobile devices, don't create a miniature version of the desktop website. Instead, reduce content and information where possible and give users the option of viewing additional information by, for example, tapping into a component. The experience on mobile should be enhanced to be more usable and consumable while still retaining the brand and style characteristics of the desktop website.

Enhancing web layout with animation

This chapter covers

- How to use animation effectively to enhance the user experience and usability of a website or application
- When to use animation and what that animation should provide for users
- How to plan animations in the design phase before coding begins

Animation is to a website or web application what the extra sprinkles are to a cupcake. The frosted cupcake is still as delicious and edible without the sprinkles, but the sprinkles (or other accouterments) create a unique experience for the person eating it. Suppose the sprinkles are gold flaked and elegantly wrapped around the cupcake frosting. This presentation would create a much more memorable experience for the person eating it. They may take more time admiring the edible gold flakes before deciding how to eat the cupcake. Perhaps even the pattern of the gold flakes influences their decision on how they choose to eat it. Extra sprinkles on top of the cupcake frosting also create a much more memorable interaction than, say, a cupcake with no sprinkles and just some frosting. The eater is less inclined to spend time with the cupcake if it's just covered in some buttercream frosting. The cupcake is edible and still good, but it may not be memorable or delight the eater like a few well-placed sprinkles would.

When it comes to websites, animation is the sprinkles on top of the cupcake. If done well, animation makes the experience more memorable and more delightful. However, bad animation can be just as memorable with the opposite effect on visitors to our website. Whether it's too much animation or it doesn't consider users' personal settings—for example, reduced motion—bad animation can make our site less usable and less accessible. The use of animation shouldn't make the site experience any worse than it would be without it. It should inform users and delight them. Just like the cupcake is edible without the sprinkles, your website should be just as usable without animation.

7.1   Why use animation?

Animation should be applied to your website with care and thoughtfulness. It shouldn't be added just because you want some motion on your website. Do you have a purpose and a plan for the animation you want to use? Is it on brand for the type of client you're building for? For example, I wouldn't expect to encounter much animation on a website for a hospital or a healthcare provider that specializes in terminal illnesses. Maybe a light scroll effect is applied, or certain buttons change color or have a subtle hover effect. However, it's important to consider your users' emotional state when they're on your website and whether superfluous animation is appropriate.

7.1.1   Improve usability

Improving the usability of your website or application is the main reason to introduce some animation and motion. The caveat is that if your website is all animation based, like a game, animation is necessary. However, animation on marketing and e-commerce websites should primarily be used to improve usability.

Animations can be combined with our design fundamentals like contrast to provide more obvious cues to users about where they may want to proceed next on the website, guiding them through an actual user flow you already planned out in your research phase. It can also demonstrate how to use the site or indicate the function of something. It should help users in their journey through using your website or web application and shouldn't inhibit them from using your site and accessing the primary content in any way. It should enhance and not subtract from the experience, which is why you should test your interactive prototypes with users.

7.1.2   Create memorable interactions

Beyond informing users of a UI element's function or purpose, animation can delight the user and create a memorable experience. One of my favorite animations is of the snow Yeti, as shown in figure 7.1, which tracks your mouse movements and then animates when you've filled out the form successfully. The animation when the user submits the form not only serves the purpose of informing the user; it also adds some playfulness to the experience before the user submits the form. I'm more likely to remember this experience with this form because it's unlike any other form I've filled out online. Find opportunities to create delight for the project, if appropriate. It will leave a lasting effect on your users and get them to return to your website or even share the experience with others, which will drive visitors to your site.

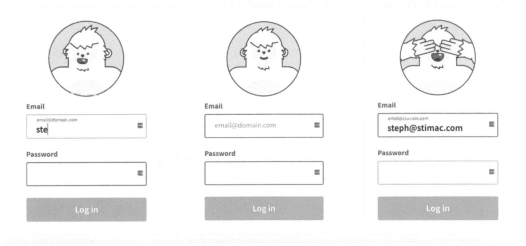

Figure 7.1   Yeti login form animation by Darin Senneff showing the Yeti in different stages depending on what part of the form you're filling out. (Courtesy of Darin Senneff)

7.1.3   Use as decoration to spark an emotional response

Finally, animation's only purpose may be decoration. However, when done in a way that isn't overwhelming, it can spark an emotional response in users of the website, which can either contribute to creating a memorable experience on the site or just add a little bit of fun. Maybe it's not enough to make a user share the site experience with someone else, but it makes their experience on the site more enjoyable.

In the past, one of my favorite retailers with physical stores and an e-commerce presence put Christmas lights at the top of their e-commerce store around the holidays in November and December (see figure 7.2). The multicolor lights would blink softly. They weren't distracting or overwhelming and didn't draw my attention away from my primary focus for being on the website. They added to the ambiance and made my online shopping feel just a bit more festive without having to deal with the crowds in a physical store.

Figure 7.2   An example of a website header of a retail site with Christmas lights, which could be animated with opacity or color changes to show subtle blinking

A personal example is my technical blog and portfolio. The hyperlinks have a thick light-purple underline that animates upward to highlight the whole word when someone hovers over it (figure 7.3). I implemented this feature for purely decorative purposes while I was experimenting with some CSS animations. Your personal website, if you have one, can be a great place to experiment. You can try things you may not normally get to implement on a client's website, and you have more time and free range to figure out what works without the stress of taking time from a paid client. I've received several comments on social media about that hover animation. I added the effect for decorative and experimental purposes but found it also does a good job of saying "I'm clickable!" thus adding a functional purpose that elicits a response from my site's visitors.

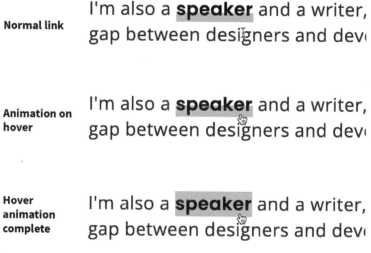

Figure 7.3   Animation progression of a hover effect on a link. The normal link is the state in which it exists without any interaction. The animation on hover shows the purple outline has transitioned upward, and then the final animation shows the link completely highlighted by the color.

7.2 When to use animation

Animation should be used to improve usability, create memorable experiences, and elicit emotional responses from our users. However, when is the right time, and what are the right scenarios to use animation to accomplish these things? Let's look at a few common scenarios to consider where to apply animation for a website or application.

7.2.1 Providing cues for navigating the site

Depending on the type and style of website you are designing, navigational cues are one way to incorporate animation. There are subtle ways to apply movement to elements to indicate the next action a user should take, such as scrolling or clicking the Next button to access further information. I've often seen a Scroll at the bottom of a web page that fades in and out or slowly bounces up and down. This movement brings enough attention to the animated element, especially on a site where all other elements are static, that the user will notice the change on the page and proceed accordingly.

If you're building a website that you expect your users to interact with more than once and return to somewhat frequently—something that provides a more app-like experience—animation can be used to familiarize your users with where to find certain actions and how to do things. For example, let's say you've built a web application for dream journaling. Your users would, ideally, frequent your application almost daily. So, on the first run experience, you may provide tooltips that appear one after the other, indicating how to complete certain actions and where to find things. These shouldn't be intrusive and should be easy to clear if the user doesn't want to see them. While a small change, the fading in and out of tooltips is a way of using animation to direct visitors to your site or application.

7.2.2 Giving users feedback when interacting with UI elements

One of the easiest and most direct ways to incorporate animation on your website is by providing users with visual feedback when they interact with UI elements on the page. For example, a button may change color or position when it's hovered over, certain form inputs may respond to interaction, and a text input's outline color can be animated when it's clicked into. All of these animations are subtle indications to the user that something has happened and they are interacting with the website.

This type of animation can go a step beyond indicating an interaction has occurred to confirm whether that action was successful. A common example is password inputs. The example I'm most used to encountering occurs when I don't enter the correct pin in my iPhone. The dots at the top of the screen move back and forth quickly, indicating something went wrong. Although this example relates to a mobile phone's operating system, the same concept applies to the web.

If I log in to a website, enter the wrong password, and see the login form shake before telling me I entered the wrong password, I can connect the dots more quickly and conclude that something failed. It takes me a bit more time to process the error if I enter a wrong password and an error message appears, but that's all that has changed on the form. Nothing out of the ordinary happened to indicate something in the flow I was working through went wrong. I then need to scan the form, look for the error message, and parse what happened. The shake animation to indicate something went wrong gives me immediate feedback and reduces my cognitive load of trying to process what went wrong, and I can more quickly start retyping my password to complete my task.

To determine potential areas where animation could be applied on your website, identify the user touch points—the user interface elements that users will interact with by clicking on or into. What kind of feedback do you need to give them? Are they filling out a form? What happens when the form is submitted? What happens if the form submission fails? If it is successful? Can animation provide useful visual feedback to the user to make their next step clear? Or if they're simply hovering over a button, what kind of state change can you provide that makes it clear that the button is clickable? Maybe it changes position slightly, or maybe there's a color fade. This sort of feedback says to the user, "I am interactive, so please click me!"

7.2.3   *Navigation and page transitions*

When a user is transiting your website or application, animating between pages is another way to incorporate motion into your website. Navigation transitions tend to be much more prominent on mobile applications when you're switching between screens. For example, say you're viewing hotel listings in an app on your phone and select a hotel to view more details. A nice transition between the list page and the individual hotel page can occur where the listing expands and becomes the details page, blocking out the listing page. Planning that animation would look something like the wireframe in figure 7.4

Animation in transitions helps orient the user in the application and gives the sense that the user is traveling deeper into the app and its subpages. If the user went back to the hotel list page, the return animation could conceivably be the page minimizing back to the list, a reverse of the original animation.

In a typical desktop experience on the web, you click a link, and a new page loads with no transition. While navigation transitions are much more common on mobile apps, a few frameworks, like React and Vue.js, make these transitions available for desktops. Adding these transitions not only helps orient the user like on a mobile app but can also make navigating a website feel much smoother. Not having an animated page transition doesn't make the experience on the website bad, but applying animation in this instance can provide user delight with how seamless it can feel to navigate through a website with these transitions in place.

Figure 7.4   A wireframe can show the progression of a transition. The wireframe on the right shows the transition after the hotel listing on the right is clicked.

7.2.4   *Indicate the status of something in progress*

Jakob Nielsen, co-founder of the Nielsen Norman Group and web usability expert, said, "When users know the current system status, they learn the outcome of their prior interactions and determine next steps" (http://mng.bz/MBM8). Keeping your users informed about where they are and what's going on when they're interacting with your website is another ripe opportunity to use animation to provide visual feedback on the status of their journey through your site.

The easiest way to use animation to indicate status is to utilize a loading animation. Whether someone has clicked into a page or has submitted a form, a loading animation is a clear way to say "Something is happening; it's just taking a moment to complete" if the page isn't loading quickly or visual feedback isn't immediate. Without a loading animation, the user has no idea whether something's going on when they see a blank screen as the page takes time to load. Is the page loading? Did something freeze? Do I need to refresh? If the page is loading content, another option instead of the typical loading spinner is to show skeleton content (figure 7.5) that looks like a wireframe of the loading content. It could also have some sort of animation. For example, the color could fade in and out ever so slightly to create a pulsing effect, so it appears something is happening to the page.

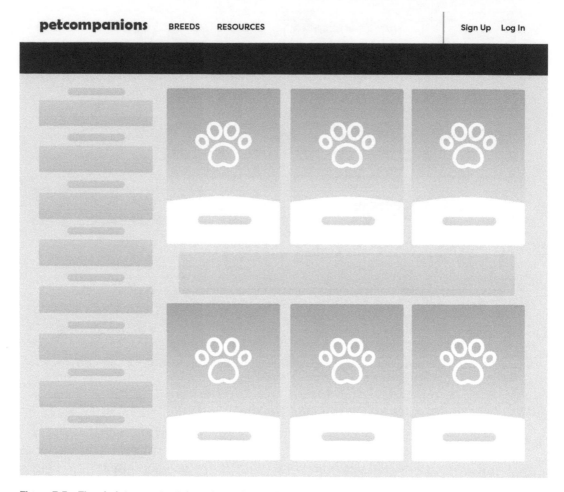

Figure 7.5   The skeleton content doesn't need to be just gray boxes. You can add some icons or use a brand color to create a less sterile experience.

The same goes for submitting a form. Let's say your user just filled out an order form and payment details, so it takes a little time for the payment to process. Say they submit the form and don't get an immediate "Order successfully submitted" (or an error message if the form submission fails). In addition, no loading animation appears between the time they click Submit Order and receive the final success or error message. They may assume that something went wrong or the order didn't go through, causing them to refresh the page or start over, which is frustrating.

The more obvious place to consider animation when communicating status is a progress bar, whether it's to show the state of uploading or downloading or to indicate a longer-than-expected process. I've seen the progress bar used a few different ways, with the most memorable being Domino's online order system. I would order a pizza and then be shown a progress page, the "Pizza Tracker." It was just a loading bar, but it was sectioned out into a few different stages like "Prep" and "Bake." Each section would animate until the step was complete. This animation added an extra layer to the experience of ordering a pizza: the animated progress bar for each section gave me the feeling that I was watching the pizza being made.

Another example of a loading screen that provides a delightful and memorable interaction is the loading screen in the German BVG app. When you're waiting for your ticket purchase to complete, a loading screen pops up with a mesmerizing animation you can watch while waiting. I never get tired of it, and it makes the wait seem short. The animation shows a few different train shapes from a head-on view. They bounce as you wait, and as they bounce down and then up, they each morph seamlessly into the next train shape. It's an incredibly smooth and well-thought-out animation that lets you know something is happening. While it doesn't give an exact status, it's clear that your ticket purchase is in progress.

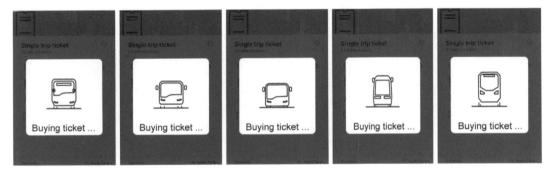

Figure 7.6   From left to right, the train illustrations bounce up and then down before morphing into the next train on the next bounce up. (Courtesy of Frank Schreier)

Keeping your users informed about the status of their journey through your website or application is just good usability. It lets your users know what action they just completed and indicates their next step. It also provides a perfect opportunity for animation to be brought into play, resulting in a good experience for your users.

7.2.5   *Consider the long haul*

One of the most important things to remember when applying animation to the experience you're building is that it shouldn't inhibit your users from interacting with your website. The amount of data necessary to display animations can cause serious user experience problems. Unnecessary animations may even add cost to an end user for data usage. Therefore, for more immersive animations, like those that show how to use your product, it's important to ensure that users with reduced bandwidth and lower connection speeds can entirely disable animation. In addition, experience-blocking animations should only be shown on the first visit to your website; the experience should be skipped for returning users, who may grow impatient or annoyed.

Users may get annoyed with certain experiences involving animation, even smaller ones, if they repeatedly encounter them. Consider the long haul when it comes to including animation in your website: how you expect your users to interact with your website and the duration of animations are important. The best way to determine whether an animation is inhibiting the experience or annoying is to test with your users.

You can build a rough, interactive prototype (it doesn't have to be perfect) and have something users can interact with. Ask them questions about the experience and how they would feel encountering this experience repeatedly. Ask them how the animation makes them feel. As designers and builders of these experiences, we can sometimes become tied to certain touches we've added, but we need to ensure we're adding value to the experience. At the baseline, if we're not adding value, we shouldn't be making the experience of interacting with the website or application we're building worse for our users.

7.3   How to plan animations

Like the rest of our website or application design, it's important to have a plan for what you're going to animate. This plan gives you a blueprint that lays out how the experience starts, what happens in the middle, and how the experience should end. These plans for animations should be cheap to produce, meaning they shouldn't take a lot of time. And, while some animators or motion designers create elaborate plans, they don't need to be elaborate for the types of animations you'll create.

Planning out animation is called storyboarding. Motion designers and film animators use storyboarding to visually plan out a sequence of events in a low-fidelity way. Generally, storyboards are sketches that depict actions or events in a series of panels. When planning animations for the web or an application, you can use storyboards for everything from a simple button animation (showing the direction of a hover) to more elaborate animations such as transitions and scrolling. The most important thing is that the storyboard gives a sense of the sequence's start, middle, and end.

7.3.1   How to storyboard

As developers, you'll most commonly animate elements of the UI. Elements will be scrolling, hovering, or sliding. Storyboarding comes into play when you want to convey this movement. Your storyboards can be incredibly low fidelity, the roughest and most unproportionate sketch; it doesn't matter so long as there's a sense of the start, middle, and end.

The benefit of storyboards is similar to that of wireframes. Storyboarding plans out each step in an animation and can benefit developers when deciding how to code the animation. They're rough concepts that are easy to sketch out on paper to get buy-in from a client or stakeholder before spending a lot of time on a polished design. In the case of animation, a polished design means time spent coding. Especially when you're on a tight timeline and have a limited budget, spending time coding and figuring out animation can be too expensive.

Figure 7.7 An example of how low fidelity a storyboard can be as long as it conveys the idea or story you're trying to animate

Exercise: Draw a storyboard for an animated object

Let's practice sketching out a quick storyboard that shows how we want to animate a button. Draw three blank squares or rectangles. These shapes will be our panels that show different states of animation for the button. In the first panel, sketch your button in its resting state, when nothing is hovering over it. In the second panel, sketch your button in the state it should be in when it's being hovered over. Ask yourself what you want to happen under this condition. Does it move in a direction? Does it get bigger? Does it change shape? Quickly sketch this state using things like arrows to indicate motion. For example, if the button moves up when it's being hovered over, draw the button higher than the position in the first panel and add some arrows to indicate which direction it's moving. Then, in the third panel, sketch the final state when the button is pressed to confirm the action was successful. Does it change color? Does something in the button itself, like the text, change? What's the final state?

This exercise should take only a few minutes. These sketches should be quick and without a lot of detail. And now you have a storyboard for an animated button!

7.4 Technical considerations of animation

As previously mentioned, animation should be applied with care because we don't want to overwhelm our users visually. Too much animation can also overwhelm our users' devices. We need to take care in both instances because animation comes with a cost to performance, affects the speed of a website or application, and can physically affect some people.

7.4.1 Performance considerations

When done incorrectly, animation can cause something called *jank* in the browser, meaning it slows down the user interface. Responding to user interaction while loading animation in the background can take time. What you animate with can also play a part in slowing down site performance.

While CSS animations can be the least costly in terms of browser performance, some CSS properties are more expensive to animate because of how the browser handles the animation. Animating some elements' properties, such as width, height, and font size, requires the browser to recalculate the position and shape and then repaint the entire element, which is costly in terms of performance. More costly properties to animate also include color, margin, and position. Less costly properties include opacity or transform because they don't require the browser to repaint them or change the layout. For an in-depth list of the different CSS properties and what the browser needs to do to animate them, check out the website CSS Triggers (https://csstriggers.com).

How animation affects the performance of your website is a key factor to consider when planning out your animations. They should add to the user experience in a meaningful way, or if they are purely for delight, they shouldn't negatively affect the user experience or create a slowly loading website or application.

7.4.2   *Accessibility considerations*

When determining animations and how they will affect the user experience of your website, you need to consider the accessibility of the animations. The Web Content Accessibility Guidelines (WCAG) developed through the W3C provide different levels of accessibility compliance for the web, including animation. When designing, we should consider two main factors when it comes to accessibility and animation: first, we should provide users a way to pause, stop, and hide animation, and second, we should include an experience for users who have reduced motion settings turned on in their system preferences. Reduced motion settings are important for people who may become ill from certain animations. Intense animations involving flashing can also cause seizures, so providing a way to turn these off or not show them at all, based on user preference, can create a more enjoyable experience.

The recommendation to pause, stop, or hide animations on a page specifically applies to any animated user interface element that doesn't require user interaction to trigger it or lasts longer than 5 seconds. An example is a landing page with a background video that starts playing automatically. To comply with WCAG guidelines, there should be a way to stop or pause the video.

Reduced motion settings are created in the development portion of the project but should be considered ahead of time and planned for when you're initially planning your animations. You can utilize the `prefers-reduced-motion` media query in your code to create a less-intense animation.

Summary

- Use animation in your website or application with care and thoughtfulness; otherwise, it can negatively affect a website's user experience. When applied correctly, it can improve usability, create memorable interactions, and spark emotional responses from users.

- Animation can be added to navigation and page transitions to orient users. These animations offer cues for navigating your website and give users feedback when interacting with UI elements to help them understand what's happening on the screen.

- Frequently, animation is used to indicate the status of a user's progress. The goal—to reflect the user's journey through your website or to indicate whether a page is loading—is to keep your users informed and oriented throughout their experience on your site.

- Consider how animations will affect the user experience of the site over the long haul. Will they inhibit the way users interact with your site? Will they get annoying or frustrating for return users? Animation shouldn't negatively affect the user experience, so consider these questions when planning your animation.

- Storyboarding quick sketches of what you want a UI element to do when users interact with it is as valuable as wireframing but, due to very low fidelity, much less time consuming. The goal is to convey movement and a start, middle, and end.

- Animations can become extremely expensive in terms of page load time, so consider what animations are essential to your experience. If you can, animate elements without using CSS properties that require the browser to repaint or shift the layout.

- Accessibility is a vital component of building for the web. Animations should adhere to the WCAG guidelines, if applicable. These guidelines include providing a way to stop, pause, and hide animations that automatically start on page load and coding in an alternative experience for people who have reduced motion settings turned on using the `prefers-reduced-motion` media query.

Choosing and working with typography on the web

8

Typography is one of the most powerful aspects of visual design because depending on the typeface, the meaning of the words can change very quickly, like in figure 8.1. "I'll love you forever" takes on a much more sinister meaning with the typeface on the bottom compared with the one on the top.

Figure 8.1   The meaning of "I'll love you forever" becomes much more sinister when we change the typeface from a script to a decorative horror-themed one.

Comic Sans is perhaps the most notorious example of a digital typeface being used to convey a meaning opposite of its intent. This childlike, whimsical typeface often appears in serious (even government) communications. First bundled with Microsoft's Windows 95, it has been used frequently in appropriate situations, like the classroom, but more often than not, it's used in inappropriate situations. For example, in 2019, a former attorney to the President of the United States wrote a letter explaining certain people's involvement in a political scandal, making headlines because the font was entirely too whimsical for the situation (http://mng.bz/gBlG). An attorney sending an official letter with a typeface that looks like a child's writing conveys a message of unprofessionalism and flippancy compared to a serif font like Times New Roman.

The visual treatment of type communicates a message beyond just the literal meaning of the words on the page. It can evoke emotion from users and, when used correctly, help visually set the tone of a design, even without the assistance of any other sort of graphic elements. You can tell a story purely through the treatment applied to lettering, and I think nondesigners often overlook its importance because they don't understand it. The choice is more than between a sans serif, serifed, script, and decorative font. Typeface conveys whether your brand is serious or playful, and it sets the underlying tone for the entire experience, even in the most subtle of instances.

8.1   Type basics

A number of different typography terms are helpful to understand before we look at how to pick type for projects. There are different classifications of type, and each broad umbrella category has a general look and feel that can influence the decisions you make when choosing typefaces. Different styles and weights are available within each typeface, which can make picking type a bit daunting, especially if you're working with a typeface that has a large family of styles and weights.

8.1.1   Distinguishing between a typeface and a font

The terms *font* and *typeface* have unique definitions, although they frequently are used interchangeably. A typeface is a set of characters, such as Avenir or Helvetica, and a font exists within a typeface. There can be many different fonts within a typeface. Font refers to the variation in weight, sizing, and style within a typeface.

For projects, you'll pick typefaces and then choose specific fonts within each typeface. You most likely won't use the entire typeface, as some typefaces can have 18 or more fonts to pick from. To visualize the difference between a typeface and a font, let's look at Google's font library website, where you can pick typefaces to use in your projects, shown in figure 8.2.

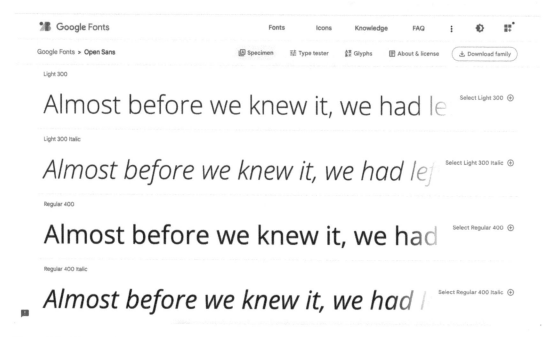

Figure 8.2   This typeface is Open Sans, and all the styles shown are the fonts within the typeface. I frequently use the Open Sans Regular 400 font for my web projects when I want a readable font for the main body text.

8.1.2   Different type classifications

At a high level, typefaces are categorized into four main classifications: serif, sans serif (meaning without serif), scripts, and decorative styles. Although several subclassifications for typefaces exist beyond these four main categories, that discussion extends beyond the scope of this chapter. The four main classifications help categorize and group typefaces that share similar characteristics. It's helpful to understand each classification when deciding on typefaces for your project. Each classification has an inherent look and feel that is important to consider depending on the message your project is trying to communicate.

SERIF

Serif typefaces get their name from the small lines added at the end of other larger strokes (see figure 8.3). These small lines are called *serifs*. Serif typefaces have been around for over a thousand years, with ancient Romans using a serif typeface when they carved words into stone.

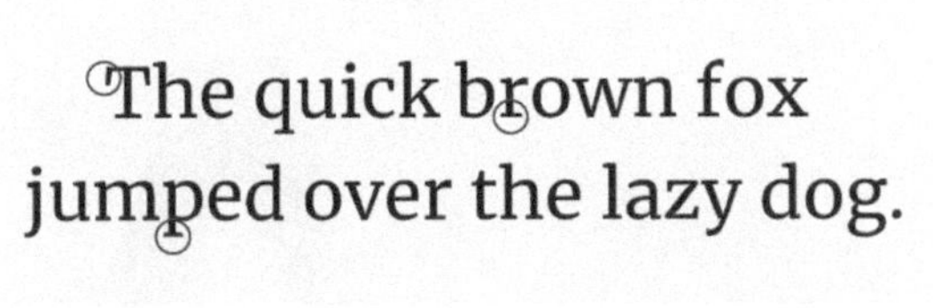

The quick brown fox
jumped over the lazy dog.

Figure 8.3 Serifs are the small lines extending off the larger main strokes of the letter.

The first printing presses, invented in the 15th century, included serif typefaces. These typefaces continue to be used in the modern day for printing newspapers and books. They work exceptionally well for body copy, which is the text that makes up the primary content of a page. However, today's tools and digital font options offer sans serif fonts that are just as legible and easy to read as a serif font. Because so many options are now available, picking a typeface comes down to the feeling it conveys.

Serif fonts overall tend to give a more professional and strict feeling to a project. At my first full-time job as a designer, the owners hired an outside agency to redesign our website. We were a tech startup, so we wanted to convey that we were modern but professional. One of the example mockups showed our website with serifed fonts. I called out this selection for not feeling modern and not really giving the vibe of a tech startup; the CFO took a moment to look between the sans serif and serif options and agreed.

Are there more modern-looking serif typefaces and a way to make old serif typefaces look modern? Absolutely! I usually look to certain print publications to get an idea of how to use serif fonts in the contemporary environment; *Vogue* is one of my favorites to reference. The best way to understand how to use type is to study what's already been done and use those examples to fuel decisions, allowing you to start experimenting outside the box. But you can also use serif fonts in a more traditional way to give a professional, refined, and classic feeling, sometimes even conveying a conservative feeling.

SANS SERIF

Sans comes from the French word for *without*. Based on what we just learned about serif fonts and this brief French lesson, we can conclude that a sans serif typeface is a typeface without serifs. While sans serifs were used in ancient times in tablet writing, they were not used in printing until the 18th century. They were often used for advertisements, but their popularity really didn't take off until the 1920s when more modernist designs started to develop. Because the letters were hard to distinguish in big blocks of text, sans serifs were used sparingly in print, limited primarily to shorter lines such as big, bold headlines. Generally, sans serifs have the same line thickness throughout a letter, unlike serifs where line thickness throughout a letter can vary. Figure 8.4 compares a letter in serif and sans serif types.

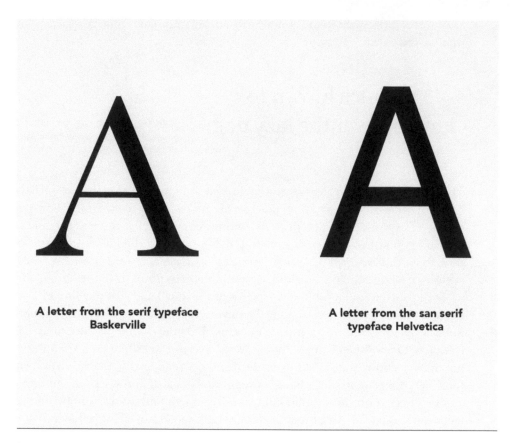

A letter from the serif typeface
Baskerville

A letter from the san serif
typeface Helvetica

Figure 8.4   Serif vs. sans serif. The serif, with one side much thinner than the other, has greater variation in line strokes than the sans serif.

The sparing use of sans serif for big blocks of text was largely due to printing constraints; with the advent of digital typography, sans serif typefaces have flourished. They work well and are readable on a screen. My personal blog, for example, uses Open Sans for the body copy. At one point, usability guidelines even suggested that sans serif typefaces were the preferred style for readability and legibility reasons on websites. Improvements in display technology now offer much more freedom in the digital space to use both serif and sans serif typefaces. However, as with all design decisions, it's important to think about your main user group in addition to the brand feeling you're trying to communicate. On lower-resolution screens, serif typefaces may still be slightly distorted, so if your product or website targets a group of users who may be using lower-end devices, you should test your choices to see how they render on a similar device.

If you want to communicate the message that you're trendy and with the times, a sans serif font is your best choice. Sans serif typefaces typically give designs a much more modern mood and clean feeling. They often have a wide range of font styles, from ultra-thin to heavy black weights, offering a lot of opportunities to create the right feeling for your project.

SCRIPT

Script typefaces are typefaces based on calligraphy and handwriting. The styles can range from a very formal script, like in figure 8.5, to a less formal and more loose script, like in figure 8.6. With the explosion in popularity of hand lettering in the past few years, the thicker, more casual-looking script typefaces have become extremely popular for events such as weddings, which use these typefaces on everything from their websites and invitations to decorations for the event.

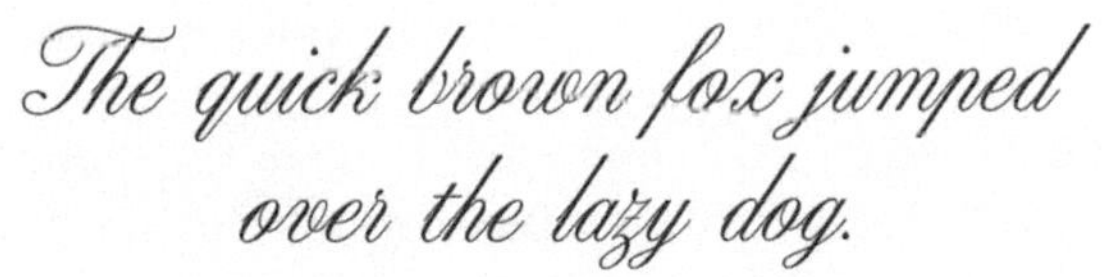

The quick brown fox jumped over the lazy dog.

Figure 8.5   A more traditional script that looks like cursive handwriting

The quick brown fox jumped over the lazy dog.

Figure 8.6   A script with a more modern, playful feel with big strokes resembling thick brush strokes

The types of projects in which you would use these kinds of typefaces are somewhat limited. I've most commonly seen them on wedding, freelance photographer, and blogger websites (including my own style blog).

Script typefaces are typically limited to large headlines and titles and should never be used for body copy. Due to the amount of detail in script typefaces and the small size of body copy on a website, scripts can be very hard to read in large blocks. It's better to keep script typefaces as large as possible with short lines of text. On my style blog, for example, I use a mix of a sans serif and a hand-lettered typeface for section titles, like you see in figure 8.7.

I keep the use of the hand-lettered font minimal to emphasize the word that indicates the section. In figure 8.7, the heading for the section is Shop Favorites, with emphasis on "Favorites" to indicate my favorite items at the moment. The heading also creates a sense of the page's hierarchy as this treatment appears throughout the page.

Figure 8.7   Using sans serif and a bold hand-lettered font for section titles on a style blog

When you scroll down to Latest Posts, shown in figure 8.8, you see the same treatment, unlike any other typography on the page. It's bold and draws the eye through the page, clearly indicating a new section.

Figure 8.8   The same heading style is repeated, creating a distinct indication of a new section.

While script typefaces are less common than sans serif and serif typefaces, they do offer a distinct personality to a page. Depending on the kind of product being sold or the kind of website, like a blog, they may be an appropriate option. As always, if you're unsure, test some design options with your users to get feedback.

DECORATIVE

Decorative typefaces have ornaments, embellishments, or other treatments that make them unique. In the early days of LiveJournal and Myspace when I was teaching myself how to use Photoshop, I was particularly taken with grunge-style fonts, like in figure 8.9.

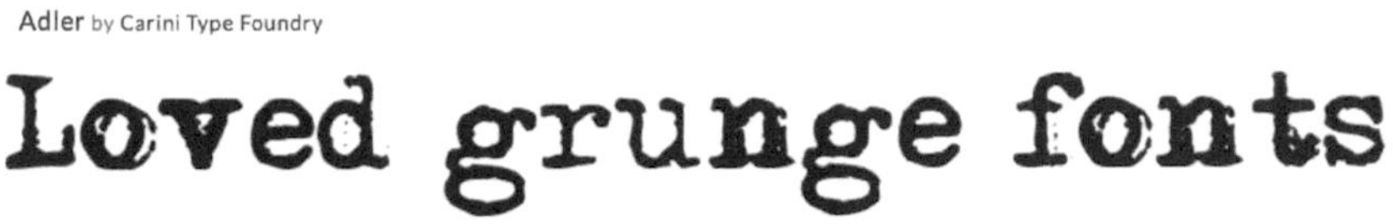

Adler by Carini Type Foundry

Loved grunge fonts

Figure 8.9   This decorative font has a rough feel to each letter and is so stylized that it doesn't fit into the classic sans serif or serif category.

Decorative typefaces, like Script typefaces, should not be used in body copy and should be used sparingly for headlines or section headings. The different kinds of subcategories for decorative fonts are extensive. These typefaces are more suited for novelty websites or even event websites like a comic book expo or music festival. They have their place in design but aren't typically used unless you're after a very specific theme for your website. If you're building an application, I'd avoid specialty typefaces and stick to a sans serif that can be read easily on smaller screens. If you'd like to browse more decorative typefaces to see what people have designed, check out the Novelty section on Font Squirrel (www.fontsquirrel.com/) or 1001 Fonts (www.1001Fonts.com), which has a Decorative category along with many other categories that would fall under this decorative style.

8.1.3   Font styles and weights

Each typeface family has multiple font styles, from italics and oblique to thin and thick bold weighted. These different style types are often used to emphasize certain words. Depending on the emphasis you want to create, you can choose italics (or oblique) or an extremely weighted font, like a heavy bold.

ITALICS AND OBLIQUE

Although italic and oblique styles are both slanted font styles, some stylistic differences exist between them and how they are designed. Italics tend to have a more script-like quality, and the characters have different design qualities compared to the normal font style of the typeface, like we see in figure 8.10.

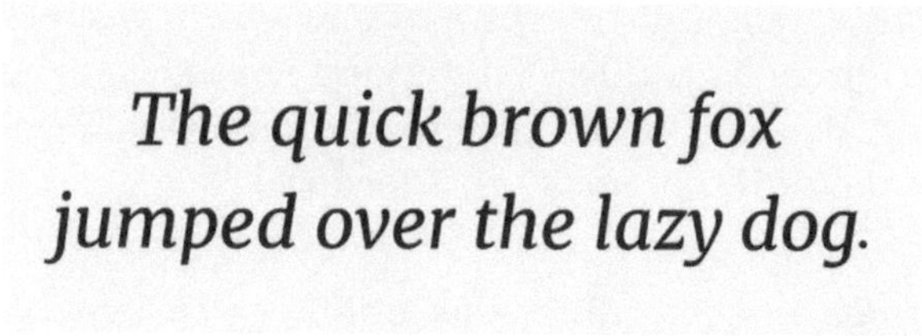

The quick brown fox jumped over the lazy dog.

Figure 8.10   Italics aren't just slanted; they have design elements added that make the slant feel more cursive and natural.

Oblique style fonts are merely fonts that are slanted with no design differences between the normal typeface and the oblique styling except the slant. Figure 8.11 shows an oblique font in the same typeface family as in figure 8.10.

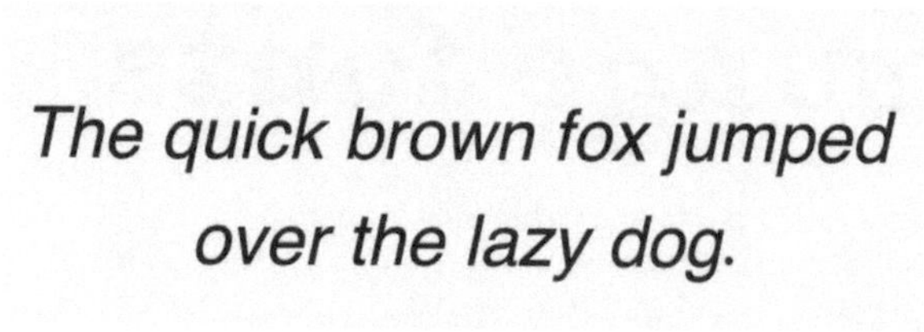

The quick brown fox jumped over the lazy dog.

Figure 8.11   An oblique font is just a slanted version of the original font.

Some typefaces, though rare, have both italics and oblique font styles, although sans serif typefaces will less often have true italics. Whether you use an italic or oblique style comes down to a stylistic choice. However, when you're coding with different font styles and need to include italics, how you choose your code to include italics is important. If you're using italics to create emphasis, the appropriate HTML tag is <em>. However, if you're using italics to convey an alternate mood or voice or to distinguish certain text from the main text—for example, for idiomatic, technical, or taxonomical reasons—then you would use the <i> tag. If you're using italics for a purely stylistic purpose, you want to wrap your word or words in a generic HTML tag, create a CSS class, and use `font-style: italic;` in your CSS declaration. When writing code, we want to keep our markup semantic and apply the correct tags for accessibility purposes, even when it comes down to something as seemingly small as how we display certain words.

FONT WEIGHTS

Most, but not all, typefaces have, at a minimum, two font weights: normal and bold. Changing the font weight is a way to introduce contrast into your typography and, especially with bold fonts, draw attention to certain words or strings of text. Many of the typeface families that I gravitate toward using on the web have many more font weights than normal and bold and, on average, have nine font weight variations to choose from. However, I never need to use all nine font weights in my design, nor should you.

Using so many font weights would create an inconsistent feeling across the design of the site or app. It would also be a pain to maintain the style guide about what to use where, and from a performance perspective, it is a bad idea. Serving up nine fonts for your users is going to take a while to load and adds to website file-size bloat, so be minimalistic and intentional with your font choices. I typically stick to three fonts: one for the body copy, one for large headings, and one for smaller headings and text that needs to stand out from the body copy. These can be from the same typeface or, as I frequently choose, one typeface for the body copy and one for anything that isn't body copy. For typefaces with nine font weight variations, you could just use one typeface and pick three distinctly different font weights so there's enough contrast between them to signal a different treatment.

Typefaces with multiple font weights typically use a numbering system to distinguish names and, on the web, use a range of 100 to 900, in increments of 100, corresponding to a common weight name, as shown in table 8.1.

Table 8.1 Font weights and their common weight names

100	Thin
200	Extra-light (Ultra-light)
300	Light
400	Normal or Book (Regular)
500	Medium
600	Semi-bold (Demi-bold)
700	Bold
800	Extra-bold (Ultra-bold)
900	Black (Heavy)

These font weight numbers are used when you're coding your CSS to indicate the font weight you wish to use with the `font-weight` property. After declaring which font family you want to use, if you wanted to use an extra-bold for smaller captions on your website, you would write `font-weight: 800;` in your CSS for the smaller captions' stylings.

When deciding what style of font to use in your design, it's best to use lighter fonts for larger text because lighter text is much harder to read at a small size. You can use bolder text for small or large lettering but be mindful of how much of the text will be bold, as bolder fonts tend to draw people's eye due to how much contrast they can create. When it comes to semantic mark-up, there is no semantic HTML tag for lighter text. Unlike italics or bold type, lighter text doesn't have an alternate meaning—it is purely aesthetic—but bold type can.

Two tags can be used to create a bolded font, `<b>` and `<strong>`. If you want to draw attention to a certain word or words, use the `<b>` tag. But if you want to indicate that a certain word or words have more importance than the rest of the text, use `<strong>`. For a visual example of how you would use `<strong>` semantically, let's look at figure 8.12.

Park visitors are often able to see bears while driving through during the early morning. **Never exit your vehicle when bears are near.**

Figure 8.12   The contents of the bolded text are extremely important, and the emphasis here is necessary to convey importance.

Just like when we use italics for aesthetic purposes only, we can use bold fonts without semantically differentiating their importance in the code. Use the font-weight property in CSS, wrap the word or words in a generic HTML tag, and apply the CSS class to the tag.

8.2   Choosing type for the web

Typography communicates more about your brand than just being the vessel that displays the words about your brand. It has its own personality and voice. The design of the typography you choose tells a visual story that needs to fit into the narrative about your brand and your product. With so many options to choose from, picking the right type for your project can be a bit daunting. But when you're picking type for the web, you can consider a few factors based on how your work is being viewed that help reduce the number of typefaces and fonts available to you.

8.2.1   What makes a good web font?

If you type "free fonts" into your search engine of choice, the first website in the list will most likely be www.1001freefonts.com, which boasts 65,000 free fonts, followed by www.dafont.com, which boasts 63,000 free fonts. Even for me, that's a lot of fonts to suddenly be faced with when I need to pick some for a project. But because we're working on a website or web app, we specifically want free typefaces that we can use on the web. Thus, we can immediately reduce the number of typefaces to pick from because chances are those 63,000 aren't all optimized for the web, and many may be more appropriately used for print design.

WHAT TO CONSIDER WHEN CHOOSING A FONT

When considering which font to use on a website, the main criteria is that it is readable and legible at the size you intend to use. The harder something is to read, the higher the chances are of your users abandoning your website. Keep long pieces of body copy in a sans serif or serif font and avoid decorative fonts, as I've mentioned in the previous section. Choose a legible font with enough contrast on the page so that users can scan quickly for the information they're looking for. Unsure if your chosen font is legible? Test, test, test! Whether it's with users or finding devices with lower resolutions, testing is the best way to ensure you've made the right choice.

Licensing is also important to consider when you're picking a font. Even though 1001freefonts.com has 65,000 free fonts, your ability to embed them and use them in a website is not guaranteed. For this reason, my go-to library for free web fonts is Google Fonts (https://fonts.google.com/), followed by Font Squirrel (https://www.fontsquirrel .com/), especially if I want something a little quirkier for a personal project. Font

Squirrel's selection of fonts has varying license types, but it links out to the typeface's owner or designer, so you can ensure you have the rights to use them on your website. Google Fonts' catalog of types is all open source, so you can choose from its library with confidence that the type is free to use and optimized for the web. Google Fonts has also started to include variable fonts, an even more precise form of typography for the web.

VARIABLE FONTS

Variable fonts are OpenType Font Variations that enable an even wider array of font styles and weights in a single file. Instead of having to pick one or two font weights, like Regular 400 and Bold 700, a variable font gives us access to all the different weights between Regular 400 and Bold 700. If I decide that Regular 400 is just a bit too light, but Medium 500 is heavier than what I want to use, I can choose something like 430 to increase the weight a bit and fine-tune the font to just how I want it to be. The advantage of variable fonts is that you get all these options in one font file. With web fonts that don't have a variable font option, you must link to each individual font file in your code, and including too many fonts may negatively affect performance. Not every web font has a variable font file, but if you're looking for good typography with a range of options that are also performant, you can filter by typefaces that are variable fonts on Google Fonts.

8.2.2 How to pair typefaces and fonts

Pairing typefaces is about creating a cohesive set of typography that helps define the hierarchy of your page, draws people's eyes through the page, and conveys the tone and voice of your brand. Just as there seem to be endless typefaces to choose from, there are endless pairings available, but you can pair in a few different ways that help guide you.

USE THE SAME TYPEFACE FAMILY

One of the easiest ways to find a font pairing is to use different fonts from the typeface or use different typefaces from the same typeface superfamily. A superfamily contains typefaces that share the same base design, but features are added to create a new classification, like a serif from a sans serif. In figure 8.13, the typefaces Roboto and Roboto Slab are examples of typefaces in a superfamily that can be paired easily.

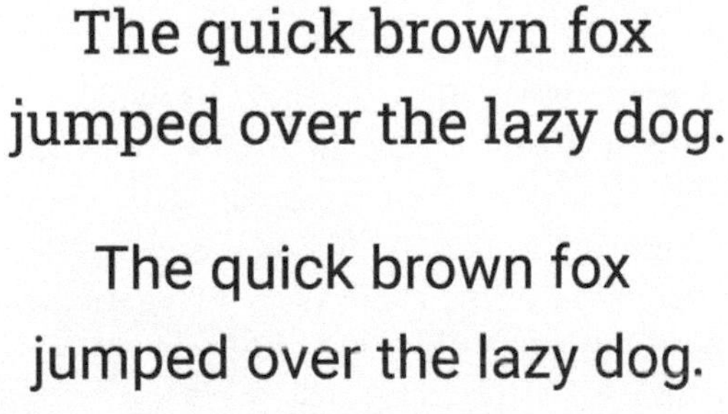

The quick brown fox jumped over the lazy dog.

The quick brown fox jumped over the lazy dog.

Figure 8.13 Roboto Slab and Roboto are two typefaces from the same superfamily, Roboto, and pair well together.

Roboto Slab is a slab serif, a subclassification of a serif, and would best be used for headlines, and Roboto is a sans serif that would best be used for body copy. Each typeface family has several different weights and styles to choose from as well, so you could play with the weight of the headings for greater contrast against the body copy, like in figure 8.14.

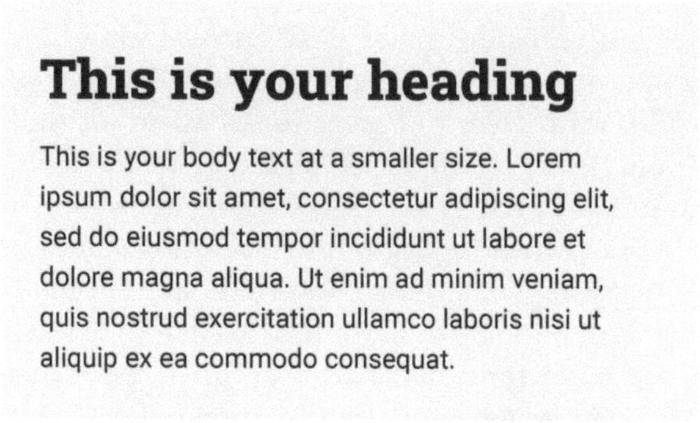

This is your heading

This is your body text at a smaller size. Lorem ipsum dolor sit amet, consectetur adipiscing elit, sed do eiusmod tempor incididunt ut labore et dolore magna aliqua. Ut enim ad minim veniam, quis nostrud exercitation ullamco laboris nisi ut aliquip ex ea commodo consequat.

Figure 8.14   When we change Roboto Slab to a bolder option, the hierarchy becomes clear, and the type pairs even better together.

If you don't have a set of typefaces from a superfamily, you can look within a single typeface family with many font styles and weights to choose a pairing. In figure 8.15, I've chosen the typeface family Fira Sans and used the Regular 400 style for the body copy with extra-bold 800 for the heading.

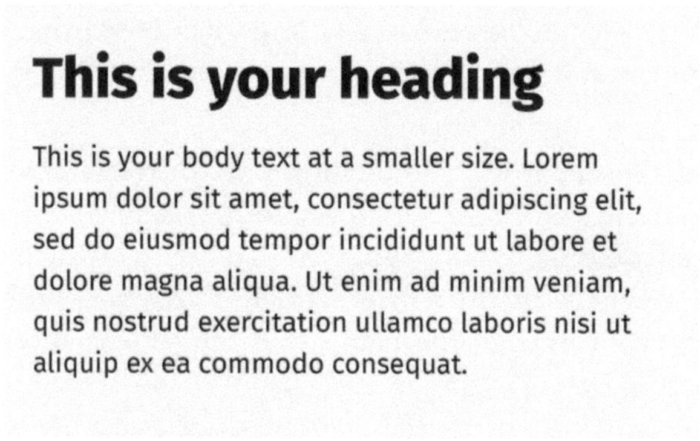

This is your heading

This is your body text at a smaller size. Lorem ipsum dolor sit amet, consectetur adipiscing elit, sed do eiusmod tempor incididunt ut labore et dolore magna aliqua. Ut enim ad minim veniam, quis nostrud exercitation ullamco laboris nisi ut aliquip ex ea commodo consequat.

Figure 8.15   You can pair very different weights from the same typeface family if it has multiple weight options.

One of the goals of pairing typefaces is to create contrast that establishes hierarchy in the content. Especially when using one typeface family to pick your contrasting fonts from, you want to ensure that there's a visible difference in size and weight between the two typefaces to create clarity. Otherwise, headlines and body copy may look too similar, like in figure 8.16. The same weighted heading, while slightly larger, doesn't create as much of a hierarchal effect as would using a bolder font from the typeface family.

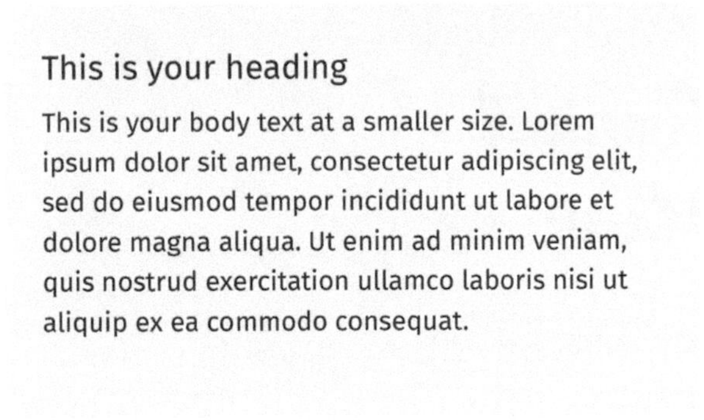

This is your heading

This is your body text at a smaller size. Lorem ipsum dolor sit amet, consectetur adipiscing elit, sed do eiusmod tempor incididunt ut labore et dolore magna aliqua. Ut enim ad minim veniam, quis nostrud exercitation ullamco laboris nisi ut aliquip ex ea commodo consequat.

Figure 8.16   When pairing different fonts from the same typeface, ensure that the fonts are different enough in size and style. Otherwise, the hierarchy doesn't feel as defined because the font sizes are too similar in size and weight.

PAIR DIFFERENT CATEGORIES

Another way to pair fonts is to pair different categories from different typeface families: sans serif and serif, sans serif and decorative, script and serif, and so on. Immediately, we have contrast due to the shapes of the letters. In figure 8.17, I pair a script type, Pacifico, with a sans serif, Red Hat Display.

All Day Tropical Happy Hour

Enjoy a selection of our best selling
tropical refreshments all day

Figure 8.17   A sans serif with a lot of round letters pairs well with a playful script.

It's important to think about the tone and message you're trying to convey on your website when picking typography. If you're going for something more lighthearted, like figure 8.17, both fonts should have an air of playfulness that comes through. In figure 8.18, if I swap the sans serif for something like Source Sans Pro, which is a bit more formal sans serif, it works, but not quite as well as Red Hat Display does with its more rounded features.

Explore and compare as many options, styles, and weights as possible when pairing different categories. Some typefaces will look and feel like they fit better compared to the ones that don't.

PAIR THE SAME CATEGORIES

The same rules apply when it comes to pairing fonts of the same category. Look for fonts that are very different looking despite being from the same classification; we're

All Day Tropical Happy Hour

Enjoy a selection of our best selling tropical refreshments all day

Figure 8.18   A more formal sans serif that is narrower and not as round feels a little too stiff and formal. We want to convey a feeling of fun through both typefaces even if one is more toned down like in figure 8.17.

always looking for contrast but in a cohesive way. Let's look at a pairing option for serif fonts. In figure 8.19, I use Playfair Display and Merriweather.

The 3 key pieces you absolutely need in your wardrobe this season

According to our stylists, these 3 pieces will tie together every piece in your outfit this season.

Figure 8.19   You can pair typefaces from the same classification but pick fonts with different design elements in the lettering to create hierarchy and contrast.

Playfair display has much harsher serifs and lines, whereas Merriweather has softer serifs and lines. These qualities contrast and are a good recipe for pairing. Now let's look at a sans serif pairing. In figure 8.20, I've chosen the typeface family Raleyway for headings and Nanum Gothic for body copy.

A farm-to-table menu that changes with the seasons

We're dedicated to sustainable, seasonal cuisine. Our ingredients are collected by our special in-house experts.

Figure 8.20   As with serif fonts, if you're choosing two sans serif fonts to pair, pick contrasting letter styles for a great effect.

The Raleway typeface is much rounder and more geometric, creating wider letters. In contrast, Nanum Gothic is more condensed. Once again, we're looking for those contrasting qualities to create a natural hierarchy on the page.

8.2.3 Establishing a type ramp

A type ramp is the set of guidelines and font styles that establishes the font family, size, style, and when and where types should be used throughout your website or web application. This set of rules immediately establishes a sense of order and cohesiveness throughout your website. Each page on your website is part of a larger story and should feel as if it belongs to the rest of the website. If I'm browsing products on your website and the product headline and body copy are all sized differently from the product page I was just on, it's going to feel off and, frankly, can look a little sloppy.

I encounter this frequently when browsing for books on Amazon.com. I still quite haven't figured out why some individual book pages have a newer web page layout than others, but when I see the same layout six or seven times and am suddenly served up with a new layout, it's jarring, and I need to recenter myself to find the information I'm looking for.

Similar pages should share styles—especially the typography you use throughout your website. Your web browser already has a type ramp with default styles built into it. If you create a list of `<h1>` to `<h6>` elements with no styling in an HTML document and load it into your browser, you will see a default type ramp provided by the browser. Each heading has its own size that decreases, signaling a step down in importance or prominence. The `<h1>` heading tag is the most prominent on the page, and the `<h6>` heading is the least prominent.

I have never actually needed to use all six heading tags on a page before, and semantically speaking, when it comes to code, those heading tags are only a portion of a type ramp. We wouldn't use an `<h6>` element to wrap our paragraphs of body copy because that `<h6>` indicates to the browser and screen readers that it is a heading of a section. So, what types of fonts do we need to consider for our website when building out a type ramp? Certain projects' type needs will vary, but a safe place to start would be the following:

- Heading
- Subheading
- Title
- Subtitle
- Body
- Caption

Heading, subheadings, titles, and subtitles would map to the `<h1>` - `<h4>` elements in HTML, body text would map to the `<p>` element, and captions to the `<caption>` tag. Any other styles you may need would most likely be applied to a `<p>` element with a CSS class. When coding the CSS for the type ramp, the HTML tag and a corresponding CSS class are often paired, such as `<h1>`, `.heading`, providing the ability to apply the heading styles to type that may not necessarily semantically be an `<h1>`.

8.2.4 Applying sizes to your type styles

You could use default sizes that the browser provides out of the box for your type ramp if you're defining it in CSS using only HTML elements. However, if you're using CSS classes, you'll need to define those sizes in your CSS.

The values you choose to define your font sizes are important. Pixels, such as `font-size: 16px;`, are not accessible, and users cannot change the base font size in their browser if they need a bigger font due to poor vision or eye strain. Using relative units such as, but not limited to, rem or em is preferred, especially if you want your typography to be responsive.

When it comes to sizing and figuring out the type scale, start with your body copy size, and go from there. Typically, body copy is 16px to 18px (1–1.125 rem when the base `font-size` is set to 16px or 1em on the `<html>` element). Once you have the body copy set up, I recommend using a type scale calculator to determine the scale for the rest of your headings rather than calculating them yourself. Start with an easy px-to-rem calculator, such as the Pixels Converter (https://pixelsconverter.com/px-to-rem) with your base font set, and pick from the sizing there to get a feel for the type sizes. For the px-to-rem calculator, if your base font is set to 16px, you get the values as shown in table 8.2 for a type scale based on that base font.

Table 8.2   Px-to-rem values and type ramp equivalents

Px	REM	Type ramp name
16px	1rem	Body (p)
24px	1.5rem	Subtitle (H4)
32px	2rem	Title (H3)
40px	2.5rem	Sub-heading (H2)
48px	3rem	Heading (H1)

If you want a type scale based on more mathematic proportions, my go-to tool is the Visual Type Scale Calculator (https://type-scale.com/). You can choose from different scales such as, but not limited to, the golden ratio, major third, and perfect fourth, and it provides a preview as well as the CSS for your type ramp. For typography, keep in mind that no two typefaces are the same. A certain font may look much larger at 3rem than another font does, so you'll have to play with different values that a calculator can give you to ensure you get the ratios you're looking for.

8.2.5 Establish a vertical rhythm

Once you've set your base font size, the next important thing to set is the line height for your text, which will establish the basis for the vertical rhythm of your website. Vertical rhythm sets the spacing between all the elements on your page in a systematic way. Your text should align along the baseline you set so the bottoms of the letters align, except for the descenders. Figure 8.21 shows text aligning along the baseline.

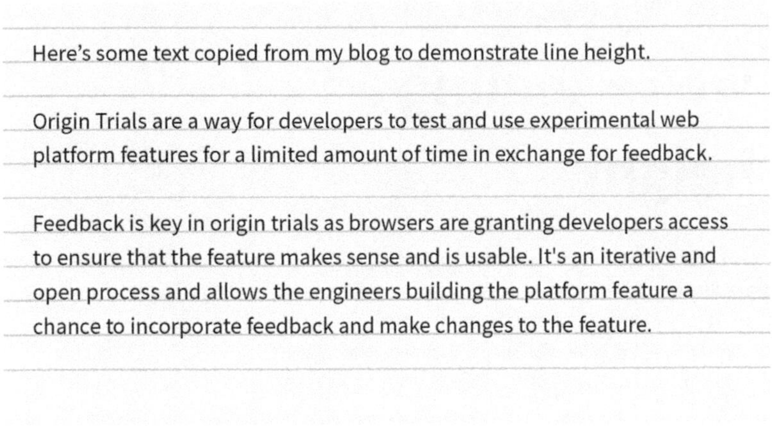

Here's some text copied from my blog to demonstrate line height.

Origin Trials are a way for developers to test and use experimental web platform features for a limited amount of time in exchange for feedback.

Feedback is key in origin trials as browsers are granting developers access to ensure that the feature makes sense and is usable. It's an iterative and open process and allows the engineers building the platform feature a chance to incorporate feedback and make changes to the feature.

Figure 8.21   The text aligns along the baseline grid of 24px.

Many examples on the web use a line height of 150% or 1.5em for the base font. This setting makes calculations for the rest of your type system and vertical rhythm easier because we can calculate our line height by multiplying the font size by 1.5 to get the value in pixels. The other benefit of using the 150% value as the line height is accessibility. If you're concerned about accessibility, the Web Content Accessibility Guidelines (WCAG) version 2.1 define a minimum line-height value of 1.5em for the main paragraph text. With larger headings, we can reduce the line height to anywhere between 120% and 140%, as a line height of 150% creates a bit too much space between multiline headings.

In the previous section, we established our base font size as 16px or 1em. The pixel value of your line height, which we get by multiplying the font size in pixels by the line height value in ems—in our case, 16px × 1.5em—is the number that our vertical rhythm will be based on. It helps us calculate margins, padding, and line heights for the different-sized fonts in our type scale. If you're using a tool that calculates your font sizes and line heights for you, you'll want to pay attention to your line height for your base font in that scale, as that will be your number to reference to calculate margins and padding on the text and images on your page.

You can start by setting your top and bottom margins to 24px on your text elements. Let's look at top and bottom margins of 24px set on our text elements in figure 8.22.

Note that the browser doesn't calculate the margin from the ascender or descender, as we can see if we open the browser developer tools, as in figure 8.23. But if we look back at figure 8.22, that's okay; our type is still aligned to the baseline, and although our heading type is aligned to the top, it still falls on the grid. Type may not always fall directly on the baseline, but as long as it sits between the baselines, you've still established a rhythm.

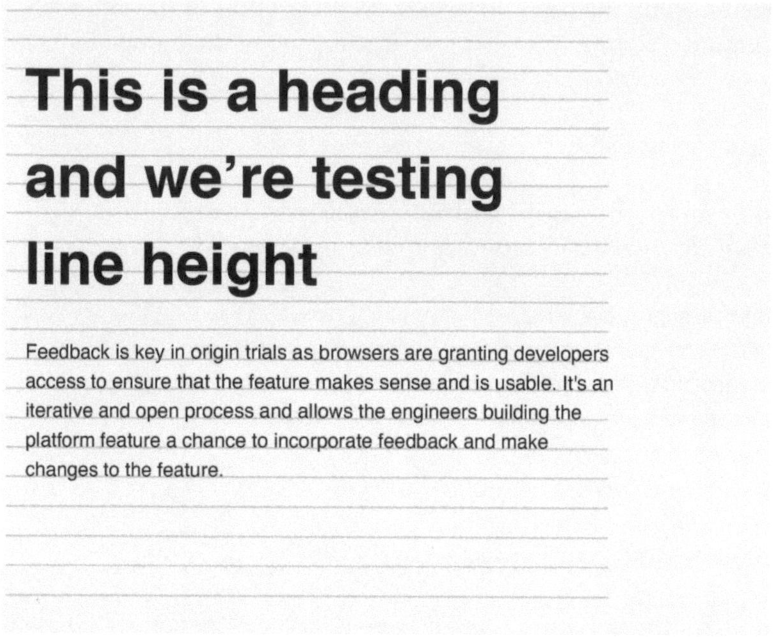

This is a heading and we're testing line height

Feedback is key in origin trials as browsers are granting developers access to ensure that the feature makes sense and is usable. It's an iterative and open process and allows the engineers building the platform feature a chance to incorporate feedback and make changes to the feature.

Figure 8.22   A margin of 24px is applied to both the heading and paragraphs, so everything is very equally spaced throughout the page.

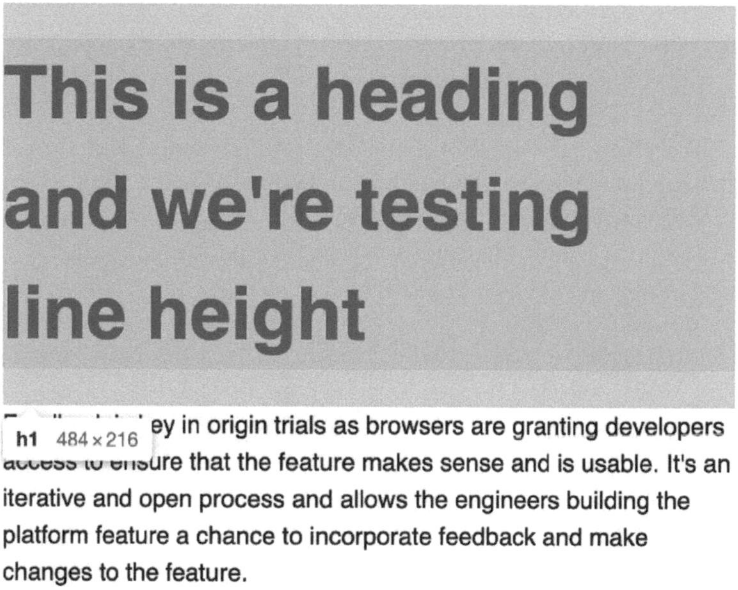

This is a heading and we're testing line height

h1   484×216

Feedback is key in origin trials as browsers are granting developers access to ensure that the feature makes sense and is usable. It's an iterative and open process and allows the engineers building the platform feature a chance to incorporate feedback and make changes to the feature.

Figure 8.23   When we highlight the text in the browser developer tools, we can see the margin applied in orange isn't directly calculated from the top or bottom of the text.

Let's look at how to calculate our margins and padding when we're using a smaller line height to make a multiline heading a little bit tighter and reduce the space between lines. In figure 8.24, we're still using the same type of sizing as we did in figure 8.22. Our body size is still 16px with a line height of 1.5em, so our number is still 24px for our vertical rhythm. Our heading is 48px, and we're going to use a line height of 1.25 because these equal a round number of 60px, which is easy to work with. However, 60 is not a multiple of 24, so we need to add some margin and padding to stick to our baseline grid of 24. The next multiple of 24 is 72, but this only gives us 12px of margin or padding to work with since our line height is 60px. Instead, we'll go to the next multiple of 24, which is 96px. We'll subtract 60px from 96px to get 36px to work with. So, for our example in figure 8.24, let's add a top margin of 24px and

Figure 8.24   Adjusting the line height of the heading prompts us to adjust the margin and padding so that we stick to the baseline grid we created.

bottom padding of 12px to equal 36px to our heading. These dimensions align to 96px, a multiple of 24, and give reasoning to our margin and padding numbers.

For paragraphs of content under the same heading, the space between should stay at 1.5em, a full space based on our number for the vertical rhythm. If we go back to our design principles in chapter 2, remember that spacing helps establish relationships, so we want paragraphs under the same heading to be grouped somewhat near each other, ideally no less than that line height number. Items spaced further apart convey that they're not a part of the same group, so take care when exploring spacing your paragraphs further apart, and instead focus on spacing between each group of content. Add spacing to the main blocks of content, such as the heading, paragraphs, and any media, so each stands out as its own group compared to the other groups of content.

Once you have the formula for vertical rhythm, you've established an organized flow of content with an actual rhythm that brings a sense of order to your site. It adds polish to the site and makes things easier to read, which is important for multiple reasons. It makes the site content easier to scan, and there's an accessibility component to it which we briefly touched on, but readability goes beyond line height.

8.2.6   *Ensuring readability*

Readability is how easy or difficult it is for people to read and understand the text in front of them. Bad typography choices can hinder the readability of the copy on your website or in your application, and we want people to use our websites with ease. We just looked at line height and now know that not having enough space between lines is an accessibility problem called out by the WCAG. There are a few other things to think about when considering how readable text is on your website.

LINE LENGTH

There is an optimal line length for text. It can be too wide or too narrow, and we want the sweet spot in between. The optimal line length is between 45 and 70 characters, give or take a few, depending on what source you're referencing. Shorter line lengths allow people to scan content more quickly, whereas longer line lengths tend to be harder for people to focus on. Limit your column width, or set a `max-width` on your heading and paragraph elements.

LETTER SPACING

You can control the horizontal spacing between letters in CSS with the `letter-spacing` property. When applied, this property adjusts the spacing between letters in a word or a block of text. In some instances, you may want to create a little more space to fill out a line of text a little bit further or reduce it so that you don't have a single and final word that gets pushed to the next line. These adjustments should be small. Adjustments that are too large in either direction, like we see in figure 8.25, leave us with a hard-to-read block of text, which will have a negative effect on the user's experience of the site.

Make small adjustments to the letter spacing if you feel it improves the readability. Because each typeface is different, always test with users or have a few people look at the spacing you've applied if you're unsure.

Text with too little spacing between letters and can sometimes meld letters together and confuse the reader.

Text with too much spacing can cause issues as well because it takes too long to read the words.

Figure 8.25 Letter spacing in either direction can cause readability problems.

Exercise: Pair the typeface with the mood it conveys

Look at the different typefaces in the tiles in the figure, and then assess the subsequent list of moods provided. What mood does each typeface convey to you? How does it feel?

EB Garamond

Museo Slab

Madre

Montserrat

Typefaces can communicate different moods.

Some of the moods or feelings that each typeface could convey (more than one can apply to each typeface) are as follows:

- Whimsical
- Friendly
- Classic
- Modern
- Formal
- Bold
- Welcoming
- Hip

EB Garamond is a serif font that has a classic and formal feeling to it. Museo Slab is a slab serif. Although it's a subtype of serif, it's not as formal as other serifs, so it feels more friendly but also bold. Madre is a script that feels welcoming and whimsical. Montserrat feels modern and hip.

Summary

- Typeface choice is one of the most powerful aspects of visual design because the message your type conveys can change depending on the typeface you choose. Informal text can become formal. Text meant to be endearing can take on a dark meaning. It's all in the typeface.

- Free tools are available to developers to pick well-designed types so that a website or web app looks modern.

- The main classifications of typefaces are serif, sans serif, decorative, and script, although other subclassifications also exist. Serif fonts generally feel more formal and classic. Sans serifs tend to be more modern. Decorative typefaces can communicate a wide range of feelings but tend to skew toward greater novelty. Scripts are popular for weddings or photographer websites—things that carry a personal touch.

- The key to picking typefaces is to think about the kind of mood and feeling your brand needs to convey.

- Accessibility and semantics should be considered when you style words as bold and italic. Ensure you choose the correct HTML tag or apply styling via a CSS class to a generic HTML tag when you want to style italics or bold for aesthetic purposes only.

- Pair typefaces to help create greater visual hierarchy on the page. You can pair typefaces from typeface superfamilies, from different categories like a script and a sans serif, and from the same categories. Be sure they are different enough to provide clarity when they're from the same category.

- Vertical rhythm creates the rhythm of the page and defines relationships of different elements via spacing. Establishing a vertical rhythm brings a mathematical component that adds sense and order to the numbers we choose for the spacing on our page. It establishes a grid and creates a cohesive rhythm across the entire website.

- Readability of the text on your page is vital to providing a good user experience. Ensure you add enough line height to your body text, don't use letter spacing unnecessarily, and limit your line length to around 45 to 70 characters per line.

Color theory

9

This chapter covers

- The color wheel and color relationships
- How to create shades, tints, and associated terminology
- The psychology of color
- How to pick and apply a color scheme, including accessibility considerations
- The different web color modes and color discrepancies across screens

If you search for "color optical illusions" in your favorite search engine, you'll get a number of results, including some that look like the image is moving. This perceived movement is due to the color choices, the structure of our eyes, and our perception. The color choices that create the illusion are a part of the subject of color theory. One of the more famous color optical illusions, shown in figure 9.1, is Adelson's checker-shadow illusion. A checkerboard appears to have a shadow cast over it by an object. The square labeled "A" appears darker than the square labeled "B," but they are actually the same color when placed side by side.

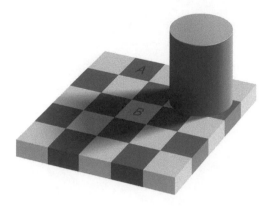

Figure 9.1   Adelson's checker-shadow is an optical illusion where squares A and B are the same color. (Source: Edward H. Adelson. Licensed under CC BY-SA 4.0)

Color theory is the science and art of applying color, how we perceive it, and the visual effects created when colors are mixed and matched, like in those optical illusions. At its most basic level, color theory has a defined set of guidelines and rules that helps us make color choices using the color wheel.

When I've spoken to web developers, one of the most common areas of design they've told me they struggle with is picking and applying colors. Understanding the color wheel and the different relationships between the colors is the key to being able to select colors for your project. If you're ever struggling to pick a color scheme, referencing the color wheel and the different color relationships is the easiest way to help you make a decision.

Color is one of the most powerful tools in design because of its ability to influence our emotions, mood, and the way we perceive it, which are all influenced by our personal and cultural relationships with color. One of my favorite examples stems from an interaction with a client on a project. I was designing a website for a technical program designed specifically to give United States military veterans the skills to transition into a role in technology after their military careers. In one of the initial mock-ups that I showed my client, who was also former military, I had used a rather vibrant red as one of my accent colors. His feedback was "I don't like the red. Red is an extremely aggressive color, particularly in the context of the military." As a designer, I appreciated this feedback because he articulated the reasoning behind why the color wasn't working for him.

Everyone has an opinion and a personal reaction to color, which can boil down to people not liking a color just because they don't like it. That feedback can be difficult to work with when choosing colors based on cultural or emotional meanings. Articulating why you chose the specific colors for a project can lead to much more productive discussions with stakeholders and target audiences when you're in the testing phase of a design and they give feedback on the color. If that feedback is simply "I don't like the color blue you chose," talk about why you chose that color blue, and ask the user what colors they associate with the emotions or feelings you're trying to convey through your design.

Sometimes, though, people will be averse to the color you selected no matter what. So, take the feedback from different users into consideration. If the colors you've chosen come up as a problem multiple times, reassess your color choices and go through another round of review. Every person perceives color differently, which is perhaps why color selection is one of the areas that developers struggle with. In this chapter, we'll learn how to approach picking colors and palettes based on relationships between colors in the color wheel, making those decisions less daunting.

Apart from the emotional aspect, color is also an incredibly powerful tool for defining relationships between things, creating contrast, and drawing the eye through a design. Picking a palette is just one step in the process of understanding color. You also need to understand how to apply it to a design so that it doesn't clash or isn't overwhelming. So, we'll also walk through an example of how to approach applying your color palette to a webpage.

9.1 Color terminology

An incredible amount of color variations can be created beyond what the standard color wheel shows. However, before diving into the primary color relationships on the color wheel, we should familiarize ourselves with some color terminology. This terminology will help you better understand the different ways to mix colors and color theory. These terms will provide you with ways to both speak about color and create variations of the color schemes you pick from the color wheel.

9.1.1 Shade, tints, and tones

Shades, tints, and tones are different variations of a color created by adding either black, white, or gray. Shades use black to darken a color, tints use white to lighten a color, and tones use gray to dull a color down. You can add these to your color palette to create a wider variety of colors based on the website's primary color or colors. Because they are derived from the primary color in your palette, you can apply color that makes the website UI feel cohesive but not overwhelming due to the muted nature of shades, tints, and tones.

All the software available today makes working with colors for the web fairly easy. I prefer to use Adobe Illustrator when I'm starting out on projects because it's the interface I'm most familiar with and I find it's easier to experiment with color more quickly.

In Adobe Illustrator, I start with the main color from which I want to create a shade, tint, or tone and create a shape with the main color as a fill. I use the HSB brightness slider in the color panel to make my shade by adding more black. For my tint, I start with the base color again and adjust the saturation slider to make my color lighter by adding white. I get the results in figure 9.2

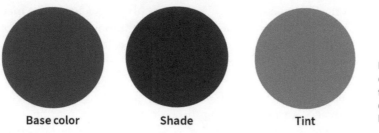

Figure 9.2   The base
color is a bright purple,
followed by a much
darker shade and a
lighter-colored tint.

Base color   Shade   Tint

9.1.2   *Warm vs. cool colors*

Colors evoke certain emotions, moods, and feelings, and the terminology that broadly covers how to talk about the emotive nature of color starts with color temperature. Colors can initially be grouped into warm or cool colors. Warm colors are red, orange, and yellow; cool colors are green, blue, and purple. Each of these two groups tends to evoke different emotions, with warmer colors associated with happier and more energetic feelings and cooler colors associated with more calm and relaxed feelings. We'll look at the different themes and feelings associated with each color in a few sections.

Even though the color wheel is split into two different temperatures, warmer colors can still have cooler variations, and cool colors can have warmer variations. Even gray colors can trend cooler or warmer, like in figure 9.3.

Figure 9.3   Although grays are neutral, they can trend cool or warm.

Warm colors stand out and are more attention-grabbing than cooler colors. As such, warm colors give the effect of being more prominent and at the front of a composition. Cool colors are more recessed or give the illusion of being further back. Let's look at the red button sitting on a blue background in figure 9.4. The button seems to sit on top of the blue, but what happens when we swap the colors? Does the blue button feel like it's on top of the red, or does it feel a bit recessed? The button on the right gives the illusion of being further back, as if you were looking down into a hole. If you were to look at a deep hole in the ground from above, the light would disappear the further down you looked until it was black. The recessive effect of cooler colors is

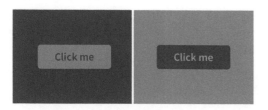

Figure 9.4   The red button on the left
visually appears more forward than the
blue button on the right.

probably more prominent in art like paintings, but a subtle effect of the same nature is still noticeable in digital UIs.

Warm colors also tend to be more aggressive or energizing, depending on the color. Red can be an incredibly aggressive color and is usually used, especially in dashboard UI, to indicate something negative like a decline, warning, or error. It can also be used simply to bring attention to something like a notification badge on a neutrally colored UI.

While a cooler color like green can be used for a positive notification badge, it won't be as eye-catching as a red icon. Cooler colors can be used for less pressing notifications that don't require the user's immediate attention.

9.1.3   Hue, saturation, and lightness

When talking about color, you'll commonly hear the term *hue* used. Hue is the term for a pure color or base color, like the red from our primary colors group, that has not had any white, black, or gray applied to it to create shades, tints, or tones. It's just the pure color.

Saturation is how vivid and intense a color is. On a scale from 0 to 100, the value 100 is when a color is at its full hue. Have you ever opened a photo in a photo editing app and seen a setting labeled Saturation? When you increase the saturation in the photo, all the colors gradually become incredibly vivid. If you decrease the saturation, the colors start to become dull and faded, the opposite of saturated. Figure 9.5 compares a saturated image with a desaturated one.

| Less saturation | Original | High saturation |

Figure 9.5   An example of reducing and increasing saturation of an image

Especially when you're building out color schemes, too many saturated colors that aren't balanced and seem to be clashing with each other can create a messy and overwhelming UI that doesn't look professional. Highly saturated colors should be used to create contrast. However, photos that are too saturated will create contrast problems on your website or app, especially if you try to overlay text. They will be the main focus and draw users' attention over and over because of how vividly they stand out against the rest of the UI. Or, if the UI is more neutral, they may feel out of place because of

how overly colored they are. Too much saturation can be overwhelming, and multiple fully saturated colors should typically be avoided until you feel more comfortable applying color palettes and creating intentional contrast.

Finally, lightness is simply how light or dark a color is or how much black or white it contains. Lightness refers to the shades and tints we discussed previously. Increasing the white in your color will make it lighter until you've reached full white, and decreasing it will make it darker until you've reached full black. Figure 9.6 demonstrates hue, saturation, and lightness visually.

Hue

Saturation

Lightness/Brightness

Figure 9.6   Hue is a color, saturation is how vibrant a color is, and lightness or brightness affects how light or dark a color is.

We now have the basics of color, so let's look at color relationships and how to build out color palettes.

9.2   *The color wheel*

The color wheel is the most basic tool in color theory and for identifying relationships between colors (see figure 9.7). It's a color chart laid out in a circular shape that displays the color spectrum. In its most basic form, it displays the colors red, orange, yellow, green, blue, and purple, although it can be further divided to include colors between each main color in the wheel.

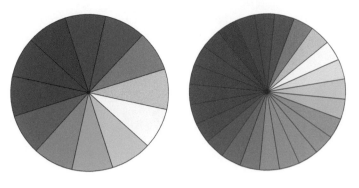

Figure 9.7   Different levels of color granularity in color wheels are common. The one on the left is a basic color wheel with 12 colors, and the one on the right has 24 colors.

9.2.1   Color relationships

The color wheel is the easiest way to identify relationships between colors and know which colors work best together. It can be used in several ways to identify colors that work together, from pairs to triads of colors.

Before we dive into the different color relationships, we need to understand the different kinds of color sets that make up the color wheel. There are three primary colors: red, yellow, and blue. These three colors mix to make many other colors in the color spectrum. Secondary colors are created by mixing two primary colors; for example, purple is a secondary color created from red and blue.

Tertiary colors are created by mixing one primary color with another color adjacent to it on the color wheel. They are in-between colors, such as red-orange (amber) and blue-green (teal). Figure 9.8 identifies primary, secondary, and tertiary colors.

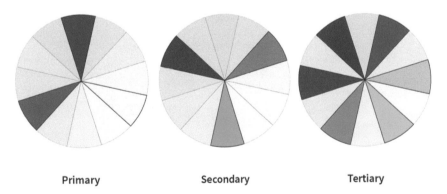

Primary   Secondary   Tertiary

Figure 9.8   The color wheel is divided to show primary, secondary, and tertiary colors.

MONOCHROMATIC COLOR SCHEMES

Monochromatic color themes are color themes that use various shades and hues of one color. These color schemes work well as a color palette because they're of the same color family—for example, all green or all blue.

This color scheme is great to experiment with when applying color because you'll avoid severe color clashing or having too many different colors to apply to a design. It can also help simplify a design or make it feel harmonious if the content already makes it feel very busy. Figures 9.9 and 9.10 are examples of monochromatic color schemes.

Figure 9.9   A monochromatic color scheme

Figure 9.10   The Web We Want website is an example of a monochromatic color scheme applied to a website.

COMPLEMENTARY COLOR SCHEMES

Complementary colors sit directly opposite each other on the color wheel and create a bold color scheme. Opposites complement each other and create a harmonious color combination.

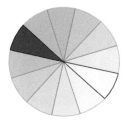

Figure 9.11   An example of a complementary color scheme with purple and yellow

From personal experience, I tend to find complementary colors harder to work with on the web because of the amount of contrast between the two colors. It takes a little more thought to apply those colors throughout your website, and the chances of you only using those two colors are slim. You'll want to incorporate, at minimum, a neutral color (black, white, or gray) and decide which of those complementary colors is your primary color that dominates the website and which is your accent color.

Complementary color-based color schemes add a lot of effects and visual contrast. Use this type of color scheme to focus users and draw their attention to particular places on your website. That extreme contrast will keep drawing their eyes back to the spots where you want them to focus.

For example, suppose you have a piece of UI in your web app or website with a notification badge you want to keep relatively unobtrusive to the rest of the UI, but you still need to draw some attention to it. You can use a complementary color scheme to create contrast and draw attention to the notification badge.

Because complementary colors are so visually contrasting, they can also be used to bring clarity to a piece of UI that contains information about vastly different states. For example, a stock market chart that displays an individual stock's price changes throughout the day can use a mix of red and green to indicate when the price rose and when the stock dropped. In a list of multiple stocks that provide an overview of the day's trends, red and green with appropriate icons or symbology, such as up and down arrows or plus and minus signs, give a quick view of which stocks performed poorly and which performed well.

ANALOGOUS COLOR SCHEMES

An analogous color scheme consists of three colors on the color wheel that sit next to each other (see figure 9.12). This scheme blends colors together in a more harmonious, less intense way compared to the high contrast created by a complementary color scheme.

Analogous colors also naturally occur together in nature, which is why we can find this scheme of colors so much more pleasing than other color schemes. When we look at a sunset, the colors are analogous: we get a rich gradient of yellows and oranges that sometimes turn to red. Even the sky at sunset, when you look to the east, away from the sunset, turns from pinks and purples to deep blues into the night sky, a reverse analogous color scheme but analogous all the same.

Analogous color schemes can be used to create a harmonious palette that feels cohesive and not as brash as color palettes with contrasting colors. Even warm colors,

Figure 9.12   This
is an example of
an analogous color
scheme with varying
shades of purple.

like red, orange, and yellow, can make a design feel elegant when used properly. Because analogous colors are right next to each other on the color wheel, the color palette is incredibly low contrast. If you're using the colors in something like a dashboard with charts, those colors should not be the only way to differentiate between something like bars in a bar chart. The color scheme will look harmonious even to those without vision deficiencies. So, especially in something like a bar chart, use additional pattern overlays rather than relying on a color key.

The colors in this scheme should be used on individual UI elements that don't overlap, again due to contrast problems. To start, pick a neutral color as the base of your website and use analogous colors on top of that neutral color to draw attention to UI elements. Similarly, you could use a shade or a tint of one of the colors in the palette to create more visual contrast between items, which would still maintain the similar feeling of a fully saturated analogous color scheme.

TRIADS

Triad color schemes consist of colors that are evenly spaced around the color wheel. The most straightforward example of a triadic color scheme is the primary colors: red, yellow, and blue. If you look at the color wheel in figure 9.13, the colors are spaced evenly, creating a triangle. This color scheme can be intense, and typically you'll want to identify one color as your primary color and use the other two as accents.

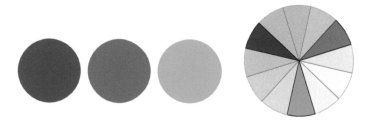

Figure 9.13   Purple,
orange, and green form
a triad color scheme.

Some designers apply an interior design color rule to graphic and UI design situations to keep color schemes balanced. It's called the 60:30:10 rule. Your primary color should be used across 60% of your space, your secondary color should be used 30% of the time, and your third color should be used as a minimal accent, covering 10% of the page. You can use shades and tints of each color to bring down the intensity of a color or to create a more neutral color like gray with a hint of the hue mixed in so you're not using pure gray to help with contrast. You can use this rule with any of the color relationships we've looked at that use three colors. This rule will particularly help with triadic and split complementary schemes to ensure you establish primary, secondary, and accent colors that don't clash or fight for dominance, especially when using bold color schemes

SPLIT COMPLEMENTARY

Similar to the triadic color scheme, the split complementary color scheme uses three colors and is the final color relationship we'll look at. A split complementary color scheme uses one color on the color wheel, and instead of using the direct complement across from it, it uses the two colors adjacent to the direct complement color. As we see in figure 9.14, our main color is purple, and the complementary colors of our scheme are yellow and orange.

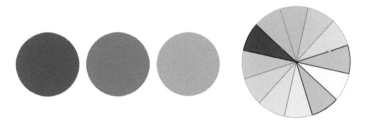

Figure 9.14   An example of a split complementary color scheme using shades and tints of yellow-orange, yellow-green, and purple.

9.2.2   *Study examples of color, and then study some more*

Color palettes shouldn't feel overwhelming or use colors that fight for dominance on the page. Knowing the different color relationships is helpful when picking your color palettes from scratch, and using the 60:30:10 rule gives you an idea of how much of each color to apply. Color is arguably one of the hardest concepts to grasp, and while this chapter sets the foundation for understanding how to build palettes and apply color (later, we'll walk through an exercise on how to apply a palette), my advice is to continually be looking at examples of websites or other UI and studying how color is used.

The website Dribbble is one of my go-to sources for inspiration. Pick a design you like, save it to your computer, open your design tool of choice, place the example in your file, and use the color picker to build out the palette the design is using. Can you identify which color relationship it's using? Is it using shades and tints? Fully saturated hues? Perhaps the ratio of colors is entirely different from 60:30:10. While I'd say it's difficult to calculate the exact percentages, you can get a feel for whether it's using a ratio like 70:15:15.

Color has the potential to make a user interface overwhelming when it isn't balanced. It also has the potential to not create enough effect or contrast to draw the eye through a design. Neither too much nor too little contrast is ideal, as both can lead to confusion, and a user may not understand their next course of action. If a user is faced with too many clashing colors when they first land on your page, they may abandon your website pretty quickly. It's the first impression your users get, and if you don't have an inherent skill for picking and applying color like some people do, studying examples and practice can help build that skill.

9.3 *Color psychology*

Entire books have been written on the topic of color psychology. The way different colors make us feel, what we typically associate them with, and how they influence us have been studied for years, with Carl Jung being a pioneer in the topic. Because it's an extensive and fascinating topic, I provide a few recommendations for further reading in the appendix.

Color in product design is especially important as it influences how people perceive your product. A bad color scheme or clashing colors in the user interface or logo design communicates more to your customers than you intended. If color schemes are poorly put together, it ultimately doesn't matter what the colors stand for because something that's hard on the eyes gives a sense of unprofessionalism. Ultimately, poor color design detracts from the message or mood you're trying to convey. But what are you trying to communicate with color? Let's look at a brief overview of the main color groups and what they typically represent:

- Red is a vibrant and bold color that falls on the warm side of the color spectrum. It's a color that symbolizes strength, dominance, power, war, danger, sexuality, love, and passion. Red attracts attention. I live in an area with many supercar owners, and a red Ferrari stands out far more than a black one. Stop signs are bright red to catch your attention at an intersection. In the movie *The Matrix*, the main character Neo is distracted by the Woman in Red while in a training simulation.
- Orange is another warm color that draws attention. It typically symbolizes creativity, amusement, being adventurous, energy, and activity. It can be an indication of danger or warning (like safety cones construction crews put out on the road) because of how visible it is against different backdrops. In the United States, I've seen orange used frequently in the logos of sports teams and fitness companies.
- Yellow falls on the warm spectrum like orange and red. Due to its high visibility, it is also frequently used to indicate caution and warning (for example, high-visibility vests). It can symbolize positivity, optimism, amusement, and happiness. Yellow is another color that draws attention and focus. However, it's a color that isn't terribly popular with people and can even be a bit overwhelming and unpleasant if overused, depending on the variation of the color. Still, yellow will grab attention, especially if used against a darker color for contrast.
- Green starts to fall on the cool spectrum in terms of color temperature. It can symbolize growth, nature, safety, healing, relaxation, and freshness. It's one of the more calming colors compared with the high energy of red, orange, and yellow. Green is commonly used in illustrations and logos that have to do with the environment, outdoor activities, and health, such as spas, to convey healing and relaxation.

- Blue is a cool color that symbolizes tranquility, calm, trust, authority, and loyalty. It's one of the most popular colors in the world due to its neutral nature and is frequently used in logos. It's typically not a very loud color and, despite its association with boys and men in the United States, is a fairly neutral color. Blue is also associated with nature because of the ocean and the sky, and it can produce calming effects when we look at it.

- Purple is typically a cool color. However, because it is created from blue, the coolest primary color, and red, the warmest primary color, it can trend cooler or warmer more easily than other colors. Purple has deep connections to royalty and is associated with power and luxury. It can symbolize ambiguity, mystery, individualism, and spirituality. It's also tied to faith and religion, particularly in Christianity.

- Black is the complete absence of light and technically doesn't have a hue like other colors. It is typically associated with darkness, power, sophistication, elegance, mourning, and evil. In movies, the stereotypical bad guy dons a black outfit. In contrast, many couture fashion houses have all-black logos because of how clean and elegant black is. It's also a good neutral color that can instantly make a website design feel elevated and high-end. It's a color that can work well on its own but can also be incredibly powerful and create dynamic contrast when used with lighter colors in the color wheel.

9.4   Picking and applying a color scheme

We've covered basic color theory, which provides us with a framework for choosing a color scheme based on relationships in the color wheel. The next thing you need to do is apply your color scheme to your user interface.

First and foremost, no matter what color scheme relationship you're using, pick one color that will be your base color. This selection will be the primary color throughout your website and show up the most in the UI, regardless of whether you're using a monochromatic or split complementary color scheme. Then pick one or two additional colors as accents. From these swatches, you can create several tints and shades to work with.

Next, you'll pick a few shades of gray. You can create grays that have a hint of your primary brand color and temperature to make the neutral palette feel more cohesive. Once you have your colors, it's time to apply them to the UI of your website or app. If you're unsure how much of each color you should use, start with the 60/30/10 rule commonly used in interior design. This simple rule can help if you're struggling to get your color combination amounts to feel balanced. Next, we'll walk through picking a color scheme and applying it to a website user interface to give you an idea of how to approach applying color.

9.5   *Tutorial: Pick a color scheme, and apply it*

For this tutorial, I will walk you through applying a color scheme to the landing page of a travel website. I've chosen a monochromatic color scheme, and to build my color scheme, I'm using the HSB color slider in Adobe Illustrator, as shown in figure 9.15.

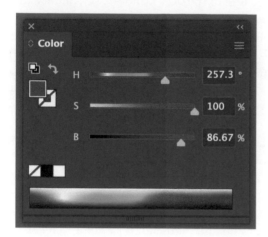

Figure 9.15   The Adobe Illustrator color tool pane with the HSB slider

To build my palette out, I start with my primary color, a violet-blue color, and then in the HSB slider in Adobe Illustrator, I adjust the saturation slider. I want two additional colors from the primary color. I reduce the saturation to 60% for my second color and to 10% for my third color. I want a medium tone somewhere in the middle and a very light tone onto which I can overlay text.

To create my gray palette, I keep the hue value the same but reduce the saturation for each new gray I pick. I also reduce the brightness value to 45%. For the first three colors in the gray palette, I start with 20% saturation because I want a hint of that violet-blue in my darkest gray. Then I reduce the next two swatches by 5% each to get rid of the hue shade. For a lighter gray, my fourth gray, I keep the saturation at 5% and bump up the brightness to 60%. And now we have our color palette built out. Figure 9.16 is my full color palette.

Figure 9.16   The color palette I apply to my landing page

Next, I apply my color palette to the landing page. I start with a high-fidelity wire-frame that is all the same color, sort of like a coloring book, as in figure 9.17. Now I've figured out the typography and the structure for the page, but I don't have any color or graphics applied.

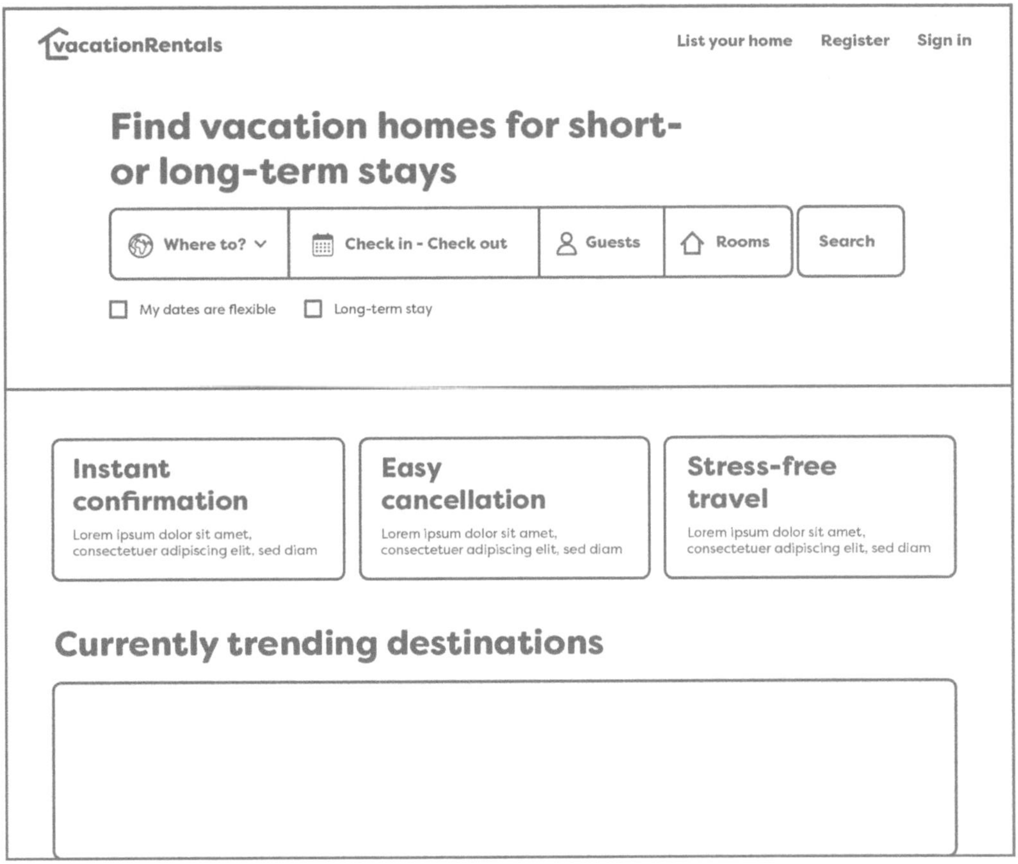

Figure 9.17 The high-fidelity wireframe for our landing page with no color applied

I start with my base color, which should be the most vibrant color and draw attention, as shown in figure 9.18. I apply it to the main headline, my search button (because that's the main call to action I want customers to focus on), and the fill for the check-boxes when they are checked so that it is crystal clear that they're checked.

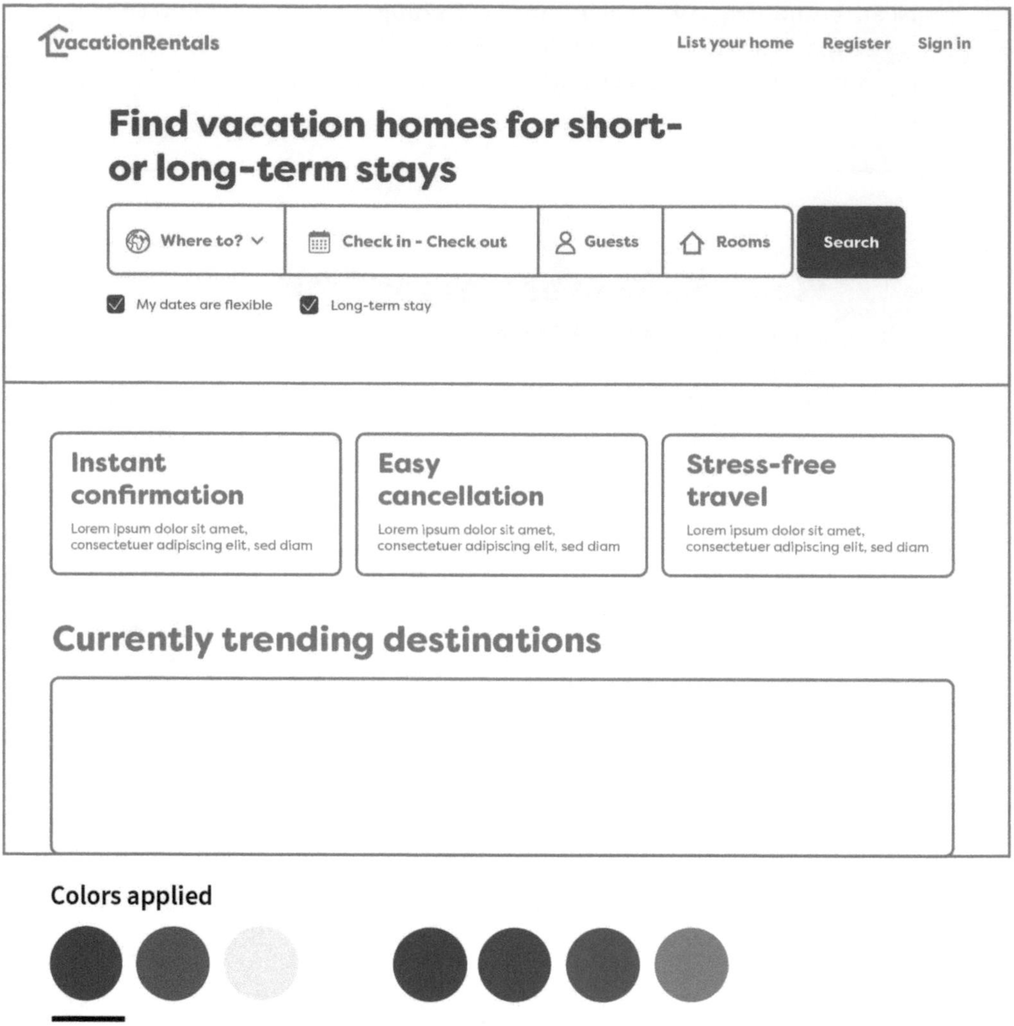

vacationRentals   List your home   Register   Sign in

Find vacation homes for short- or long-term stays

| Where to? ⌄ | Check in - Check out | Guests | Rooms | **Search** |

☑ My dates are flexible   ☑ Long-term stay

Instant confirmation
Lorem ipsum dolor sit amet, consectetuer adipiscing elit, sed diam

Easy cancellation
Lorem ipsum dolor sit amet, consectetuer adipiscing elit, sed diam

Stress-free travel
Lorem ipsum dolor sit amet, consectetuer adipiscing elit, sed diam

Currently trending destinations

Colors applied

Figure 9.18   The primary color is applied to the UI.

Next, I apply the accent colors and some of the gray swatches. For the sake of this exercise, the logo contains no color, so I use my secondary color to do that as I don't want it to draw attention from the main call to action and headline. Then I use the third color as the background for the tiles with secondary information that I want to highlight. Again, I don't want to draw attention away from the main call to action, but these should be the next thing that people are drawn to.

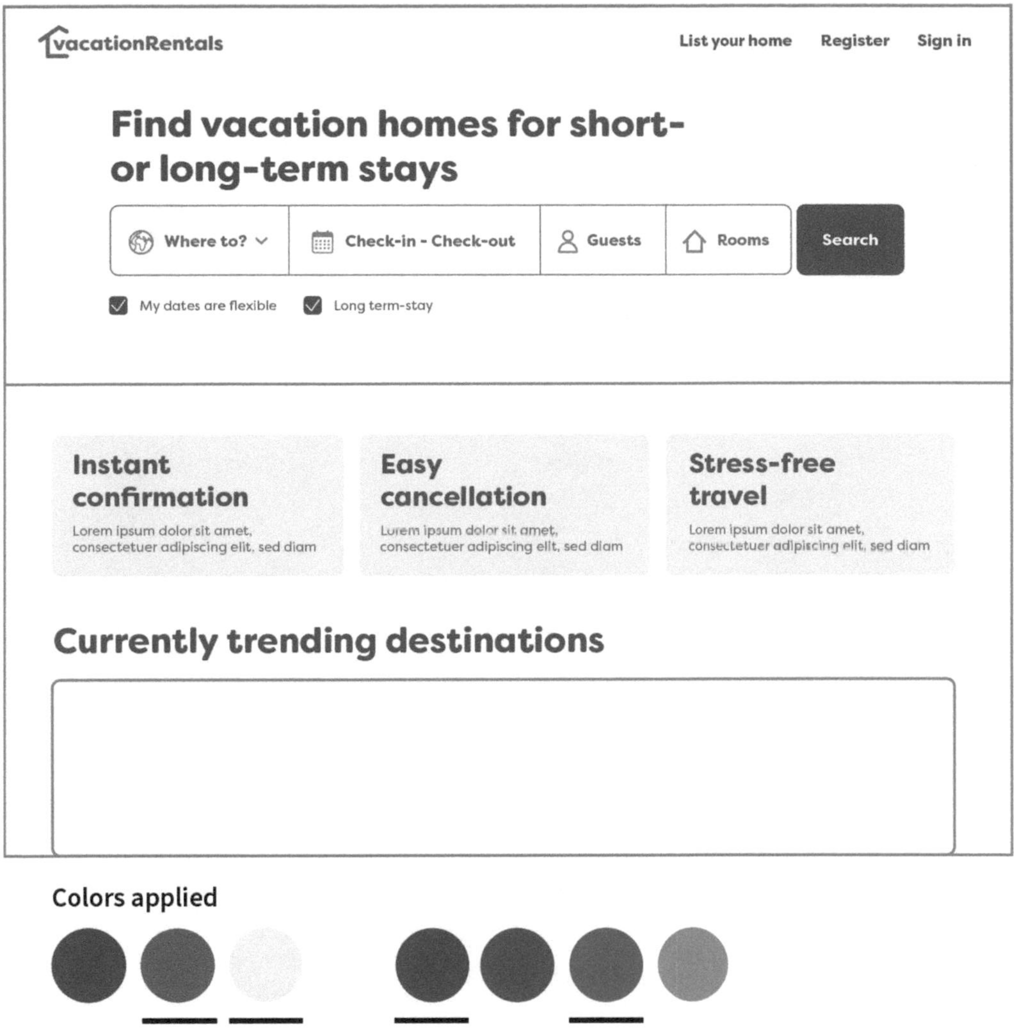

Figure 9.19 I've applied the accent colors and gray shades to our fonts.

For font colors, I use two gray colors. I use the darkest grey with a hint of the primary color for the headlines, navigation, and subheadings and a more neutral gray for the smaller font sizes in the form and body copy, as shown in figure 9.19. In figure 9.20, I color the icons in with just a slightly darkened grey for some subtle contrast.

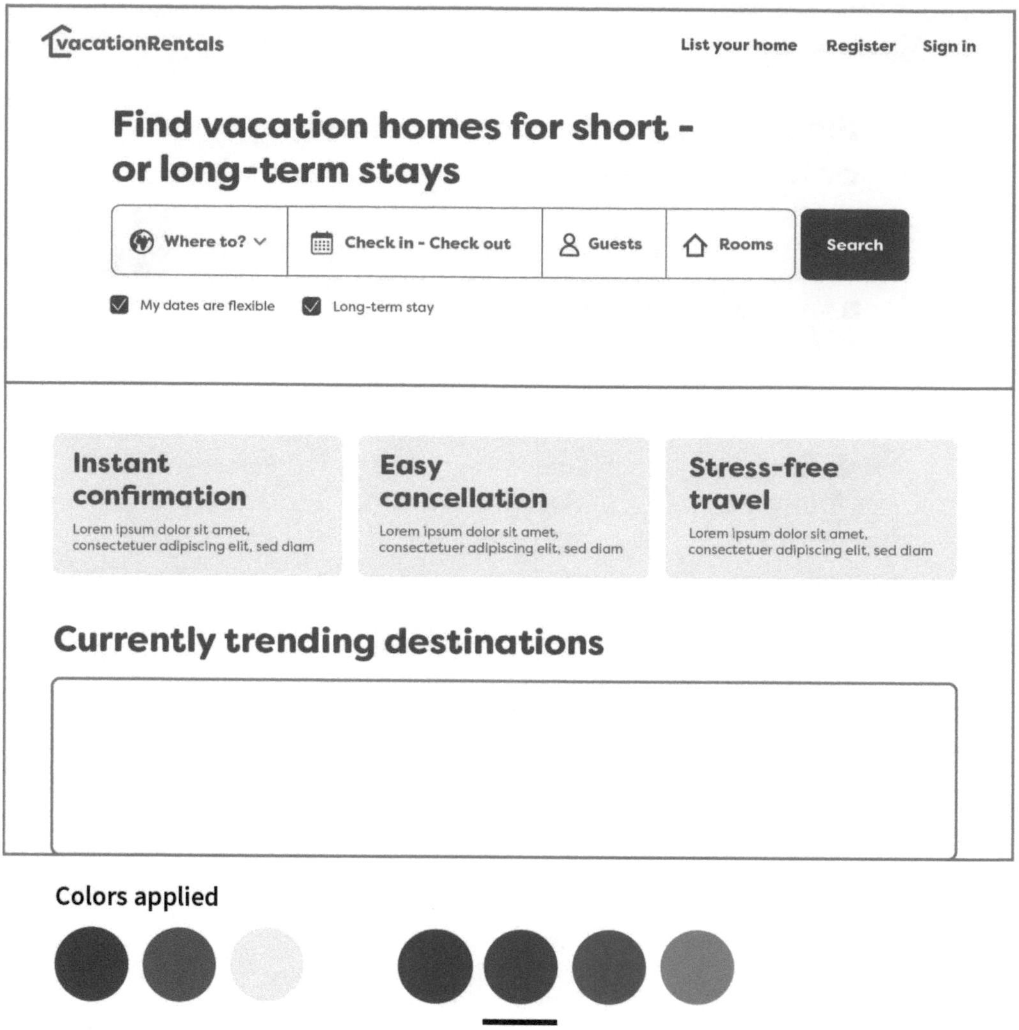

Figure 9.20   The icons are colored with gray that is slightly darker than the form text.

Finally, I include an image to bring some contrast to the website's main hero section and create more visual interest further down the page (figure 9.21).

By adding an image with an opacity treatment to the hero section, I create contrast with the following section, which has a white background, thus bringing even more attention to the form to search for rentals. When adding background images, it's important to think about the readability of the text against the image, which is why I added a white layer and slightly reduced its opacity.

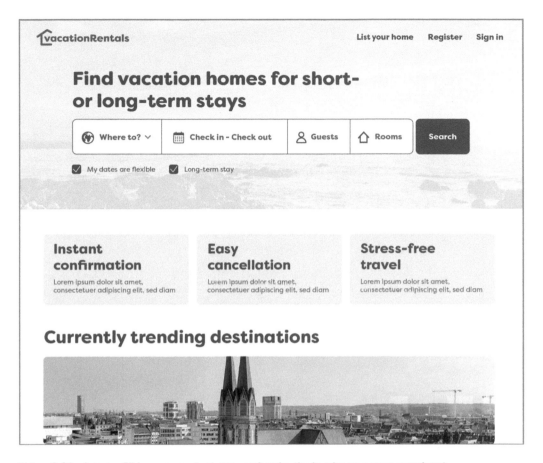

Figure 9.21 Images fill in some content gaps and make the header area more prominent.

The image itself doesn't add any content value other than hinting at a tropical getaway. However, it makes the hero section more prominent and visually interesting while helping to break up the page. If I don't add that opaque layer, I would have to reconsider multiple color options in the hero and navigation area of the site, as in figure 9.22.

Without that white overlay treatment on the image, the text becomes unreadable, even to people without visual impairments. Picking and pairing colors that are readable and accessible is key to ensuring a good experience for everyone using your website or web app. Color is one of the most basic items to check off your list when making your experience accessible. Next, let's consider some factors that go into color accessibility.

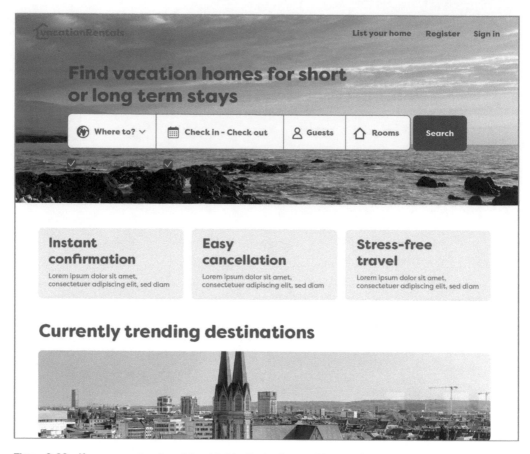

Figure 9.22   If no opaque treatment is added to the background image, the text is rendered unreadable.

9.6   Accessibility considerations

When picking colors for the web, you need to ensure they are accessible to those with visual impairments. In the United States, you are legally required to make your web experiences accessible. Accessibility spans more than color contrast, but using colors that meet contrast requirements is one of the easier things to check off your accessibility list. The color contrast requirements apply to text, graphical objects, and user interface components like an HTML input form's outline or background color. For example, an incredibly light grey on a white background with no outline on an input form will be hard to see, even for people with no visual impairments.

9.6.1   Testing color contrast

Once you pick your color schemes and know what color your fonts will be, run those color combinations through a color contrast checker. Make sure they meet color contrast requirements before applying them across your design mock-ups so you don't have to make extensive color changes further down the road.

Multiple tools exist that make checking color contrast easy. Depending on your tool of choice, a plugin may be available to check the contrast of your colors while you're working. For example, there's a plugin for the Figma app if that's how you're building out designs.

Online tools are also available that tell you what level of WCAG you're passing or failing when you input your background and foreground color codes. My go-to for the last several years has been the WebAIM contrast checker (https://webaim.org/).

Check your colors early, and make this a part of the process. You want to flag potential problems, particularly with colors related to your brand. Accessibility checks beyond color should also be integrated into the process of designing your website, not after all the pieces are in place.

9.6.2 *Don't rely only on color to indicate a state or status*

In the parking garage elevators in the Seattle-Tacoma Airport, the button for the floor with direct access to the terminal is a faintly colored bronze. It's incredibly worn and old and, depending on the elevator, is barely noticeable. In some other airports, two lines of different colors are visible on the floor, and a sign indicates that you should follow the red or blue line to get to certain spots in the airport. There are no other indications on those lines on the floor where they lead to.

In both these instances, I often think of people with color blindness or a visual impairment that makes discerning the bronze button from the other buttons or knowing which line is which color to follow in the airport difficult. Color should not be the only indication or tool to inform people of something's function or importance. For example, if you need to indicate the severity of a warning or an error message, simply using a yellow or red background isn't enough. Include icons or a text label where possible to accompany the color. Not everyone sees color the same, so adding additional clarity with more context is key to building an accessible and easy-to-navigate experience.

9.7 *Web color modes*

You can define your color choices in your code in several different ways. Working with color in digital spaces is different from working with color in the analog world using pigments and dyes. On digital screens, all of our colors are made up of variations of red, green, and blue light, or additive color. When red, green, and blue are all mixed together in equal amounts, we get the color white.

However, if we mixed red, green, and blue pigments, we wouldn't get the color white; we'd get a muddy mix of colors. Using subtractive color and primary colors to create other colors is different from using additive colors. Subtractive colors mix cyan, magenta, yellow, and black to create colors. This color mode is referred to as CMYK, with K standing for *key*, which is black. If you're working in Adobe Illustrator and change your document color mode from RGB to CMYK, you'll see a noticeable difference in color because of the different methods of creating color. A monitor display will display CMYK colors differently because a monitor inherently uses RGB.

If you've ever bought ink for a color printer at home, the ink cartridges are cyan, magenta, and yellow. However, we want to focus on additive color since that's how we define our colors for the web, but it's helpful to have a basic understanding of the two different ways to create color.

9.7.1 RGB and RGBA

RGB stands for red, green, and blue, which are each defined by three numerical values on a scale from 0 to 255. The addition of the A, which represents the alpha channel, controls a color's opacity; it is defined by a number on a scale of 0.0 to 1.0.

Previously, when defining a color with `rgba()`, each color value needed to be separated by commas like this: `rgba(255, 255, 255, 0.8)`. However, as of the CSS Color Module Level 4 specification, the commas are no longer needed between the red, blue, and green values and a solidus (`/`) is used to separate the alpha value like the following: `rgba(255 255 255 / 80%)`. At first glance, this feels easier to read and to discern what is what. CSS does not support what the specification refers to as "legacy color syntax," notably the syntax with commas.

When using the RGB syntax, you alter different values of red, green, and blue to get the color you want, and you'll most likely need to reference a color tool to make adjustments or build out a palette. Both RGB and RGBA are supported color modes in all major, modern browsers. However, defining your colors with RGB syntax feels less intuitive than the HSL syntax, which we'll look at in section 9.6.3.

9.7.2 Hexadecimal

Hex color code values are another way to define your colors and are probably the most common color notation used on the web. They declare RGB values that are mapped as #RRGGBB. The first two letters are the red channel; the next two, the green channel; and the last two, the blue channel.

Whereas the six-value hexadecimal notation has no way to set the opacity of the color, an eight-digit notation can be used that sets the alpha channel at the end of the notation with another two digits. However, although supported in major, modern desktop browsers, the eight-value notation has less support on some mobile browsers and browsers with lower market share. A three-digit notation provides a shorthand way to write a color instead of using the six-digit value, but the values must be repeated. For example, you would write the value #11EECC as #1EC.

9.7.3 HSL and HSLA

HSL stands for hue, saturation, and lightness—not to be confused with Hgh-Level Shader Language (HSHL)—and is a much more intuitive way to modify colors without constantly referencing a color tool. HSL is written in the same notation as RGB, but the values are different. Hue is your color and is set on a range from 0 to 360. The value is based on the color wheel, with a numeric value applied to each degree around the circle. Saturation and lightness are percentages from 0% to 100%. The final value, the alpha, allows you to change opacity and is a number between 0.0 and 1.0. So, you would end up with, for example, `hsla(210, 60%, 20%, 0.5)`. The previously mentioned specification change regarding commas (see section 9.6.1) on RGBA also applies to HSLA. Thus, the value can be written as `hsla(210 60% 20% / 0.5)`.

HSLA is a more intuitive way to create colors because once you set your hue, you can change the saturation and lightness of that hue to create different shades and tints by adjusting those two percentage values. You can also set the saturation and lightness and change the hue to create a few different colors within the same tint or shade range. HSLA is supported by all major browsers, including Internet Explorer 9 if you have to support a legacy browser.

9.7.4   *CIE Lab and LCH*

CIE Lab and LCH are new color modes introduced into the CSS Colors web standards specification. Lab and LCH are device-independent color spaces designed to align with all the colors humans can see. They also give us access to many more colors than the RGB space.

Lab is a color space defined by the International Commission on Illumination (abbreviated to CIE). "L" specifies the lightness in the CIE color space, and "a" and "b" respectively represent the distance along the *a* and *b* axes in the Lab color space. Thus, a color defined in CSS code would look like, for example, `lab(32.556% 19.2835 30.0664);`.

Michelle Barker covers these new color spaces in the *Smashing Magazine* article "A Guide to Modern CSS Colors" (http://mng.bz/e1Aq). She suggests Lab as a color mode to use in Photoshop and that would be the best if you want a color printed on a t-shirt to look the same as on a screen.

LCH stands for lightness, chroma, and hue, and while similar to HSLA, the lightness of colors is handled very differently. Depending on your hue, when you adjust the lightness in HSLA, the perceived lightness of the hue isn't uniform. You can apply two different hues with the same lightness settings, and one may look much darker than the other. Chroma is the amount of color we want to display, and due to restrictions based on monitors, we can't actually see the full color value displayed. But the technology now exists to give us access to a wider range of colors so we can have a more colorful web in the future.

CIE Lab and LCH are both new color spaces, and the support and information available about them outside of the CSS Specification is limited. I list some available articles in the appendix, including Michelle Barker's *Smashing Magazine* article, which provide links to demos to test these color spaces. Note that you must use a browser that supports the color modes.

9.7.5   *Which color mode should I use?*

The three most common color modes are HSLA, hexadecimal, and RGB. Which one you choose to work with is up to you. However, if you want to adjust opacity or animate colors, HSLA and RGBA are typically easier to work with, but you can still animate with hex. So, again, it comes down to what you're most comfortable working with!

9.8 *Color discrepancies on screens*

I usually code and design in software on macOS machines and occasionally switch back to a monitor that isn't an Apple product. I've encountered instances in a user interface where the color varies so greatly between settings that even the user interface in some well-known applications, like Microsoft Word, loses certain features. On one screen I own, when paging through the different color settings, the normally gray background of a Microsoft Word document gets so washed out that it blends in with the white of the page on the screen.

Different screens will look different based on their resolution and bit depth, which is the number of bits that indicate the color of a single pixel (higher bit depth means more pixels on the screen and better colors). If you're able, test your design on a lower-end monitor. Or, if you're using a monitor with multiple display settings that you can page through, see whether anything with your color drastically changes when you page through them. Especially for critical elements that require user interaction, ensure that a display setting change doesn't make them less visible.

Summary

- Color is one of the most powerful tools in visual design because it can evoke emotions and change people's moods. A poor color scheme can immediately drive someone away from your website or web app if it is too intense and causes a visceral reaction.
- When picking color schemes, use the color wheel to identify color relationships. Color relationships, including monochromatic, complementary, analogous, triad, and split complementary, can help you pick a color scheme.
- You can easily create shades and tints from a base hue by adjusting the lightness and saturation in your design tool of choice.
- Different colors mean different things and convey certain types of emotions and feelings. If you're stuck trying to decide on a color scheme, think about the kind of feeling you want to evoke from your design and pick primary colors based on that.
- Accessibility should be considered when picking color schemes, so use a contrast tester to ensure your text color is readable. Also, avoid using solely color to convey information, and include additional context like icons or labels along with the color.

Building a website

10

This chapter covers

- Building a landing page based on the requirements given to us by a client
- Organizing content using user experience fundamentals
- Making visual design choices and applying them in a step-by-step process

Thus far, we have covered the basics of user experience design, the need to understand business requirements before starting to wireframe, how to wireframe, common web layouts and whitespace, typography choices and how typography conveys the tone of a brand, and how to use and apply color. Now we'll apply what we've learned by walking through how to build a landing page for a travel agency. This process is only one way to approach design, and different people have different workflows. You'll find what works for you, but the goal is to give you a blueprint to approach design step by step, from wireframe to a full-color design.

10.1 The website requirements for our project

We are designing a website for a new travel agency that wants to target people planning a luxury vacation but without the luxury price point. The travel agency wants its website to feel modern, hip, and luxurious while still maintaining a professional feel that inspires confidence. The goal of the website is to drive potential customers to book a vacation package as well as highlight some of the other services it offers, such as guided tours and group travel.

The travel agency team has provided us with a list of items to focus on with its redesign in mind. It wants to achieve more bookings from repeat customers and has conducted its own initial research to establish what needs to be done to its landing page to achieve this business goal. Specifically, the agency wants to highlight

- The ability to easily search for travel packages and destinations
- The benefits of booking with their agency
- Trending packages and destinations
- The group travel service it provides, although this is lower priority
- The ease of signing up, without being too pushy about it until it makes sense for a customer to sign up
- Testimonials
- An air of confidence and a feeling that customers will get a luxury experience at a lower cost without compromising other services like customer support

This list gives us more than enough information to start wireframing the landing page for the agency.

10.2 *Figuring out content placement with a wireframe*

We can start the project's design stage with wireframes now that we have our requirements from the client. With the very first wireframes, we're focused on content organization and placement. We're not worried about precise measurements and spacing or having any design details down. The client's requirements give us the pieces to the puzzle that we want to solve. And while we don't want to copy our competitors, researching what's already being done by others can help inspire our design decisions. Figure 10.1 is our initial wireframe.

The client wants to convey a sense of luxury and high-class travel and wants users to be able to quickly search for vacation packages. At the top of the page, we'll plan to put a big hero image below the navigation and logo that make up our header, and we'll highlight the ability to search for travel packages.

Next, immediately under the search bar, we'll highlight the benefits of using the company so that the value of using this particular travel agency is easy to see. Following that, we'll place a section for trending destinations. With a travel website, imagery will be vital to draw users in, so we'll plan to use some high-quality images of locations in this section. The final section before the footer will be for group travel, which is one of the specialties that the client specifically called out as something they want to highlight on the home page but with a lesser priority.

This wireframe is the first stage of the design phase. We would then take a wireframe of the homepage and a few subpages back to the client for review and approval

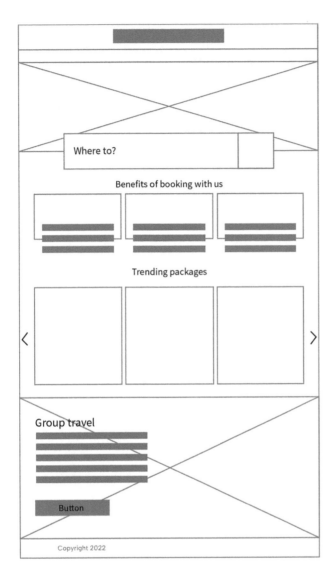

Where to?

Benefits of booking with us

Trending packages

‹   ›

Group travel

Button

Copyright 2022

Figure 10.1 We loosely place our blocks of content to figure out how we will group content and the basic hierarchy of the page.

before starting to refine our wireframes into polished design mock-ups with precise measurements for our developer.

10.3 Establishing the grid system and spacing

Once the client signs off on the sections and general placement of content, we can safely start to refine the website's structure. For this website, we will stick with a 12-column layout for larger screens.

Our 12-column layout has a max-width of 1220px, which we've chosen because it accounts for extra-large viewports, with a gutter of 16px (the space between the columns). That leaves us with 12 columns that are 87px wide. We do not have any margin applied on this grid. Our content will line up with the edge of the grid container.

Remember, there is no correct value when picking a max-width for your container. It will vary depending on the design and the type of device you're targeting—for example, whether you are designing for a large display or an everyday laptop or mobile device. Check out the resources in the appendix for more information on picking a container width.

Figure 10.2 shows our wireframe with our grid overlaid on top. We won't add a margin to the outer container's left or right side for our desktop size. The main content below the hero image will fill the space of the container. With our grid in place, we can make minor adjustments to each piece of content to find the dimensions of

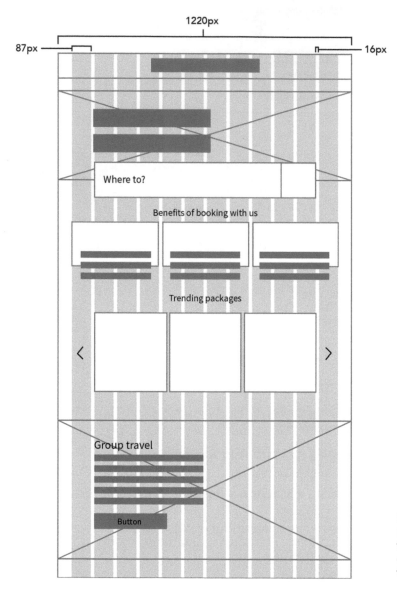

Figure 10.2   We use the grid system to adjust the widths of our content to align to the edges of the grid.

the different user interface pieces. For example, the edges of the search bar that over-laps the hero image will be adjusted to align with the grid.

The grid helps keep structure in place even if the width of content varies between sections. For example, the three placeholders for the Benefits of Booking With Us section fill the entire width of the 12-column grid, while the search bar above it doesn't. The Trending Packages section below the Benefits section will be a carousel that needs navigation buttons on both sides. So, while the main content doesn't feel like it spans the whole 12 columns, the component with icons does. Because the icon isn't as tall as the boxes next to it, an invisible line runs from that point to the edge of the box above it.

The varying content width between sections helps move your eye through the page and groups content establishing relationships between the sections. The search component and the combined width of the boxes in the carousel are the same and help tie the design together. Everything is organized and laid out on the grid, as shown in figure 10.2.

10.4 Choosing typography

If you look at luxury brands, many of the newly branded logos use sans serif typefaces. Sans serif fonts are typically indicative of a modern design and are more aligned with the present. They're on trend and with the times. Different kinds of sans serif typefaces with rounder letters feel more playful. Because we want to avoid those playful typefaces, we'll stick to one that is a bit more rigid but feels modern. For our brand, we will use a sans serif, Montserrat, that I've chosen from Google Fonts.

We will use this typeface for our headings and titles. Now we need to find a good body font to pair it with. Body type needs to be easy to read, so the letter shapes should be differentiated. Again, sans serif fonts with more rounded and geometrical shapes are harder to read. Our body font also shouldn't be a specialty font, like a handwriting font. Although these work well for headings in a larger size and a short line of text, they don't work well for larger segments of type, like paragraphs, especially if they are small in size. The weight of our font is important, too. Hairline or thin fonts won't work well at smaller sizes, and very bold fonts will be too intense. We want a regular or medium-weight font. The Albert Sans typeface, also available on Google Fonts, is a good neutral-style sans serif. It's not overly geometric but also not as rigid or condensed as something like Open Sans. It has a hint of personality.

Now that we've picked our fonts, let's build out our type scale and vertical rhythm. We're keeping things simple with our grid system. We will use a 4pt grid system to easily create our margins and padding in multiples of 4 to keep things uniform. Using a 4pt grid system gives us more flexibility by allowing us to make size adjustments in smaller steps. When your spacing and even typography is a multiple of 4, they fit more cohesively on the grid.

Using an 8pt grid will reduce our flexibility as we get much larger numbers when multiplying by 8. We go from 8 to 16 to 24 to 32, as opposed to 4 to 8 to 12 to 16 with a 4pt grid. The main benefit is flexibility. Additionally, most screen sizes are multiples of 4 or 8, so our designs will scale in line with our screen sizes.

10.5   *Establishing vertical rhythm*

To help pick our font sizes, we want to set our baseline. Our baseline is the line on which all our typography sits, no matter the size, and is the guide that gives your pages consistency. Because our grid system is 4pt, our baseline should be a multiple of 4. We'll use 12px as our baseline and set our body font size to 16px, which is a good size to start with; we can then adjust up or down depending on the font family we choose. As a multiple of 4, it is easy to calculate line height, margin, and padding (add multiples of 4) to keep it on the baseline.

Figure 10.3 shows what our baseline would look like spanning the whole page. We are going to create a type ramp for three types of headings and our body font. These

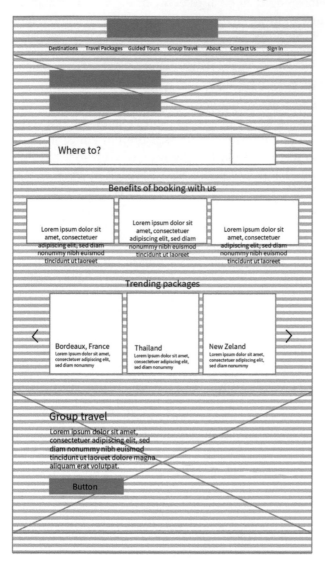

Figure 10.3   **Our baseline for typography is 12px and doesn't change at all. This baseline will establish our vertical rhythm and influence margin and padding for the rest of the UI components.**

types are all we anticipate needing for the website, but our math for vertical rhythm can help us later if we need to create more type variations.

We want our text set as H1 (main heading), H2 (subheadings), H3 (subtitles), and P (body copy). I will pick the font sizes I want to use for each and then calculate margins after deciding on a line height. Our H1 will be 48px, H2 will be 36px, and H3 will be 28px. Let's look at this breakdown in table 10.1 and see how we can scale up.

Table 10.1   Font sizes

Type	Informal naming	Font size	Font size (scale 1.25)
H1	Main heading	48px	25px × 1.25 = 31.25px
H2	Subheading	36px	20px × 1.25 = 25px
H3	Subtitles	28px	16px × 1.25 = 20px
P	Body copy	16px	16px (base)

Remember, we can multiply our font size by a unitless number to get a line height value (see table 10.2). For example, 16px × 1.5 = 24px line-height value.

Table 10.2   Line height

Type	Font size	Line height	Font size × line height value = line height (px)
H1	48px	1	48px × 1 = 48
H2	36px	1	36px × 1 = 36
H3	28px	1.25	28px × 1.25 = 35
P	16px	1.25	16px × 1.25 = 20

The line height for our body copy feels a bit too spaced out, as we see in figure 10.4, so let's decrease the line height to 1.25 for a line height of 20px. This change will throw our baseline grid alignment off since 20 is not a multiple of 12. We'll fix that with the margin and add 16px of top margin to any of our body copy that is wrapped in a <p> tag: 20 (line height) + 16 (font size) = 36, which is a multiple of 12. Figure 10.5 shows a comparison of the two different line heights.

Lorem ipsum dolor sit amet, consectetuer adipiscing elit, sed diam nonummy nibh euismod tincidunt ut laoreet dolore magna aliquam erat volutpat. Ut wisi enim ad minim veniam, quis nostrud exerci tation ullamcorper suscipit lobortis nisl ut aliquip ex ea commodo consequat. Duis autem vel eum iriure dolor in hendrerit in vulputate velit esse molestie consequat.

Figure 10.4   The body copy line height feels a little too spaced out for our design.

Lorem ipsum dolor sit amet, consectetuer adipiscing elit, sed diam nonummy nibh euismod tincidunt ut laoreet dolore magna aliquam erat volutpat. Ut wisi enim ad minim veniam, quis nostrud exerci tation ullamcorper suscipit lobortis nisl ut aliquip ex ea commodo conse- quat. Duis autem vel eum iriure dolor in hendrerit in vulputate velit esse molestie consequat.

Lorem ipsum dolor sit amet, consectetuer adipiscing elit, sed diam nonummy nibh euismod tincidunt ut laoreet dolore magna aliquam erat volutpat. Ut wisi enim ad minim veniam, quis nostrud exerci tation ullamcorper suscipit lobortis nisl ut aliquip ex ea commodo conse- quat. Duis autem vel eum iriure dolor in hendrerit in vulputate velit esse molestie consequat.

Figure 10.5   We reduced the line height on the left to the line height on the right.

There is no magic number for the perfect line height. The more you work with typog- raphy, the more you will develop the skill to pinpoint what is or isn't readable. In addi- tion, other factors besides line height—notably, line length—can affect readability. Some studies on readability indicate that a longer line length is less readable for big blocks of text.

Looking at the H1 and H2 sizing, a line height of 1.5 is still too big for our font choices. As shown in figure 10.5, H1 is 48px; if we multiply 48 × 1.5, we get 72px. How- ever, as we can see in figure 10.6, this creates too much spacing between each line. Thus, for H1 and H2 headings, we will use a line height of 1.

We don't anticipate having very long copy for our H1 and H2 headings, so the close gap, which is a whole baseline between each line, works well for these two head- ings. Therefore, the line height is equal to the font size, and our H1 and H2 sizes are multiples of our baseline. So, extra margin or padding isn't necessary to get anything back on our baseline grid. However, we do want to add margin and padding to create space between headings and other UI elements. Again, we want to stick to multiples of our baseline grid. For our H1, let's use 60px as a top margin. The H1 is the main headline that tells us what the page's content is about. Typically, each page should have only one H1, considered a best practice on the web.

If a page has two H1 tags, the large top margin ensures that they are spaced ade- quately apart to indicate that they are different topics. Spacing between objects estab- lishes relationships. On a webpage, the H1 will probably be the first piece of content below the header. You need to find that balance between acknowledging that the con- tent of the page and the header are separate pieces but still related. Sixty pixels is a nice place to start and appears to work well for our vertical rhythm.

For our H2 tag, we'll set our top margin to 48px, which, again, is a multiple of our baseline grid. Because of our line-height value, we don't have to do any math to add extra margin to stay on our baseline grid.

Looking at the H3, our subtitle, we know that 1.5 hasn't worked for any of our headlines, so we'll try 1.25, which is 28px × 1.25 = 35. However, 35 is an odd number and just shy of 36, a multiple of our baseline. We don't want to apply 1px of margin to get on the baseline grid. All our headings will need a margin added to create spacing between sections. We could add a margin of 13px to the top, but that is a very small

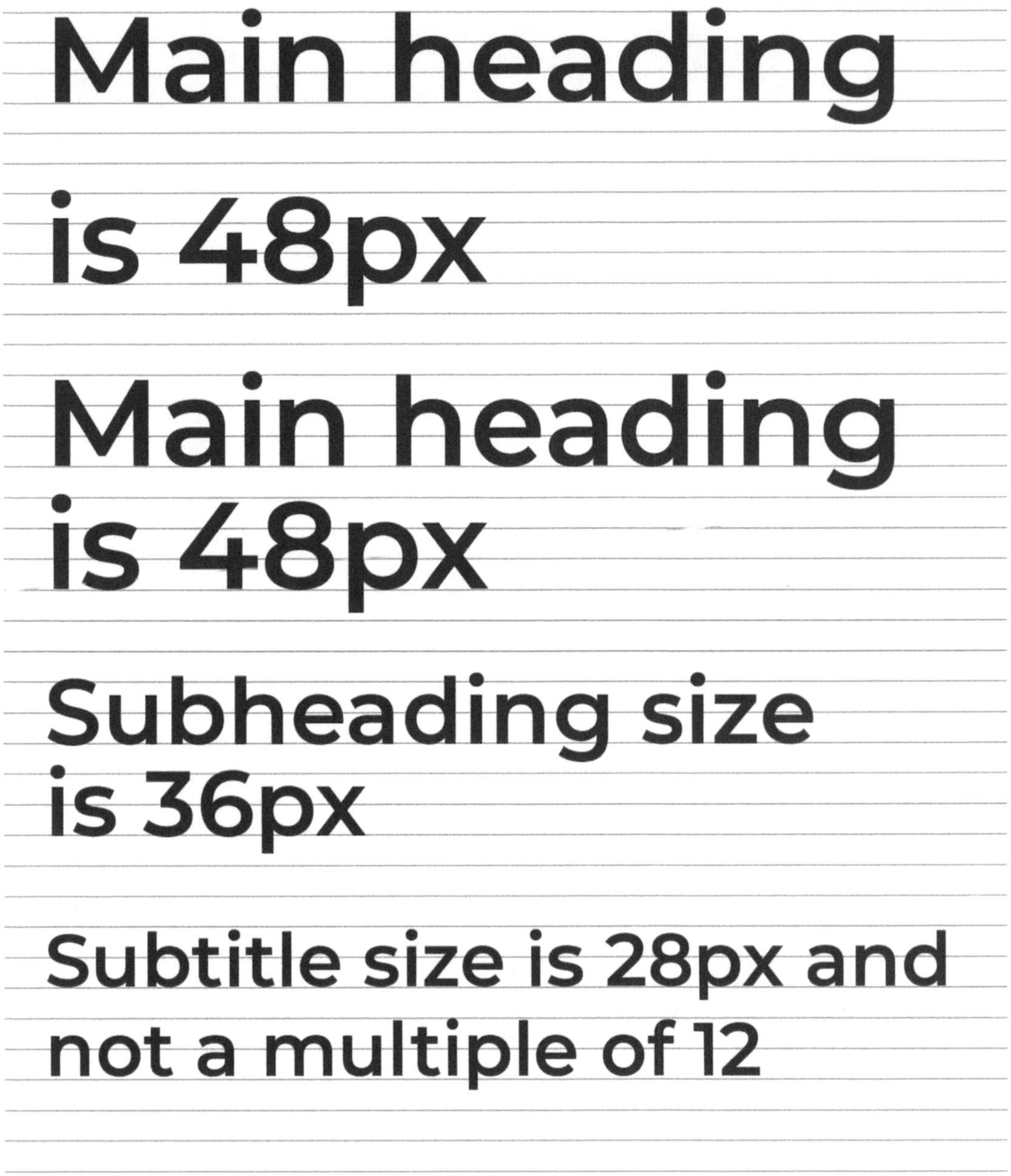

Main heading is 48px

Main heading is 48px

Subheading size is 36px

Subtitle size is 28px and not a multiple of 12

Figure 10.6   The first heading has too much space between lines, so we adjust the line height to be more compact.

gap above a heading, so the next multiple we want to aim for is 60px. If we add 25px to 35px, that gives us 60px. Let's look at our vertical rhythm numbers in table 10.3.

Table 10.3　Vertical rhythm

Type	Font size	Line height	Font-size × line-height value	Top margin
H1	48px	1	48px × 1 = 48	60px
H2	36px	1	36px × 1 = 36	48px
H3	28px	1.25	28px × 1.25 = 35	25px
P	16px	1.25	16px × 1.25 = 20	16px

Figure 10.7 shows our type ramp as we've defined here but built in the browser. We can then use our baseline of 12px to help us with margin and padding between elements that are not type. Margin and padding combined should equal multiples of 12. The principle of proximity comes into play here. Use less margin and padding for items that are a part of the same group, and space them further apart if they are not.

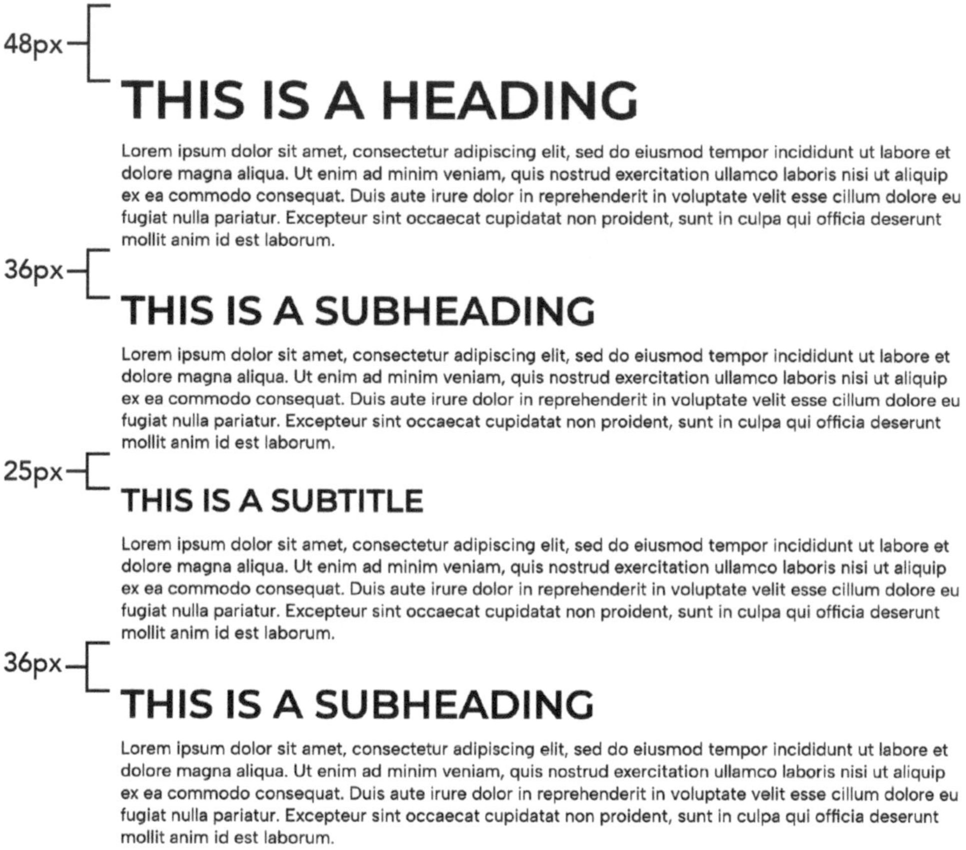

Figure 10.7　Our type ramp as rendered in the browser. We use more space above the subheadings to make it clearer that a new section of content is starting. The subtitle under the subheading is a bit closer and indicates it's a part of the content under the subheading.

We can apply our typography choices to the text in our mock-up to see how it aligns with the baseline (see figure 10.8). We can then make any necessary adjustments to the margin and padding to keep it on the baseline.

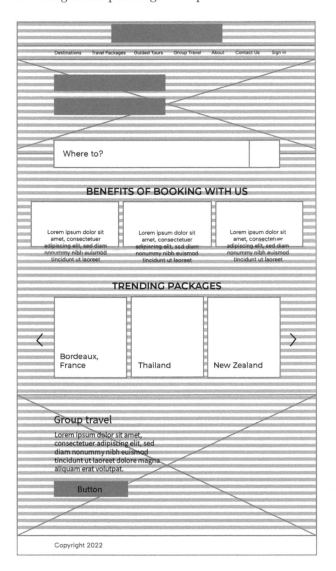

Figure 10.8   We've applied our heading type to some headings that we know we want to stand out. We'll assess where else we may want to use that heading font as we build out the page.

Using Flexbox for CSS, we can easily space our menu items in the header with the following:

```
#menu {
    display:flex;
    justify-content: space-between;
}
```

Flexbox will handle the spacing between items for you, and once you get to a smaller viewport size, you'll usually have a mobile menu implemented that opens in a vertical direction.

10.6 *Choosing imagery*

When picking imagery for any website, you want to use high-quality sources if you're not using a brand image library. Nothing degrades an experience or reduces a brand's credibility more than a website filled with pixelated and blurry images. It doesn't feel like a high-quality experience. Whether or not it's intentional, it can also convey a message that attention to detail isn't a priority for the brand.

10.6.1 *Using imagery to set the tone*

Even if you source high-quality imagery, a mismatch of photography treatments and filters applied to photos can disrupt the cohesive look of your website. Some images have a faded look, some are incredibly vibrant, and others have cooler tones or brighter shadows.

Many different photo filter treatments are available to change how a photo looks. The Instagram filter option for your photos is a perfect example of how different settings change the look of an image. You wouldn't want to apply three different filters to three images and place them all on the same page because they would clash.

For our website, we want imagery that is bright but doesn't contain a lot of different colors so that it feels busy. Figure 10.9 shows the added imagery on the site. The header image we've chosen is mostly blue and white. It feels spacious, and the content of the image feels luxurious: a private pool overlooking the ocean. It's simple but elegant and effectively conveys the feel of the brand and the type of travel our users book.

The images for the Trending Packages section bring attention to individual locations. Each photo is focused, and colors do not clash. However, instead of focusing on city imagery, the photos highlight a particular aspect about a location. For New Zealand, it's a mountain; for Bordeaux, grapes; and for Thailand, hints of a luxury spa with the distinctly shaped mountains in the background. The Group Travel photo also needs to be light and bright, and the use of a desert image here works well with the accent color in our palette and helps break up the amount of blue tones in the rest of our images.

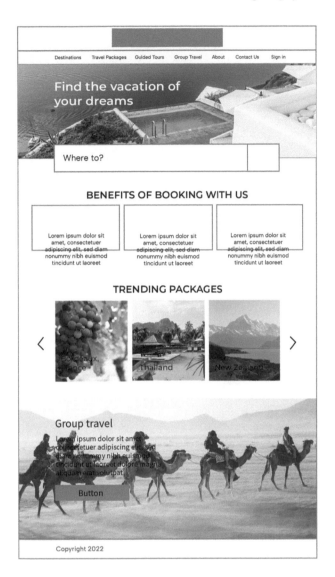

Figure 10.9 We've added bright-colored imagery that isn't overpowering and conveys a sense of luxury and adventure.

10.6.2 *Text over imagery*

When you put text over images, the readability of the text is important for accessibility reasons. It also has a positive effect for users who don't necessarily have an issue with their eyesight. Over the years, I've encountered thin white text over images that are not dark enough, or the subject matter is too busy, and the text is hard to read. If you want text over an image that is not dark or light enough, you can increase the readability in a few different ways.

You can apply a color treatment over your image to increase darkness. I often default to using a dark gradient with a "layer style" in Illustrator or Photoshop applied to the image. Figure 10.10 shows the gradient without a layer style applied, and figure 10.11 shows the layer style applied. The layer style overlays the gradient onto the image, making it brighter or darker with more or less contrast, as shown in figure 10.12. With a gradient, those effects can be partially applied to an image to make overlaid text more readable. In Adobe Illustrator or Photoshop, you can access these treatments via the opacity tool in the toolbar. The same functionality is available in Figma in the Layer UI.

Figure 10.10   **The gradient is a black-to-white gradient with no opacity settings applied at first, as shown in the Illustrator interface for gradients. The position of the black point on the gradient is adjusted so that the full black color extends further into the gradient before we move on to the next step.**

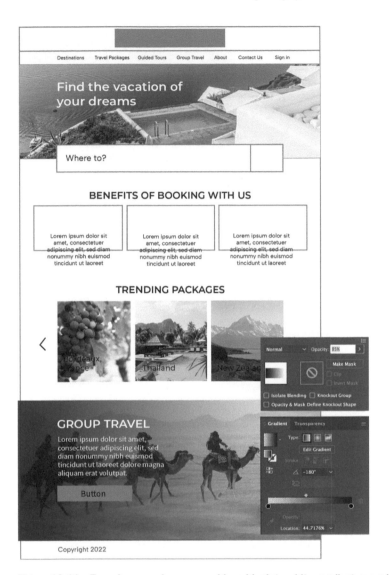

Figure 10.11   To reduce any haze caused by a black-to-white gradient, we will make our gradient points both black. We'll reduce one to an opacity of 0% and keep one at 100%. After we adjust our gradient, we can adjust the opacity of the entire gradient and choose a layer style. We'll keep a layer style Normal and reduce the overall opacity to 85% to achieve our desired effect.

Otherwise, you can add a solid-color shape behind the text and check the color contrast between the text and background color. This method is the easiest way to ensure your text is readable.

Layer style: Normal, opacity 85%

Layer style: Multiply, opacity 85%

Layer style: Color burn, opacity 85%

Layer style: Overlay, opacity 85%

Figure 10.12   We can apply different layer style treatments to a black gradient over an image for varying effects.

10.7 *Pick and apply the color palette*

Our client wants to use some color, rather than a neutral palette centered around the color black. Many luxury brands tend to have a color palette scheme that is strictly black, white, and grey, but our client is in the travel industry, and travel is colorful! They want a color palette that is still a bit muted and not overwhelmingly bright or loud.

Blue is a neutral color in the context of people's emotional response to it. It's the safest bet if you're unsure of a brand color. Our primary color will be a muted blue with some saturation reduced. Using the technique from the previous chapter to build out a color palette, we create some tints from the primary color. Blue is complementary to yellow; in this case, our complementary color is a golden yellow. It's not bright and harsh, but it creates a good accent color that will draw the eye through the website's design. It also brings attention to the pieces of UI that we want the user to engage with, like searching for travel packages. Figure 10.13 shows our color palette.

Now let's apply the color. We have a lot of imagery, so we don't want to apply too much color to the background of sections because it will muddy the design, particularly if we're using either the primary blue or accent color at full strength. There aren't too many pieces of UI on the home page that we'll apply color to.

We'll apply the primary blue to the header and footer since that's the brand color, and we'll place the navigation in a separate bar below the header with a muted blue background. This placement will prevent the header from feeling too heavy or overbearing with its height. We'll apply the accent color to the search button and the Trending Packages card UI. This placement will draw the user's eye down to the next

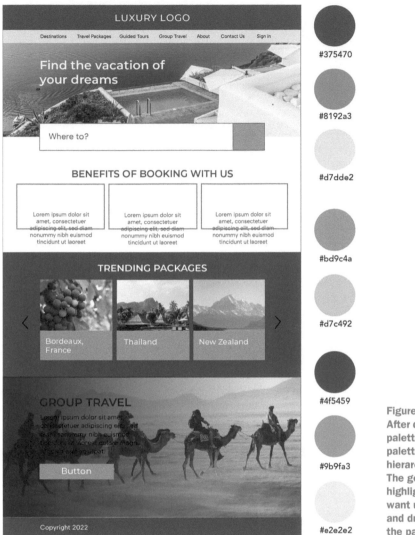

#375470

#8192a3

#d7dde2

#bd9c4a

#d7c492

#4f5459

#9b9fa3

#e2e2e2

Figure 10.13
After defining our color palette, we can use our palette to bring more hierarchy to the page. The gold accent color highlights the areas we want users to focus on and draws them down the page.

section of the page. We'll do the same with the button in the Group Travel section. This final pop of color will continue leading the user through the end of the page.

Next, we want to separate the Benefits of Booking With Us and Trending Packages sections a bit more, so we'll use the lightest of our blue tones as a background for that section. Finally, we can't forget the color of our typography. We'll use our primary blue for headings and dark gray for our body text. For text on different pieces of UI, like the button, we'll use white as the final touch for color on the home page.

10.8   *Finishing touches*

With the color palette applied, we mostly have our website together. To polish up the design, we want to find some icons to add to the Benefits section along with a search icon. Picking iconography is similar to choosing imagery. If you select iconography from the same set that so that they all share the same line stroke width or design treatment, they will be cohesive rather than being mismatched. Figure 10.14 shows our finished desktop design.

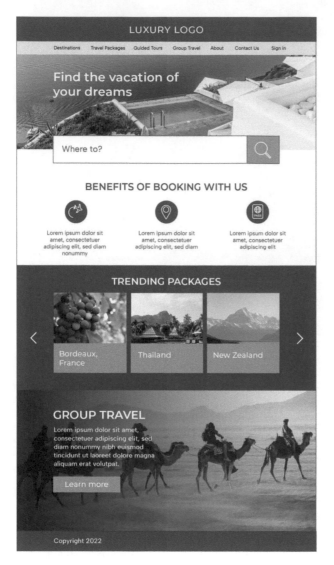

Figure 10.14   Using everything we've learned throughout the book, we now have our finalized design for desktop.

10.9   *Responsive design*

We used a 12-column grid for our desktop design; we can use an 8-column grid for our tablet mock-up and a 4-column grid for our phone. The mock-ups for tablets and phones should be a guideline for developers as to what a design should look like at certain sizes. Those viewport widths can also be the breakpoints defined in the CSS file to indicate when a layout should change depending on screen size.

Web platform technology for building layouts has come so far that, depending on your website needs, you may not need to use strict breakpoints in your media queries, such as @media (min-width: 768px), for layout. The browser and CSS can easily create fluid and responsive layouts with CSS Grid and Flexbox. If you have a lot of UI components beyond text and images (for example, analytics charts), you may want to define those breakpoints for more control. Andy Bell, who leads Set Studio, has a good conference talk on using the browser's capabilities to make layout more fluid. You can check out this talk on YouTube at https://www.youtube.com/watch?v=5uhIiI9Ld5M.

10.9.1 Tablet design, the eight-column grid

Designing for a tablet can be tricky because some tablet screen sizes are the same as a small laptop, while some are just a little bit larger than some of the biggest phones on the market today. For our design, we will focus on the larger tablet size because it can be a bit awkward. We want to ensure that if we squish our design into a small horizontal space, it's still readable and doesn't need to be altered heavily to make it more usable.

Our client wants a mock-up of what the design will look like on a tablet and a mobile phone, so we'll build out an eight-column grid for our tablet and adjust our design. We'll use a tablet with a viewport width of 768px and a height of 1024px and set the margin on the left and right of the main container to 32px. We will set our gutter, the space between each column, to 16px. Our website scales down easily on the tablet, so we don't have to make many adjustments to it. Figures 10.15 to 10.17 show the tablet design.

Figure 10.15 We overlay our eight-column grid and make just a few adjustments to the width of the tiles and the search bar.

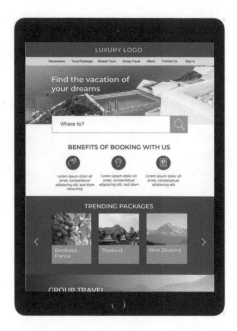

Figure 10.16   The design without the grid overlaid

Figure 10.17   The bottom half of the page on a tablet

10.9.2 *Mobile design, the four-column grid*

When designing for a mobile phone, I find it incredibly helpful to build out the grid system within a screenshot of a phone. It helps to put in perspective what experience you're designing for, especially since it's so compact compared to a tablet or desktop. When designing in an artboard in whichever tool you're using, even with the correct dimensions, you can lose some perspective about what context you're designing for. On a large screen, just scaling down your design may look okay, but it's not very usable, as shown in figure 10.18.

Figure 10.18 If we scale our design down without any adjustments, it's not very usable or readable.

On mobile phones, we want to create a design that is easy to navigate with our thumb. The touch points in your design should be large. A user shouldn't have to zoom in to click on a link or press a button. Bigger is better in this scenario.

For our mock-up that we'll show the client, we'll use a phone with a viewport width of 360px and a height of 640px. We will set our margin to 16px and the gutter to 16px. We can use our 12-column layout with these dimensions to easily make four groups of three columns to form four large columns to simplify the process, like in figure 10.19.

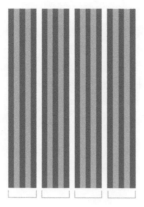

Figure 10.19   We can create a 4-column grid from a 12-column grid. Be sure to omit the outside margins from the four columns.

Figures 10.20 to 10.22 show our four-column grid and our adjusted layout. The primary goal of our design is to get users to search for a vacation package. We'll make the search bar larger, and to keep things balanced, instead of trying to squeeze three columns into a small screen for our Benefits and Trending Packages sections, we'll stack each section. Stacking will create more space and be easier for users to click on with just their thumb. We'll also make the Benefits section a slider that people can navigate, like the Trending Packages section. We want to streamline the process as much as possible for mobile phone experiences and make it easy to navigate. Content that spans the viewport makes that easier to do.

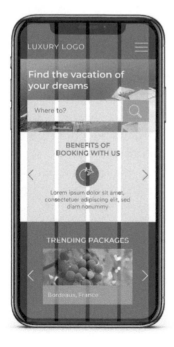

Figure 10.20   We adjusted our content to span the reduced space and four-column grid.

Figure 10.21   The mobile design without the overlaid grid

Figure 10.22   The lower half of the website on the adjusted grid

10.9.3 *Mobile-first design*

One technique that many people use when designing a website is called a mobile-first design. They start with designing the smallest screen first and work their way up to the desktop design. This approach allows designers to focus on the most important bits of a website's user experience. What are visitors to your website trying to achieve? When designing for a small screen, focus on that content to help your users achieve their goals, and then work up from there.

Summary

- Business and content requirements from the client help get you started with grouping and laying out content in a rough wireframe. Once you get sign-off from a client on these wireframes, you can start to refine the design.
- For desktop, 12-column grids allow greater flexibility for design. Many grid generators are available online if you're having trouble coming up with dimensions for your grid layout. These tools will give you the container width, margin, and gutter values. I've provided a few suggestions in the resources in the appendix.
- Establishing a baseline is the first step in defining a website's vertical rhythm. This baseline affects your type scale's line height and can be used to calculate margin and padding for the rest of the site. Use multiples of your baseline to find these values.
- You should pick images and icons with the same treatment or design style. Don't mix images that have different photo effects, and don't choose icons with differing styles.
- Typically, a website will adapt to a tablet without much hassle, but your design for a mobile phone will require more thought and precision about what needs to be prioritized on the smaller screens.

Part 4

After visual design

Now that we've conquered the fundamentals of design and built a website, we will consider whether our design is good enough to hand off to development and how we can be sure it's ready. And once we reach the development stage, we will consider how our development choices affect the user experience. The design cycle doesn't just end with our mock-up: development is part of the cycle.

Chapter 11 re-introduces more user experience fundamentals and the iteration of the design cycle. It provides guidance on when a design is good enough to test, considers a few of the most common types of testing, and discusses how to apply the results from the test.

Finally, we close with chapter 12, where your expertise comes in with web development. Web development is the technical design of your visual design. It is a crucial part of the user experience. It's where users finally get to interact with your website. If you plan to make continuous updates, it's the start of a new cycle. You can now head back to the research stage to validate that the design is meeting the requirements and start the next iteration of the design.

Test, validate, iterate

This chapter covers

- Gauging when you can start testing a design
- Understanding the differences between types of tests and when to use them
- Prioritizing the most important test results

If we go back to chapter 4 on research in the user experience stage, we discussed how the design process is iterative. The chapter focused on the iterative process within the early stages of a design before mock-ups are refined into the pixel-perfect designs that you, as a developer, will turn into a live website. You were focused on working out the different user flows to complete tasks. This early testing is important and can be done with lower-fidelity designs.

However, early in the design process isn't the only time to conduct testing. Testing after designs are pixel perfect or nearly complete is just as important. What you should focus on with later testing depends on where you are in the iterative design process and what you're trying to achieve from your test results.

11.1   *The cycle of design*

Like the entire project cycle, testing the design process should involve designers, developers, and your product manager, who will define what analytics need to be tracked to draw customer insights. If you are working solo throughout the entire design and development process, you'll want to implement analytics on the pages users are visiting and actions in their user flows to figure out how they are using your product.

For example, you may have data from your client that shows a consistent spike in sign-ups or users logging in at a certain point in the user flow. After implementing a new design, you would want to track the number of users who sign up or log in. If the number starts to trend down or grow stagnant, this indicates a problem in the new user experience. The problem may be related to a usability or discoverability problem that wasn't considered with the new design. Great, but when should I start testing?

11.1.1 *Replacing an existing design*

If you've already conducted a full project cycle through web development and have a website out in production, testing should focus on how usable a new experience is compared to the old one. This testing ensures the experience isn't degraded. A degraded experience can cause an uptick in negative customer feedback, hinder users' ability to complete tasks easily, and, if the website is selling something, negatively affect sales and revenue.

You can test a replacement design by bringing in users to complete task flows in a staging environment, observing how they use the product, and asking questions. You can take the feedback from these sessions to prioritize any problems and update the design before pushing the new experience to the live site.

The other option is to implement A/B testing. A/B testing offers different designs to users on the live website. We'll talk about A/B testing in section 11.2.3.

11.1.2 *Minimum viable product*

The minimum viable product (MVP) is an early iteration of a project that fills the most basic requirements. I've encountered the term *MVP* in two different career paths, and they mean different things depending on what you're doing. As a product manager in tech, MVP refers to a functional product. It may still be buggy and is usually a beta version, but it satisfies the minimum requirements so that customers use it and provide feedback.

When I worked in design, an MVP was the first iteration of a pixel-perfect mock-up. After the client signed off on the wireframe, I applied the visual elements and brought a website to life. You can start putting these mock-ups in front of users for testing. Tools are available to make your mock-ups clickable without any code to simulate a user flow. They provide an easy way to test your visual design MVPs.

11.1.3 When is a design good enough to start testing?

Coming from someone who has designed everything from infographics to developer tools, it's hard to ever feel that your design is done. You can continuously make small design changes. The joke among designers is that we try out 10 to 20 different designs before we think we have something to put in front of a client—probably because we are our own worst critics.

The easiest guideline to follow when you're trying to figure out if something is ready to test is to ask whether the design meets all the initial requirements laid out at the beginning of the project. If it does and you're still making small adjustments here and there, the best thing you can do is stop adjusting and start testing. Get feedback, and then adjust designs as needed; otherwise, it is incredibly easy to think your design needs to be perfect before anyone sees it. There is no perfect in this line of work, though. There will always be ways to improve and different ways to do things. Make sure the project requirements are met and your client has approved your MVP, and then start testing and building.

11.2 Types of testing

You can test your design in several different ways. Determining the right time to test depends on what you're evaluating, which affects the type of testing you can conduct. The types of testing discussed next are just a handful of the available ways to evaluate the visual design or the usability of a design that has been built and is live on the web.

11.2.1 Customer interviews

Interviewing your customers and having them provide feedback on visuals and user flows is the primary way you can test static designs—ones that aren't coded and live on the web yet. This step is important to determine whether you have a good user experience or one that needs improvement.

Figure out what you want feedback to focus on. Is it how users feel about the website or product while engaging with it? How do different design aspects, such as color, fonts, and imagery, make them feel? Do visual elements hinder their ability to navigate through the website? Does anything feel overwhelming? Is the hierarchy clear? The answers to these questions can help you improve the user experience.

Also ask questions about user flows. Are users confused about where to look? Are design elements used effectively to guide them through the page? Do they find their way to the primary call to action and click through to the next step in the flow?

Build out an interview script focused on the type of feedback you're looking for. For interviews on visuals, you may want to include specific questions and follow a strict script, although you don't necessarily need to. User flow testing can be more free flowing. Ask your tester to walk you through how they would complete a task based on the mock-ups in front of them. Then, ask questions based on the steps they take, and ensure you get detailed notes (or record the session with permission so you can refer to it later).

11.2.2 *Testing in a production environment*

Sometimes you may work on a project that doesn't allow for time to test a static design. Instead, you must launch what you have and then conduct testing once the content is live. In these cases, you need to ensure you have some sort of data instrumentation enabled to track key measures that show you're successful or that something is hindering users on your site.

Many types of analytics are available, with Google Analytics being a fairly common tool that can provide a huge amount of insight into behavior on your website. Be warned, though: it does have General Data Protection Regulation (GDPR) problems. You want to ensure that you are enabling analytics in a way that is compliant with local laws, which depend on the region you are in.

Tools such as Netlify provide anonymous data tracking. Netlify is GDPR compliant but doesn't drill into metrics like clicks and the bounce rate of visitors. Other providers like Segment and Amplitude drill down into user funnels, so you can see the path users are taking through your product. They can also be instrumented to tell you what buttons are being clicked.

If you're building a project for a client in a freelance capacity, talk to them about their ongoing needs for data analytics. It may be up to you to set up the instrumentation. When working with a team, you may have a separate data and analytics team to help set up these tools. It's still important to define what success looks like and when you need to start assessing changes to achieve it. Let's look at some types of testing that focus on the design and usability of a website or a feature.

11.2.3 *A/B testing*

If you're taking a project straight from mock-up to a functioning MVP without testing, you can perform A/B testing to determine which design experience helps achieve the business goals. A/B testing involves implementing different designs of a particular part of the interface and showing those designs to different segments of your audience. For example, a certain call to action may be designed in a few different ways, but it's unclear which will perform better and drive more click-throughs on the call to action. You can implement two designs that people would encounter. Using analytics, you can track which design performs better and make user experience decisions based on those results. For example, you could show different headers or hero sections to two different audiences and track which design gets more engagement, as in figure 11.1. You can then implement the changes based on that design so that it's shown to everyone.

A/B testing is also a good option if your project is replacing an existing design. While the results of early user experience research should give a good indication of how users expect an experience to work, there's no better feedback than tracking how a design performs in production. Rather than rolling a new design straight out, you can conduct A/B testing to ensure it performs at least as well as the current design.

Figure 11.1   An A/B test consists of two unique designs shown to different users on a live website.

Gathering data about how people are using the new design is key when determining whether to fully implement the replacement design or make updates and do more testing. Numerous tools are available to help you conduct an A/B test. Check the appendix for a list of some of these services.

11.2.4 Staged rollouts

Like A/B testing, staged rollouts are another way to test projects in production. This type of testing is most beneficial in an environment where you're designing a product that is continually being improved. For regular or new website launches, a staged roll-out won't provide much value. You need an existing user base engaging with your website or product so that you can incrementally roll out an update. For example, you could have an experience that's been overhauled on your website. To catch any problems before the experience is fully implemented, you could roll it out to 5% of your user base. You would then monitor the rollout and increase the percentage of people who see it.

Based on the results of the tests you've conducted, you can assess how to move forward. The results can be based on the number of clicks you're seeing or the number of visitors to your site who leave quickly (which would be a good indicator to check for performance problems) or who make it to the checkout page and then fail to complete the transaction (which could be a performance or payment problem). All of these results can be used to determine your next step, which may be to continue to investigate or move straight into redesigning.

You may need to go back to the drawing board and conduct more research with users to gather more data before you roll it out even further. Or maybe you're not getting the results you need from your testing to make a good decision about whether to continue the rollout. For example, you could push out a new feature that doesn't result in an uptick in usage. The next step is finding out why your feature isn't getting used as you expected. Maybe the feature isn't as discoverable as you thought. You could then circle back with customers and do more interviews or tests around discoverability.

Although done in the development phase and not strictly visual-design focused, staged rollouts and A/B testing are still available to you to validate that a design is performing the way it should. The entirety of a project is an interconnection between design, development, and product teams, and the testing phase is where all three of those teams really intermesh.

11.2.5 *Initial user research methods*

Even though we've focused on testing methods to gather results after you've spent time designing, the initial user research methods discussed in chapter 4 are still just as valuable at this stage. If you're working on a product that is in continuous development, user interviews are a constant source of data for you to tap into. They're not just tools for the beginning of a project; they can be used to keep iteratively testing your project with your target audience.

11.3   *Applying the results of testing*

After you've conducted testing of your design, whether in production or not, you'll want to evaluate the results. With A/B testing, the analytics will speak for themselves as to which design did better, and the decision on which design to implement should be clear. If the designs perform about the same, the results are still valid and should tell you that you need to go back to the drawing board and produce a new design that drives the results you want to see.

When you're testing features or a website in production, analytics are key to measuring success. Depending on the tool, you can see the flow someone clicks through to perform a task and evaluate where they encounter problems. Analytics can also help inform more testing through user interviews about user experience. All these tools are connected and help you reach the results you're after.

When evaluating visual design aspects, filtering out the noise can be difficult if you don't know what to look for. Everyone has a personal preference for things like size and color (especially color), and feedback such as "I don't like purple because I just don't like it" isn't helpful. Asking people why they don't like something can help produce more actionable results. One person who doesn't like the color you've chosen wouldn't be something I would act on. However, receiving repeated feedback from the interview group about the color indicates it's something to dig into.

With visual design, look for common themes in interview responses, and form decisions about your next steps based on those themes. How you prioritize feedback will depend on the project. As a guideline, prioritize any feedback from multiple group members that shares a common theme and focus on any feedback that indicates the visual design choices hinder the user experience of the product or website.

Summary

- When a design is ready to test can be difficult for a designer to determine based on how we view our own creations. It's important to remember that a design can always be improved because design is an iterative process.
- You can start testing a design as soon as you have an MVP, whether a static mock-up or a functioning website that isn't necessarily bug free or completely refined.
- A design is good enough to start testing as soon as it meets the requirements established at the beginning of the project.
- Customer interviews are best for getting feedback on visual design aspects. You can evaluate qualitative feedback by looking for common themes on how visual design treatments cause users to feel and making design refinements based on those evaluations.
- Visual design feedback often includes some feedback based on personal preferences. Distinguish these personal preferences from actionable feedback that affects the user experience by digging into the "why" when someone voices something negative about visual design treatments.
- A/B testing uses two design treatments implemented in a production environment, with different users seeing different designs simultaneously. This testing tracks whether one design performs better than the other.
- Staged rollouts can only be implemented if a design is already in production. You incrementally roll out updates to a small percentage of users and evaluate how the update is performing before rolling out more.
- Evaluate the results of your tests by looking for common themes in qualitative feedback to decide on any changes needed to visual elements. For quantitative feedback, if results are inconclusive, you need to conduct more testing or re-evaluate the design to achieve better results.
- Prioritize feedback that shares a common theme trending negatively in the testing group, as well as any data or feedback that indicates a design is hindering the goals it's designed to achieve.

Developer choices and user experience

This chapter covers

- Viewing code as a part of the cycle of design
- Making key code decisions based on how they affect user experience
- Assessing how you can build resilient web experiences with an HTML base

From the start of a project's planning phase, developers should be given a seat at the table. The code developers write is what brings a design to life. Without the code you write, there would be no user experience to focus on improving. Without code, our designs for our apps and websites would be static pieces that we could look at but not interact with. Development is a part of the design process because the technical choices you make as a developer critically affect the user experience being built.

Knowledge of the visual design fundamentals and user experience gleaned from a project's research and planning phases can help make you a better developer by enabling you to communicate effectively. You'll be able to discuss technical limitations or how certain user interface features or animations can negatively affect user experience because of the code. And you'll be able to do so with a more solid understanding of the design choices being made. This understanding will help you mediate discussions and come to a compromise when certain designs can't be implemented (and be able to explain why.) The choices you make as a developer are design choices, and your code should be written with as much care as possible when shipping a product.

12.1   The effect of the code written

There would be no experience or users to conduct usability tests with if you didn't write the code to bring a design to life. The choices you make with your code are just as critical to user experience as defining user flows and ensuring a design is usable.

The tools and frameworks you choose can affect a website's performance and load time. If the page's content becomes unresponsive or takes too long to load, your users will be more likely to abandon the experience out of frustration. This outcome affects revenue when the experience has been built to sell a product.

Implementing functionalities dependent on a third party, which are out of your control if something goes wrong, can affect the experience. Third-party tools can also expose security vulnerabilities, which, although unrelated to the design, affect the overall experience with the brand and can have harmful results.

You can pick from endless libraries with prebuilt components and patterns to speed up development time, but you're using someone else's solution. Are they optimized for the experience you're building? Do the designs of those components and patterns solve the needs of your users? They might, but you'll need to test them out. Are there dependencies you need to consider when implementing a library? Can they hinder the experience you're trying to build?

All these factors affect a user's experience with your product, on your website, or in your app. The code is the skeletal system and internal organs of the experience that keep everything alive. Even the outer layer, the visual design, is controlled by CSS code, giving everything a visual appearance.

12.1.1   Why writing good HTML matters

User experience goes beyond visual design and user interfaces. Some people don't use a mouse and keyboard to navigate the web. Perhaps they use screen readers or other assistive technology. You're also designing and building your code for this subset of users. And designing and building for these users starts with HTML.

SEMANTIC HTML

I don't know how many times I've seen the same meme on Twitter asking what kind of developer you are. In one column, there's a graphic of a wireframe with each box labeled with <div>, and in the other column, the same wireframe, but each box is labeled with an appropriate semantic HTML tag, such as <header>, <article>, or <section>. Using these elements instead of <div> and applying the correct heading tags to your content ensures that people using assistive technology to access your website or app can do so in a manageable way. Assistive technology parses your code using semantic HTML tags to accurately transcribe it to the end user.

Using semantic HTML has several other benefits. For example, maintaining SEO and the codebase becomes easier and clearer for other developers who may pick up your codebase. At the end of the day, you can't know how every user will access and use your website, but using semantic HTML will ensure that you have designed the best experience for all users.

IMPLICATIONS OF USING JAVASCRIPT VS. HTML AND CSS

If you wanted to, you could build an entire site in JavaScript and put it on the web. Developers have and will continue to do so. However, using JavaScript can have a detrimental effect on the user experience of your website or web app. If a user has JavaScript turned off in their browser, they may have a broken experience, depending on how much JavaScript is used in your project.

Heydon Pickering, a developer and consultant, demonstrated such a pitfall with JavaScript in 2020. When you visited his website (www.heydonworks.com) with JavaScript turned on, it wouldn't load until you turned JavaScript off, as shown in figure 12.1. If you kept JavaScript turned off after leaving his website, many people, as noted in his Twitter replies, found that a large number of their most frequented websites were completely unusable without JavaScript turned on. Not the best user experience for most of the web. While some experiences require JavaScript for more robust interaction capabilities, the fact that no fallback experiences exist for these sites with JavaScript turned off showed a lack of consideration for the different types of people who may be using your website or web app.

When bringing a design to life and considering the user experience your code will deliver, it's important to think about those edge cases. Build with HTML and CSS and add as little JavaScript as possible. The core

Figure 12.1   In 2020, consultant Heydon Pickering developed his website so that it wouldn't display if JavaScript was turned on in the browser.

functionality of your website should work and use JavaScript to progressively enhance the experience for users on modern devices. This way, those users who are not on modern devices or who need to turn off JavaScript to save data still get an experience that isn't broken.

Progressive enhancement starts with your semantic HTML. If your CSS doesn't load, the content is still delivered with the user-agent styles applied to the semantic HTML tags out of the box. Thus, those users will still get the baseline experience, with an outline of content that has a visual hierarchy provided by the browser—the same as if the JavaScript doesn't load. An experience still loads, and even a minimal experience is better than none at all.

These matters should all be considered early in the design process with a designer. What happens if the CSS doesn't load? What happens if the JavaScript doesn't load? Including a plan for something failing from the beginning will provide a better user experience and can leave users feeling less frustrated if something does go wrong.

12.1.2   *Performance and page load*

Have you ever opened a web page that took too long to load? Have you ever waited for it to load all the way and then found the rest of the experience slow, clunky, and frustrating to navigate? How many times have you abandoned a site altogether because you just couldn't be bothered?

One of the most critical things about the user experience you can test yourself is the performance of your website. How quickly does your page load? Do elements on the page take too long to load and cause the layout to shift just as someone is trying to click on an element? I've encountered this problem often. I load a page and mean to click on a button or link, but right as I do that, the layout shifts because some element finally loaded, and now I've clicked on something I didn't want. The result is a poor user experience that will frustrate your users and increase the probability they'll leave your site or app.

Low performance isn't just about a frustrating experience for your users, which can negatively affect the business if they abandon your website before purchasing a product or completing the task they came to do. Poor performance can also affect search engine optimization and where your website or app falls in a search engine's results. Poor performance can put you further down the list, and that means less visibility and fewer users visiting your website.

Google provides many tools that can test your performance and provide feedback, including its Core Web Vitals report, on how to improve the user experience of your website. For example, having a responsive website that loads quickly is a mark of a user-friendly experience. The Core Web Vitals report and categories are much more extensive than just responsiveness and page load, and they're a good place to start if you're trying to get stats on your overall user experience as it pertains to how the site is built.

12.1.3 Web technologies without cross-browser support

Just as you should plan for what happens if JavaScript doesn't load or some core functionality fails, watch out that the core experience doesn't degrade when using web technologies not supported in all browsers. Using new web platform features as they are introduced to browsers is a great way to keep up with modern features and enhance an experience. However, the keyword is "enhance": the entire experience should not fall apart if a feature isn't supported.

Again, the concept of progressive enhancement should come into play here. Be sure the core functionality is still available in your website or app, and then layer on the new web platform features to provide an even better experience. You can layer features in multiple ways, depending on the specific feature. You can use a polyfill or, for CSS and Styles, the @supports feature query, which allows you to define whether a browser supports a certain CSS feature. You should use this set of CSS; otherwise, the web browser will fall back to using the CSS outside of the feature query. This layering is a great way to try out new features, which helps advance the web platform while still providing a good experience for those using a browser that doesn't get new platform features built quickly.

While these techniques focus on the development portion of a project, they are vital to the user experience. The work that goes into creating a well-designed website or application means nothing if the site or app isn't usable.

12.2 Developers building for developers

Depending on the product or service being built, developers may be a subset of the audience you're building for, particularly when selling technology or code. The developer experience should be planned for in addition to the core experience for consumers. If developers use your API or your tool, what will their experience be? Where does the documentation live? Is it branded, and does it follow the same design principles that the core experience was built on? The experience you give developers is important too. Documentation should be easy to find, the value your product provides should be clear, and code or APIs should be well-documented for adoption.

A poor developer experience can mean a poor user experience. Take custom HTML form controls. They are currently being rebuilt by web browsers and web standards groups after 25 years because they were implemented in such a way that modern developers cannot simply style or customize them the way they want and need to. The hours developers spend recreating these components from scratch for the sake of styling mean less time focused on improving other experiences.

If you're designing and building for developers, ensure that features are well-documented and that there is a thoughtful approach to designing for the developer's experience on your website, whether it's on the core website or on a subsite that provides developer information. Building a good user experience starts with a good developer experience.

Providing a good user experience for developers means providing good documentation. Whether that's in the format of in-line documentation in code, thorough documentation in a tutorial or walk-through form, or both, documentation is vital to ensuring that the product's user experience is maintainable long after you've handed the code off or left the company.

I have seen what happens when an API isn't documented and the engineers who built it have long left the company. Hours upon hours are spent going through the code, testing, and attempting to document. Think about how you would feel if you were new to a role or a project and were handed a framework or an API that had no documentation. Instead of being able to ramp up quickly and start building, you'd be looking at someone else's code and trying to understand what it does. What if you edit something, push it to production, and take the website offline? Poor developer experience has now affected the user experience, and that, at its core, is what we want to avoid.

Summary

- Design and development are not separate workstreams in a project. Without code, our mockups for the web would be pointless. They would be pretty interfaces with no function.
- The way you write code is the foundation for ensuring the design you just created is actually a good and usable experience for people.
- Good web experience starts with semantic HTML. Writing semantic HTML ensures the people accessing your website with technology such as screen readers also have a good user experience.
- JavaScript has its place for building on the web, but too often, it is unnecessarily used in place of HTML and CSS, which can have a detrimental effect on the user experience if JavaScript fails to load or is turned off in the browser.
- Good performance and page load speed are critical to a good user experience. If a page takes too long to load, the probability that someone will abandon the site altogether grows. Poor performance can affect both search engine optimization and revenue if people abandon the site.
- Use progressive enhancement to ensure your website is functional at the most basic level and continue to progressively layer new features on top for enhanced experiences.
- Ensure the experience for developers is just as well thought out as the main experience, especially if developers are a subset of your consumer base.
- Write and maintain good documentation for developers so that they can use your service or code without frustration.
- Good developer experience is a vital part of building a good user experience and the experience that was initially designed.

further resources

User experience

Atlassian, "Customer journey mapping," Atlassian Team Playbook, https://www.atlassian.com/team-playbook/plays/customer-journey-mapping.

Basalmiq wireframing resources, https://balsamiq.com/learn/.

Dickson Fong, "The S.M.A.R.T. user experience strategy," *Smashing Magazine*, September 13, 2011, https://www.smashingmagazine.com/2011/09/the-s-m-a-r-t-user-experience-strategy/.

Sarah Gibbons, "Journey mapping 101," Nielson Norman Group, December 9, 2018, https://www.nngroup.com/articles/journey-mapping-101/.

Chris Gray, "Better user research through surveys," UX Mastery, November 20, 2014, https://uxmastery.com/better-user-research-through-surveys/.

Kara Pernice. "User interviews: How, when, and why to conduct them," Nielson Norman Group, October 7, 2018, https://www.nngroup.com/articles/user-interviews/.

Wireframe tooling, https://wireframe.cc.

Grid structure and layout

Andy Bell, "Be the browser's mentor, not its micromanager," All Day Hey! (YouTube), May 5, 2022, https://www.youtube.com/watch?v=5uhIiI9Ld5M.

Nicolai Doreng-Stearns, "Using F and Z patterns to create visual hierarchy in landing page designs," 99designs, 2016, https://99designs.com/blog/tips/visual-hierarchy-landing-page-designs/.

James Gilyead and Trys Mudford, Fluid grid calculator, https://utopia.fyi/grid/calculator/.

Ethan Marcotte, "Responsive web design," A List Apart, May 25, 2010, https://alistapart.com/article/responsive-web-design/.

Karen McGrane, "Rolling out responsive," A List Apart, November 24, 2015, https://alistapart.com/article/rolling-out-responsive/.

Nicolaj Kirkgaard Nielsen, Grid calculator, http://gridcalculator.dk/.

Kara Pernice, "Text scanning patterns: Eyetracking evidence," Nielson Norman Group, August 25, 2019, https://www.nngroup.com/articles/text-scanning-patterns-eyetracking/.

Stephanie Stimac, "Building web layouts for dual-screen and foldable devices," *Smashing Magazine*, March 3, 2022, https://www.smashingmagazine.com/2022/03/building-web-layouts-dual-screen-foldable-devices/.

Animations

CSS Triggers, https://csstriggers.com/.

Val Head, "Accessible web animation: The WCAG on animation explained," CSS Tricks, September 22, 2020, https://valhead.com/2020/09/30/accessible-animation-the-wcag-on-animation-explained/.

Val Head, "Designing 'invisible' UI animations," May 7, 2015, https://valhead.com/2015/05/07/getting-to-invisible/.

Val Head, "Including animation in your design system," *Smashing Magazine*, February 21, 2019, https://www.smashingmagazine.com/2019/02/animation-design-system/.

Val Head, "UI animation and UX: A not-so-secret friendship," A List Apart, February 11, 2014, https://alistapart.com/article/ui-animation-and-ux-a-not-so-secret-friendship/.

Mozilla, "Animation performance and frame rate," MDN Docs, October 5, 2022, https://developer.mozilla.org/en-US/docs/Web/Performance/Animation_performance_and_frame_rate.

Typography

Adobe Fonts (search by image functionality), https://fonts.adobe.com/.

Jeremy Church, Type scale generator, https://type-scale.com/.

Font Squirrel, https://www.fontsquirrel.com/.

Google, Google Fonts, https://fonts.google.com.

Hayden Mills, Dakota Weatherford, Sydney Mills, Font Pair, https://www.fontpair.co/.

Laurence Penny, Axis-Praxis Variable font playground, https://www.axis-praxis.org/.

Jason Pamental, Typography tips, https://rwt.io/typography-tips.

Nick Sherman, Variable fonts v0.2, https://v-fonts.com/.

TypeType Foundry, https://typetype.org/.

Mark Wilson, "Trump's old lawyers really, really love Comic Sans," Fast Company, October 8, 2019, https://www.fastcompany.com/90414127/trumps-old-lawyers-really-really-love-comic-sans.

Colors

Adobe Color, https://color.adobe.com/create/color-wheel.

Michelle Barker, "A guide to modern CSS colors," *Smashing Magazine*, November 18, 2021, https://www.smashingmagazine.com/2021/11/guide-modern-css-colors/.

Color Designer, Color palette generator from an image, https://colordesigner.io/color-palette-from-image.

Colorkit, Color palette generator, https://colorkit.co/color-palette-generator/.

Lea Verou, "LCH colors in CSS, what, why and how," https://lea.verou.me/2020/04/lch-colors-in-css-what-why-and-how/, April 4, 2020.

Ollie Williams, "The expanding gamut of color on the web," CSS Tricks, May 27, 2020, https://css-tricks.com/the-expanding-gamut-of-color-on-the-web/.

Testing design

Nic Chan, "A complete guide to accessibility tooling," Smashing Magazine, June 16, 2021, https://www.smashingmagazine.com/2021/06/complete-guide-accessibility-tooling/.

Google Analytics, "Create an A/B test," https://support.google.com/optimize/answer/6211930.

Tim Kadlec, "Understanding the true cost of client-side A/B testing," https://timkadlec.com/remembers/2021-01-12-cost-of-client-side-ab-testing/, January 12, 2021.

Launch Darkly (A/B testing), https://launchdarkly.com/.

Kathryn Whitenton, "How to test visual design," Nielson Norman Group, June 17, 2018, https://www.nngroup.com/articles/testing-visual-design/.

index

RELATED MANNING TITLES

Web Design Playground
Second Edition
by Paul McFedries

ISBN 9781633438323
400 pages *(estimated)*, $39.99
Printed in color
Fall 2023 *(estimated)*

CSS in Depth
Second Edition
by Keith J Grant

ISBN 9781633437555
450 pages *(estimated)*, $59.99
Spring 2024 *(estimated)*

For ordering information go to www.manning.com

RELATED MANNING TITLES

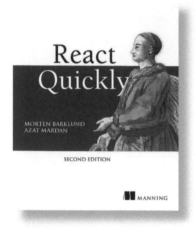

React Quickly
Second Edition
by Morten Barklund and Azat Mardan

ISBN 9781633439290
456 *(estimated)* pages, $59.99
August 2023 *(estimated)*

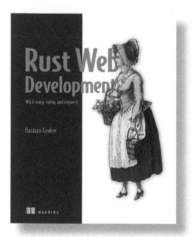

Rust Web Development
by Bastian Gruber

ISBN 9781617299001
400 pages, $49.99
December 2022

For ordering information go to www.manning.com